APPLIED COGNITIVE PSYCHOLOGY

APPLIED COGNITIVE PSYCHOLOGY

An information-processing framework

Paul Barber

London and New York

First published in 1988 by
Methuen & Co. Ltd.
Reprinted in paperback in 1990
by Routledge
11 New Fetter Lane, London EC4P 4EE

Simultaneously published in the USA and Canada
by Routledge
a division of Routledge, Chapman and Hall, Inc.
29 West 35th Street, New York, NY 10001

Typeset by AKM Associates (UK) Ltd.
Ajmal House, Hayes Road, Southall, London
Printed in Great Britain by
Biddles Ltd.

British Library Cataloguing in Publication Data

Barber, Paul J.
 Applied cognitive psychology: an information-processing framework.
 1. Cognition
 I. Title
 155.4'13 BF311

Library of Congress Cataloging in Publication Data

Barber, Paul J.
 Applied cognitive psychology.
 Bibliography: p.
 Includes index.
 1. Cognitive — Mathematical models. 2. Cognitive —
 Data processing. I. Title.
 BF311.B283 1988 153 87-20411
 ISBN 0-415-05119-3

To my parents

CONTENTS

FIGURES

PREFACE

Some topics in psychology are popular because of their appeal to the endlessly intriguing, deeper, and seemingly darker aspects of mental life. Others strike a chord because of their relevance to the caring aspect of human nature. In contrast there is much in psychology with little immediate fascination for many people, but which on reflection often turns out to be compulsively interesting. This includes the far-flung enterprise of cognitive psychology. Psychology as taught as an academic subject normally embraces all these aspects – the covert, the caring, and the cognitive.

  Cognitive psychology possibly has a less instant appeal because it relates to the apparently superficial here-and-now of experience, the mental accompaniment of everyday perceptions and actions. And when the subject matter is brought to one's attention, it may not be obvious what the problem is, why the issues are not transparent. A hint that they are less than obvious is contained, for instance, in the persistent mistakes made in designing equipment that fail to take account of human limitations as processors of information. Perhaps cognitive psychology will impinge more successfully on the public awareness when its practical achievements are more widely known. Perhaps some non-specialists will read books like this which present an account of some of these achievements. In fact, it is intended not as a popular text for the lay reader but as a course text for the undergraduate student who has to study psychology as a main subject. The emphasis on the 'relevance' of cognitive psychology will reassure students seeking evidence of its applicability to real-world problems. It will also provide students of other disciplines, such as ergonomics and sports science, in which psychology plays a prominent part, with some illustrations which they can relate to their own special concerns. And while intelligent lay readers may find the exposition too dense and detailed for their purposes, I hope that their interests have not been entirely overlooked.

This is not intended to be a comprehensive survey of the applications of cognitive psychology. In the space available it would be possible only to log the practical achievements of cognitive psychology, and it would be difficult to do justice to its foundations. I have preferred instead to illustrate the scope and the depth of the field by giving a quite detailed account of a selection of the basic topics and practical problems that have been addressed. I have concentrated on the 'information processing' approach, and I have sampled the activities that interest cognitive psychologists. Thus Chapter 3 considers a perceptual-cognitive activity that the enormous majority of sighted people carry out with impressive efficiency – that of perceiving and remembering faces. This is a domain that has attracted an increasing amount of attention in the past decade, and which has been marked by solid theoretical advance and useful practical achievements. While Chapter 3 deals with a topic that emphasizes the person as a perceiver, Chapter 4 places the stress on the selection of actions, such as are required to operate equipment, either in response to signals or to achieve a particular outcome by the manipulation of controls. Chapter 5 focuses on the performance of people subjected to a heavy mental workload, for example, in the form of tasks in which several sources of information have to be monitored under severe time pressure. In Chapter 6 a range of aspects of fluent reading is discussed, emphasizing the contributions of visual and contextual factors.

Chapter 1 is devoted to a brief review of some aspects of psychology as a discipline, and Chapter 2 puts in place an outline model of the human as an 'information processor'. The model serves to hint at the scope of the explanatory problem faced by cognitive psychology. It has a thematic role in the book, not as a piece of received wisdom but as a device to illustrate the shortcomings, and the strengths, of the information processing approach. Suitably prepared readers may go directly to Chapters 3 to 6, but others with little or no background may begin either at Chapter 1 or 2, the choice being decided by how radical is their need for basic knowledge. The final chapter is a brief overview of the progress made in the application of cognitive psychology, in light of the evidence of Chapters 3 to 6. It also raises the neglected question of how psychology is applied. While this may seem a little late in the day, it should be noted that guidelines for the application of a science are rarely formulated and psychology is not unusual in this respect. However, some analytical effort to understand the process of applying psychology might increase the success rate of the process, and enable it to be brought into contact with an increasing range of problems.

ACKNOWLEDGEMENTS

I should like to thank David Legge and Peter Herriott for their encouragement and their useful comments on an earlier typescript. I am very grateful to Detective Sergeant Peter Bennett of the Photofit Section of Scotland Yard for discussing the use of face recall aids, and for help in producing Figures 3.1 and 3.2. Permission to use Figure 4.5 was kindly granted by Taylor and Francis Ltd.

1 ON THE APPLICATION OF PSYCHOLOGY

General introduction

This book deals with some practical and theoretical matters in the field of human performance, embracing aspects of human activity that in general textbooks on cognitive psychology are referred to as perception, skill, memory, and attention. This is an area which has intimate connections with applied psychology and ergonomics (the study of the interface between the human organism and the environment). Applicability is of central interest throughout this book, and it will be dealt with in relation to a set of general problem areas within cognitive psychology.

Relation between theory and applications in psychology

Theory before practice?

Our interest in the application of psychology compels us to develop a view about the relation between theory and practice in psychology. A traditional view of this sees the research of the pure scientist motivated by theoretical considerations with no concern for its practical applicability. It is the business of the discipline's practitioners to seek out and identify applications. The view is of a gentle and productive flow of ideas from the domain of basic theory and research, continually being brought into register with practical issues by applied researchers.

This, then, is the conventional view of scientific progress; knowledge is first developed by experiment and theory, and is only subsequently applied to concrete problems. It has been characterized by Bakan (1980) as the two-step vision of scientific development, a notion so conventional and so firmly entrenched that it is hard to imagine that the conduct of science might be otherwise. Evidence in general for the two-step view includes the development of the use of electricity, the discovery of penicillin, the invention of radar, the proximity fuse for bombs, and most dramatically the atom bomb; all were preceded by theoretical advances. The two-step view of scientific progress was institutionalized by the contribution of scientists to the war effort between 1939 and 1945, with theoretical and laboratory research transferring from the laboratory with great effect. Indeed the two-step view has been partly accepted because of the great productivity of applied science in times of crisis; in particular, the extraordinary fertility of the psychological scene during the Second World War supports this analysis. Bakan (1980), however, expressed a sour opinion about this mode of applied science, considering the isolation and insulation of basic research from human problems as a factor in what he saw as a growing disillusionment of the public with science and technology. His preferred approach was one which centres on the problems, and gears the research effort in general to solutions to these problems.

Theory driven by practice?

Whether science is or can be practised on a two-step basis, and whether this is how it should be practised, is open to question. As a matter of historical fact, as Bakan (1980) noted, technology has frequently been in advance of theoretical understanding (e.g., photography was developed without a grasp of the underlying chemical processes). One alternative to the two-step view, to start one's enquiry with practical problems, is taken by Broadbent (1980), for several years the director of one of Britain's most influential research units specializing in applied experimental psychology. Addressing the question of the role of models in psychological thinking he expressed a set of priorities that also relate directly to the matter of the application of psychology:

> What follows is the credo of an applied experimental psychologist. Briefly, I do not believe one should start with a model of man and then investigate those areas in which the model predicts particular results. I believe one should start from practical problems, which at any one time will point us towards some part of human life.

Experiment and observation follow, leading to a model which 'can be used as a guide for action', and 'may make other practical problems more tractable'. The emphasis on the focus of this activity, the practical problem, could not be clearer.

In discussing the need to 'start from practical problems', Broadbent (1980) described examples of how such problems have led to important theoretical developments. He noted that it was only recently noticed that human performance is influenced by the time of day when it is measured, a fact that had eluded psychologists until they were called to work on 'continuous flow processes'. The operation of such processes has to proceed around the clock with shifts of workers succeeding one another. Research contracted by industrial and military authorities into these conditions of work revealed the time-of-day effects. Other research of an applied nature was responsible for restoring the important concept of 'attention' to psychological respectability in the 1950s. This concept, which is so familiar in everyday usage, fell into disuse at the turn of the century because of its mentalistic connotations. It was not until applied psychologists, foremost among them Broadbent himself, were called to enquire into the problems of communication between, for example, air-traffic controllers and pilots, that it was realized that the function of 'attention' was not among the theoretical ideas of the day. Theoretical accounts were accordingly modified, and one of the first models of human performance was formulated by Broadbent (1958). The important point about this development in psychology, and there is no gainsaying its significance even though it has since been radically amended, is that it was precipitated by discoveries in an applied setting.

The problem-oriented approach will be accepted here as appropriate to psychology's current priorities. The attempt will be made to establish connections between research dealing with practical issues and the theoretical efforts that basic psychology is more directly concerned with. It will be apparent from an examination of the applied psychological journals, however, that references to the theoretical underpinnings of applied research are often very loose and even merely allusive, as if in a rather forlorn attempt to preserve the link with an increasingly remote theoretical source. There is an abundance of applied psychological research, but a relatively small proportion of it consists of theory-driven research relating to a real-world problem. The connections between basic and applied psychology may therefore be somewhat indirect, and we consider in the next section what the potential contributions from the former to the latter might be.

It would nevertheless be a mistake to suppose that there is a one-way flow of benefits and contributions. Indeed, we can view applications-based research as a particularly demanding testbed for psychological theory. It cannot of course be the only one since it is in the nature of some psychological issues that they are delicate plants which simply do not readily transfer to the rough soil outside the laboratory. The direct consequences of some psychological investigations may be too marginal in terms of the magnitude of the changes in the dependent variables used (time taken to respond, number of errors committed, etc.) for there to be any material consequences to be taken note of by the applications researcher. Such issues, which may have considerable theoretical consequences and have an important bearing on how the field of enquiry is conceptualized and developed, need to be settled in the confines of the laboratory. With this proviso, and all else being equal, there is a strong case for those involved in pure research to ensure that they are concerning themselves with those aspects of psychology that bear most prominently on the everyday functioning of human beings.

For some twenty years psychology (along with other disciplines) has been subjected to an unprecedented degree of arm-twisting regarding 'relevance' and 'usefulness'. Students' expectations of the subject reflect this concern, so that an 'ivory-tower' stance is more difficult than ever to sustain and justify; and to a degree psychology has responded to these pressures. However, they have been pressures operating on a long-range basis and it is arguable that they have been applied more as a form of gentle persuasion. What seems to confront us today, on the other hand, is a very different matter. The current crisis for psychology is to respond to the blunter and more urgent problems arising from changes in the world at large. In particular, there is the looming challenge of the information technology revolution, and there are related changes in the nature of work, the emancipating spread of literacy to developing nations, and a seemingly unending list of other factors that generate problems of increasing urgency for psychologists and other social and biological scientists to tackle. Aside from being socially irresponsible it would – because of the fundamental psychological issues that are raised – be foolish to ignore these changes in the world outside the sphere of 'pure' research. Hence, whether one takes a traditional two-step view, or a more radical problem-oriented view, the application of all branches of basic psychology is a topic of importance and urgency.

What psychology has to offer

To give an introductory account to the application of experimental, cognitive psychology, it is helpful to supply some indications of what might be applied. The intention in this section is to provide a rudimentary means of identifying the nature of what it is in a given instance that has been applied, and the aspects that are noted are not by any means exhaustive, and often overlap. The brief sketch that follows serves the purpose of raising a few flags, a detailed presentation being inappropriate at this stage since this is more effectively supplied by the applications described in later chapters. What is on offer then?

Theory

At the head of the list are the *theories* that psychology, ever so tentatively, offers. They come in all shapes and, particularly, sizes. There was a time when psychologists were not so tentative and went in for theories on a grand scale (e.g., Hull 1943; Skinner 1938), and broad reaches of human behaviour were intended to be accommodated within their theoretical horizons. It is often considered to be the mark of a good theory that it is refutable, and the grand theories of experimental psychology turned out to have this desirable property. They were, however, so comprehensive that they could withstand the impact of failed assumptions and as complete theoretical systems they took many years to fade away.

The fashion has in recent years been the specification and development of what are termed 'miniature models', concerned with the detailed and closely focused examination of limited aspects of behaviour and mental functioning. Larger enterprises will no doubt be undertaken in due course as overlap and consistency between these relatively small-scale theoretical efforts increase, and perhaps also as accounts emanating from work on artificial intelligence become influential in the mainstream of psychology.

The best of these contemporary approaches to theorizing also have the merit of falsifiability of their assumptions, and it is possible to discern definite progress in certain areas of research as assumptions are modified or abandoned and ideas clarified. This is not always so and some theoretical accounts persist simply because of the lack of any clear alternatives. But durability is also the mark of a theory which stands the test of time, not because of any particular merit or validity of its assumptions but because they are not stated with sufficient specificity to be subjected to a crucial experimental test. Such theories have been attacked (e.g., by Newell 1973) for their ability to respond on an *ad hoc* basis to more or less any empirical twist or turn, by appealing to some previously unconsidered variations in the weighting given to this or that factor, to the possibility for subjects to discover another unforeseen permutation of their mental resources, all within the current rules contained in the experimental procedure. It should be noted that this criticism is aimed at many of the theoretical endeavours that are undertaken in the very areas focused on in the present book.

A superficial examination of the applied psychological literature may give the impression that there are close connections between theory and practice, simply judging this on the frequency with which theoretical papers are referred to. For a theory to be able to accommodate the results of empirical studies in the way suggested indicates either that Newell's (1973) critique has even wider force, or that the references to theory are noncritical and are more in the nature of preserving a connection with the global ideational origins of the research than of demonstrating a real point of contact. This does not mean that the quality of applied psychological research is low, though some undoubtedly is, but that there is little glue between theory and practice. In any event the connection with theory is spurious when the applications research itself is not driven by theoretical considerations, and the theory is unmoved by the outcome of the investigation. A test of the latter possibility is the low incidence of references to the applications literature in the journals which publish basic psychological research studies, though it has to be admitted that this could be a reflection of an ignorance of applied studies on the part of pure scientists, or their unwillingness to accept the relevance of such research to their own endeavours.

Method

It is often said that what is applicable is not so much the theoretical stuff of psychology as its elaborate repertoire of methods of investigation and discovery. In any event much psychological theory is so highly circumscribed that the possibilities for applying it outside the laboratory are limited. Indeed it could be argued that an applied version of the discipline should develop its own accounts of limited aspects of real-world psychological activities and tasks. While there may be considerable ground in common between the laboratory and real-world versions of the subject, and there may be mutual benefit to be gained by parallel investigations of particular issues, the real traffic in ideas may for some time to come be of a methodological kind. This is liable to be to the advantage of applied psychology because the relatively unhurried nature of laboratory-based 'pure' research provides more opportunities for techniques and investigative procedures to be developed, explored and perfected. This is not to say that applied researchers will not make substantial contributions of a methodological kind – indeed they have a vested interest in developing whatever variations in methods and procedures are required for *field* experimentation. The point is that they do not, on this analysis, need to feel this as a primary call on their resources, and they can frequently look elsewhere, to the pure experimentalist, for methodological inspiration. How far one might be prepared to press this case is for the reader to judge. It is clear, however, (and this book will incidentally demonstrate this) that applied psychology makes extensive use of the *methods* developed in 'basic' psychological research, so something of the division of labour that has been suggested does already implicitly exist.

In drawing attention to psychology's methodological offerings, we should be sensitive to the echo of Maslow's (1946) strictures against psychology, that it should not allow itself to be driven by obsession with method to the exclusion of the human problems that are its province. It remains the case, without abdicating responsibility for problems, that basic psychology is methodologically very well equipped and offers a sophistication in this respect that augurs well for applications research. There are thousands of published studies on any number of topics that signal to the intending applications researcher what experimental procedures might be appropriate, what statistical methods have been found to be useful, what options there are for the overall design of an experiment, what nuisance variables the investigator needs to be on guard against, what dependent variables might need to be measured, and how this may be achieved, what technical resources in the way of scientific equipment may be used for controlling the experiment and the environment to which the subject is to be exposed, and what characteristics of the subject population need to be controlled, balanced, or partialled out statistically. By no means all the snags of implementing an investigation will be found in the pages of the scientific journals of psychology, and much goes unsaid which novice investigators will stumble over. But in the course of a basic psychological training they will be made aware of much of what needs to be taken into account in the planning and conduct of an investigation, and this collective wisdom is to be found described in the open literature of psychology.

The methodological expertise relevant to the applied researcher in mainstream experimental psychology can be illustrated from areas such as psychophysics, and reaction-time studies. Psychophysics is the study of how sensory experience is related to the physical characteristics of stimulation. It is, for example, concerned with what may be described as the boundary or 'threshold' performance of the senses, e.g., how faint a tone can be heard, how dim a light can be seen, how small a change in the intensity of either can be appreciated. It is also concerned with how changes in the properties of stimuli of an above-threshold magnitude are mirrored in the sensation produced in an observer. Appropriate to these kinds of questions a collection of techniques has been developed, known as psychophysical methods, to estimate the way in which the observer's performance tracks changes in the physical parameters manipulated by the investigators (Dember and Warm 1979; Scharf 1975).

Problems with the classical psychophysical methods – including the failure under certain circumstances of different methods to produce equivalent results – led to the development of alternative methods, falling under the general rubric of signal detection theory (SDT) (Green and Swets 1966). As with some other psychological methods SDT comes equipped with a considerable theoretical capability. In practice, however, it is often applied with little explicit commitment to a theoretical position, other than an acceptance of its central assumption of the importance of obtaining separate measures of an individual's sensory competence and judgemental bias. One observer may, for example, be well able to detect a warning signal, yet for whatever reason (perhaps natural caution) show hesitancy in reporting its occurrence, while another may respond at the merest hint of alarm. Analyses based on the SDT approach have been widely applied outside the area of psychophysics, to research on memory, attention, and personality (Clark 1969; Long 1975; Parks 1966; Price 1966). The use of SDT means that in a given task a subject's performance is characterized by measures separating the efficiency of his or her sensory, attentional, or memory systems, from the readiness of the subject to make the different responses required.

Another widely used method is the reaction-time technique, involving the recording of how long a subject takes to initiate a response to a stimulus, to solve a problem, to answer a question, to search for and find a target, to make a decision as to whether something has been encountered before, and so forth. The assumption may be made that the time taken will reveal something about the underlying mental processes. This is an assumption that has been utilized in psychology for over 100 years (e.g., see Donders 1969), and has in recent times been implemented with the added potential of a formalism such as the additive-factors logic of Sternberg (1969, 1975), illustrated in Chapter 4. Other developments of reaction time methodology include the application of information theory (see Chapter 2).

It is customary in reaction-time experiments for subjects to be asked to respond as fast as possible. As a result the subjects have the option of responding faster but at the cost of making more errors (choosing the wrong response when there is a choice, or responding prematurely when there is none). Indeed the requirement by the experimenter for the subjects to respond fast may therefore be accompanied by the request not to make too many errors, which may make matters ambiguous for the participants. But investigators are usually satisfied if the subjects then keep the error rate below 5–10 per cent or so. Proposals have been made that it should be a matter of routine for speed and error rate both to be monitored and for the tradeoff between them to be investigated (Pachella 1974), and appropriate methods have been described that allow this relationship to be estimated.

Two other related offerings of a methodological kind should be noted. First there are the considerable advances that have been made in the general field of psychological measurement (e.g., Ghiselli, Campbell, and Zedeck 1981). This work has general application to psychology (and to related areas such as educational research, which has proved inspirational for many of the developments). This field of study is called psychometrics and is most commonly illustrated by tests of psychological functions such as intelligence and personality tests. Concepts such as reliability and validity of measurement are well-known as requisites of a psychological test, and they apply quite generally to all psychological measures. It remains to note the importance in psychology of statistical methods. Psychology has developed a heavy reliance on statistical methods and many psychological researchers (though not all to be sure) show great sophistication about this aspect of the discipline. In the context of a psychological investigation, statistics is a decision-making aid. Its proper role is not as a means of offloading the burden of inference as to the outcome of a piece of empirical research, but as an indicator of its reliability.

Evidence

For reasons which have been outlined above it would be unsafe to consider that *psychological data* obtained in the course of a laboratory-based study should automatically be valid and generalizable to external circumstances. Differences in the subject population (including ability level, motivation, and experience), and the likely intrusion in the outside world of variables the investigator had taken pains to control or exclude from the laboratory study, or had taken no account of at all, serve to illustrate the need for caution. Absolute and relative levels of performance may be expected to differ as a consequence of these factors. Moreover the nature of the task in the laboratory is likely to differ in a number of ways from that which is of interest in practical circumstances, so the question of generalizability may not often seriously arise. It will often be prudent for the applications researcher to conduct an investigation to establish performance levels and characteristics that are typical in working and other realistic environments. Nevertheless the evidence base that is available in the scientific psychological literature is very broad, and there are certain well-established and clear regularities in performance across a wide range of studies, and it would be foolish and wasteful to ignore them.

While the levels of performance that may be achieved inside the laboratory may be higher or lower than those obtained outside, there are some tasks for which the laboratory environment has been deliberately optimized, and performance in the experimental situation may then be treated as an index of the achievable limits for that task. This is the case for certain experiments in psychophysics, designed to discover the smallest stimulus intensity that an observer can detect, or discriminate from another. It is intrinsic to such research that the most rigorous experimental control is exercised over the environment, the production and presentation of the stimuli, and the physiological and psychological state of the observer, so that the performance is optimized. The interest in such studies for the applied psychologist is that they elicit what may be thought of as boundary performance. The only caveat attaching to such a concept is that human performance always seems to be improvable (for instance, through extended practice, and often via incentives), but in the circumstances we are considering the improvement is unlikely to be of material significance.

The shortlist of theory, method and evidence of course represents what one might expect any basic science to offer to the applied branch of the discipline, although their importance relative to one another in psychology seems to be different from the physical and other biological sciences. There will be occasion to draw attention to specific cases relevant to each of these aspects in the ensuing chapters.

Two points remain to be made. Firstly, there are no explicit guidelines for the application of psychology, so that a close analysis of how basic psychological ideas are used in practical applications may be of great value. What principles might emerge is not clear but it does seem to follow that criticisms of psychology which point to the failure or lack of conviction of its applications (Allport 1975; Chapanis 1967; Newell 1973; Westland 1978) must hinge on their having breached some principle of application, albeit an unwritten one. And if a principle may be breached, then it may be successfully implemented. Beyond this the challenge is to identify and make explicit these principles. Secondly, it will be found that what psychology has to offer is often said to be less tangible than our list of theories, methods and evidence, that it consists of 'a way of looking at problems'. This is a highly unsatisfactory piece of information for the novice psychologist and the outsider alike, since it implies a mystique and a mastery that are beyond analysis and inspection. There is all the more reason, if such statements continue to be issued (aside from questioning the motives of their authors), for us to look even more closely at the actual connections between basic and applied psychology.

Summary

The issue of applicability is one of the sore points raised by the critics of psychology, who have complained about its lack of connections with and application to real-world issues. A traditional view of the relation between the theory and application of a science is for basic research and theory to precede the application of the ideas of the science. Other views of scientific progress were considered, recognizing that psychology should be concerned with practical issues. The urgency of calls for psychology to take a more applicable approach to real-world questions was noted.

Some preliminary indications were given of what it is about experimental cognitive psychology, the focus of this book, that might be applied. This includes the small-scale theories that have been preferred for the past twenty-five years, the wide-ranging methodological repertoire that psychology has developed, and the burgeoning evidence it continues to accumulate.

2 THE INFORMATION-PROCESSING APPROACH

Picking an apple off a tree, tying a shoelace, answering the telephone, signing a cheque, sewing on a button, reading a letter, following the instructions for an unfamiliar washing-machine, viewing a film, telling someone the time, playing a video game, mending a fuse, listening for a familiar voice, identifying a flower, hammering in a nail, finding the exit in a department store, driving a car, spotting a friend in a crowd, using a telephone directory, recognizing someone's accent; life consists of incidents and ordinary activities like these. They are nearly all uniquely human activities and they variously implicate psychological operations referred to by labels such as perception, attention, memory, and skill. Their complexity is not to be underestimated, nor is the difficulty of supplying a satisfactory, indeed *any*, psychological account of any one of them. They are also influenced by the background against which they proceed – of emotions, needs, interests, and motivations, physical environments that vary hugely on a multitude of dimensions, and physiological conditions inside the individual that range over wide extremes.

Each of these activities can be analysed, using the perspective of information-processing theory, in terms of component processes. For example, finding a number in a telephone directory can be thought of as a visual search activity in which the successive entries in the directory are compared against some internal record of the subscriber's name. A closer specification of the task would include the preliminary narrowing down of the search activity to the relevant alphabetic section, then locating the subscriber's name, and finally reading off the required number and perhaps memorizing it. The terminology of a more detailed analysis might refer to the 'encoding' of the names on a given page in terms of 'elementary features', their 'comparison' with some 'internal representation' of the 'target' name, the 'decision' as to whether or not a 'match' was achieved, and the 'selection' of the relevant 'response'. A similar analysis could be provided for the processes underlying the use of the subscriber's number for whatever purpose was in mind. All of this is to use the terminology and conceptual framework of 'information processing'. It is in particular to assume a *model* of information processing, in which successive 'stages' of processing are organized in a particular way.

Why is a model of performance needed?

The role of models is viewed differently by different psychologists, and it is appropriate to state briefly the position on the issue to be adopted in this book. Although the approach is broadly influenced by the ideas and analytical apparatus of information processing, it would be premature to become committed to a particular point of view, and relative to applications of psychology it would be misleading. It seems appropriate to survey some of the points of contact between the general thrust of the information-processing approach, its concepts and accounts, and the applications of experimental psychology, and to provide the opportunity of assessing the influences between theory and practice. No commitment to a particular model is intended, and the book is not intended as propaganda on behalf of the information-processing approach. My view is perhaps best expressed by Broadbent's (1980) comment that 'an excessive use of models is a highly inefficient strategy for advance in a science and may delay achievements which could have been reached sooner by other means'. Particularly with respect to practical applications it seems wise to avoid becoming so enthralled by the model that one overlooks the practical problem.

Some of the activities mentioned at the start of the chapter seem to require so little effort, to occur so automatically, and to be so immediate, that we may need some persuading that there is something to explain. Others may be dimly reminiscent of childhood struggles (learning to tie a shoelace), so that it will be more easily appreciated that since their performance is capable of improvement (at least at one time of our lives), some consideration of what they involve would be of interest. Yet others (playing a computer game, using instruction manuals, mending a plug or fuse), often demonstrate human performance at its more fallible. Optimization, or at least improvability, of performance can be seen to be a reasonable objective. Moreover it will be recognized that the cause of poor performance is not always to be attributed to the incompetence of the individual. Instruction manuals may omit crucial information, or simply be incomprehensible because they get the facts and operations in an inappropriate order. A piece of equipment may be designed for self-assembly so that one has simultaneous need of a surgeon's fingers, the strength of a lion, and the timing of a professional juggler. Account is not always taken of the limitations and capabilities of the human operator or user, so it is important to delineate them, and a useful adjunct to this is a model of human performance in the relevant context. Such a model could be formulated in the light of these abilities and might serve as a device for summarizing them in a convenient framework. More generally the model may be used for communicating to the psychological community a viewpoint regarding the structures and processes that are currently considered to underpin and mediate the performance of an activity.

Yet there is no point in pretending that psychologists at large feel confident in proposing a detailed general model that will apply across a wide range of operational contexts. There are some interesting attempts in this direction (see, for example, Broadbent 1984; Welford 1976) though not surprisingly what these models possess in generality tends to result in a lack of predictive power for specific circumstances, which is what concerns the applied researcher. Most accounts, however, tend to focus on smaller models geared to suitably circumscribed conditions. The common features and framework of such 'miniature' models will become clear below. This chapter seeks to set in place this kind of general theoretical framework, before proceeding to the practical issues and problems. What follows therefore is the developmental unfolding of a general purpose model in outline form, calling on experimental support where this can be done with brevity. It is not intended as a model to be tested to destruction or otherwise, or to be slavishly applied to practical problems. It is, however, meant to provide a conceptual context representative of the information-processing approach to human performance.

Background to information-processing theory

The contemporary emphasis on the component processes underlying human performance stands in complete contrast to the behaviourist philosophy that dominated psychology until the 1960s. The view was that the functional relations between stimuli and the resulting observable responses were the principal business of psychology, and that this precluded questions about intervening central mechanisms or processes. Psychological enquiry about the internal workings of the brain was considered to be misguided. The development of information theory in the 1950s was consistent with this standpoint because it provided a system of measurement that was well suited to the characterization of functional relations between stimuli and responses. Ironically it also proved to be one of the means by which the behaviourist perspective was radically enlarged, and eventually undermined.

Information theory and psychology

Information theory was developed by communications engineers but was quickly adopted by psychologists, intrigued by the prospect it seemed to offer for supplying a metric for assessing human performance across situations (see Welford 1968). Information measured in the way proposed by the theory (Attneave 1959; Garner 1962) has no immediate or useful connection with meaning (but see Dretske, 1983). It is a measure based on the probabilities of the entire set of possible events in a given situation. An experimenter may, for example, present a series of visual signals to a subject, each to be responded to as fast as possible. The subject will see one signal at a time and there is a unique response (typically a key to be pressed) for each of the alternative signals. According to the basic axioms of the theory, the information represented in the signals is specified as $-\sum p \log p$, where the values of p correspond to the probabilities of the various signals and the summation (indicated by the $\sum$ sign) is carried out over the complete set of signals. For equiprobable signals, the value of H is log n, where n is the number of possible signals. It was found experimentally that average reaction time to a set of equally likely signals increased in direct relation not to the value of n itself but to its logarithm (Hick 1952). Thus, to illustrate, there was a constant increase in the reaction time each time the set of stimuli doubled in size. This served to establish that in this case reaction time varied directly with information H (see Figure 2.1).

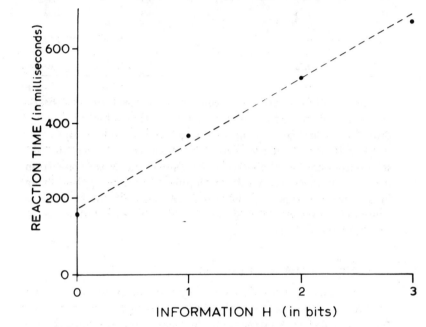

Figure 2.1   Typical relationship obtaining between reaction time and stimulus information H

But the general expression for H (see above) refers to stimulus probabilities without restriction, and investigators asked next whether reaction time would also vary with H more generally. In the event the linear relation between reaction time and H was also obtained when H was varied in other ways, for example by manipulating the probabilities of a fixed set of signals. For instance, suppose we choose to present a series of four alternative signals. Let us call them A, B, C, and D. We may now choose the probabilities to decide the presentation sequence for our experiment. Some examples are shown in the table below, with the corresponding values of H in each case. Using a probability manipulation of this sort we should be able to obtain confirmation of the direct relation between reaction time and H (as did Hyman 1953).

Examples of probability combinations and associated values of information H (in bits)

Stimulus				Information
A	B	C	D	
0.01	0.02	0.02	0.95	0.362
0.05	0.05	0.10	0.80	1.022
0.1	0.1	0.1	0.7	1.357
0.1	0.2	0.2	0.5	1.761
0.2	0.2	0.2	0.4	1.922
0.25	0.25	0.25	0.25	2.000

Findings such as these were followed by a period of enthusiastic application of the information measure, partly no doubt because it provided researchers with an economical and general description of the relationship between certain types of performance and the stimuli to them. But there was a more significant contribution from information theory since this development was accompanied by an increasing acceptance of the associated view of the brain as a communications system. A simple model of a basic communication system is shown in Figure 2.2.

Figure 2.2   Components of a simple communications system

It is not hard to see how the brain can be seen as analogous to such a system, though we shall not explore this issue closely. It is, however, important for our purposes to see that this represented a speculation about the inner workings of the brain. It is seen as a system for transmitting information, and subject to the intrusive contribution of 'noise' internally generated or externally imposed. Performance on a task requiring the faithful mapping of a set of stimuli onto a set of responses, each uniquely specified by a particular stimulus, will be degraded to the extent that the central channel is noisy.

The way was opened by such discussions for speculation about the central mechanisms responsible for the functional relationships that emerged in experimental work. For example, the linear increase in reaction time with information was discussed in terms of the way stimuli might be *internally* coded or classified (Hick 1952; Smith

1968; Welford 1960). As a possible explanation of this effect, it was suggested that when a member of a set of stimuli needs to be identified, this is achieved by means of a series of decisions successively narrowing down the possibilities by half each time. A sequence of 'binary' decisions such as this would lead to an increase in reaction time as the number of possible stimuli increased. But more to the point, if each binary decision took the same amount of time, then reaction time would increase by a fixed amount when the size of the stimulus set doubled, in line with Hick's (1952) experimental evidence. We shall not consider the fate in particular of any of the hypotheses advanced to account for the findings of research using information theory. More significant for our purpose is to note the very important shift in the intellectual climate of the time. While one focus of interest was on the methodological possibilities offered by information theory, there was at the same time a significant revival of interest in the mental processes underlying behaviour.

Computing and psychology

This interest was greatly stimulated by the rapidly developing field of electronic computing. Ever since its early days the science and technology of computing has provided a most effective service discipline for psychology. Applications to psychology have included data processing (for statistical analyses, for example), the automated control of experiments, and the computer simulation of complex psychological processes. The last of these is closely linked with the field of artificial intelligence. Both areas encourage the detailed analysis and specification of psychological activities in terms of component processes and procedures. Moreover the very concepts of computing have proved to be highly influential in psychology. Psychology has always found inspiration in the conceptual substance of its intellectual neighbours (disciplines such as physiology, linguistics, and cybernetics), borrowing where it could find a useful analogy (Valentine 1982). And so it has been and continues to be with computers and computing. There was a short-lived but still influential controversy about whether the computer could serve as a model of the brain. Part of the controversy was settled quickly; if it is taken strictly to refer to the question of 'hardware', the analogy is not a very good one even though similarities do exist between computer and brain. It is a rather better analogy when considered in terms of software, the idea being that both the computer and the brain may be conceived as carrying out a task as a series of programmed steps. Indeed it is the goal of computer simulation to do a task in the guise of a computer program which produces outputs as like those of a human as possible, and via a series of steps and operations closely resembling those assumed to be used by humans. In this sense the *program* specifies a model of the processes of the mind.

At the same time the concepts and terminology of computing had a less direct but even more pervasive influence on psychology. A fund of ideas became available in the form of the structural components of computers such as buffers, memory stores, content-addressable registers, secondary storage systems. So did a range of ideas relating to the way information is handled by computers, such as serial vs parallel processing, top-down vs bottom-up processing and so forth; and psychological accounts quickly drew on this repertoire of ideas. The fundamental assumption is and continues to be that the brain may be considered as a processor of information. A corollary of this is that it is profitable to make an analysis of the constituent processing stages and mechanisms that underlie human performance.

Basic components

Cursory analysis of the activities listed at the beginning of the chapter suggests that a model of human performance might need at least three basic components: a means for ensuring that information is picked up, a mechanism for then deciding what action this information calls for, and a third system for putting the action into effect. Broad divisions of this type are to be found in models proposed by various writers (Smith 1968; Sternberg 1969, 1975; Teichner and Krebs 1974; Theios 1975; Welford 1960). Each was formulated on the basis of a considered examination of a wide-ranging experimental data base. In particular, in Sternberg's case, it was associated with a formal methodological treatment of the data designed to aid in the 'discovery' of stages of processing (see p. 33). Yet even though he had resorted to the use of a formal procedure for this purpose, Sternberg was prompted to comment on the arbitrary nature of the labels attached to the processing stages incorporated in any model. Figure 2.3 attempts to summarize the main recurring features of the models, though it inevitably misrepresents all of them to a degree.

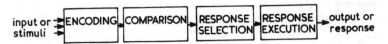

Figure 2.3   Basic stages of information processing

The choice reaction-time experimental paradigm will serve as the vehicle for explaining the workings of the summary model; an example of the task was used in the discussion of information theory in the preceding section. In this paradigm the subject is presented with a series of stimuli presented consecutively and drawn in an unpredictable manner from a set of alternative stimuli. The task is to make the corresponding response as fast as possible. The stimuli may be an array of lights, a collection of tones, digits on a screen, spoken words, pictures, and so on. The important thing is that only one of the set of stimuli occurs at a time. The subject is usually called on to respond by pressing one of a set of keys or to say the name of the stimulus. The experimenter may decide to study performance when the relationship between the stimuli and the responses may be quite obvious (e.g., giving the name of each digit as it is presented) or when an arbitrary relationship applies (e.g., the names of the stimuli and the responses to them are assigned on a random basis).

What is represented by each of the boxes in the sequence depicted in Figure 2.3 is a processing stage, at which the information supplied to it is transformed in readiness for the next stage. The processing operations in Stage 1, which we denote by the shorthand term 'encoding', include the acquisition of the stimulus and the formation of an internal representation of it. Subsequently, the internal version of the stimulus is compared, in Stage 2 ('classification'), with the memorized representations of the possible stimuli. The advance achieved by this stage is completed by the forwarding to the next stage of an indication of which member of the memory set matches the incoming input signal. (Stage 2 is characterized as the 'classification' stage, not 'comparison' as would be appropriate for the choice reaction task, in order to recognize the generality of demands at this stage imposed by different tasks. This applies too to other stages but there seems to be more uniformity about them and their labels seem adequate.)

Stage 3 ('responses selection') is responsible for translating the input from Stage 2 into a response code, by reference to the mapping rules which associate the possible stimuli with the appropriate responses. Having thereby selected the code of the relevant response, this is passed to Stage 4 ('response execution') which deals with the organization of the response, the movements necessary, and their execution. Each of the stages takes an amount of time (generally thought to depend on the complexity of the operations to be performed), and each is initiated on the completion of the immediately preceding stage. The flow of information is unidirectional, and the time taken by each stage, in the strongest version of this kind of model, is unrelated to the time taken by preceding stages. In short, the model involves the independent operation of sequentially ordered stages of information processing.

Investigation of the limits to which such simplified models can be pushed has to a large extent focused on the mode of operation of particular stages (and it remains the case that after some twenty-five years little research has been directed at the response-related processes). For example, the classification stage, being responsible in the choice reaction task for the comparison of a single item against a set of alternative memory representations, could complete its job by making the necessary comparisons one at a time (serial processing) or more than one at a time (parallel processing). Moreover the endpoint of the comparison operation could be the discovery of a match, in which case the mode of operation is described as 'self-terminating'. But this is not the only way of doing this, and it is thinkable that the operation is carried out for all members of the memory set. This seemingly uneconomic method (for which there is supporting evidence in at least one vein of research: Sternberg 1975) is referred to as 'exhaustive' processing. The issue is discussed in more detail in Barber and Legge (1976).

Clearly such a model has limitations, and this can be seen without reference to an experimental literature. It is limited, for instance, in relation to its scope. It is intended only to deal with a particular set of findings, and a particular set of simple activities, namely those resulting from choice reaction time and like studies. We should bear in mind that this is to a large extent a self-imposed limitation, not because of the ivory-tower pretensions of the modellers, but because of the implicit view that it is sensible to begin with the most unencumbered type of task, and that in any case this single-stimulus/single-response paradigm is not wholly unrepresentative of certain realistic situations (e.g., reacting to traffic signals).

In the context of this research it has been suggested that this sort of theorizing, even with its limited aspirations, is wrong. For example, McClelland (1979) has proposed an alternative to the assumption of the independent serial operation of stages. He argued that the stages may be capable of operating as an *overlapped* sequence. Thus a later stage is thought to be capable of being initiated prior to the completion of all preceding ones. Another criticism of the sequential-stages assumption concerns the one-way nature of the influence between stages. It is argued that the possibility should be acknowledged that later stages may exert an influence on earlier ones. This is referred to as 'top-down' processing, in contrast to the 'bottom-up' processing assumed for the basic model. Such criticisms are illustrated in later chapters.

Extending the basic model

The basic model has to be modified in a number of ways if it is to do service in a useful variety of circumstances. It has some blatant shortcomings and there are many ways in which it can be added to or amended with the objective of broadening its scope and its sphere of application. The attempt will be made in the following to steer a moderately consensual course through the variations proposed in the psychological literature. There are two principal aspects of the model which call for development and qualification. They relate to what in textbooks are referred to as attention and memory. These are the two most heavily researched areas related to that from which the model has emerged, but there are others undoubtedly as important which have yet to come into effective contact with the information-processing approach. Topics with a long psychological heritage such as learning, emotion, and motivation should be included in our coverage, but they unfortunately sit somewhat beyond the pale most of the time in the contemporary research effort. The facile assumption that they could be represented in an extended model as external parameters to be tweaked one way or another to vary the efficiency of the information-processing system will not be made and should be resisted. It is more than likely that the whole perspective of the information-processing approach will need to shift to accommodate these factors, and we should be frank in admitting the tentative nature of the present conceptual framework. But while we must therefore accept the highly limited scope of our present universe of discussion, we shall make the effort to extend it and our model at least to include the contributions of attention and memory.

Attention

Because of the flood of information received by our sensory systems it has been argued that there must be some sifting and selecting among the various sources of information (or inputs) available to us at any instant. As presented above the basic model assumes that this job has already been achieved, and that a neat flow of information in convenient packages (such as can occur in laboratory experiments) has already been arranged. But this avoids the key issue of just how the information-processing system manages this problem in normal circumstances, with different inputs 'competing' for attention. To introduce a realistic dimension into the model we could include a component responsible for selecting information, and this will be considered later in this section. First, however, it is necessary to examine and explain the concept, attention, which has been brought into the discussion. It will be helpful to see the concept in a historical perspective.

It is a widely held view among cognitive psychologists that the study of cognition was more or less in abeyance for some thirty or forty years following the rise of behaviourism at the beginning of the twentieth century. This terminated with its decline in the 1950s and 1960s when cognition re-emerged as an important topic of study in the context of the development of information-processing analyses of performance. This is illustrated in particular by the fate of 'attention', a concept central to cognitive psychology and arguably representative of its repertoire of basic terms. Writing of the period between the First World War and the 1960s, Neisser (1976) stated that 'there was no work on attention'. This exaggerates the demise of the concept since some seminal work was done on attention during the reputedly dark ages of behaviourism (Lovie 1983). It is, however, fair to say that contemporary psychology relies extensively on concepts, including attention, that were once referred to in a disparaging way by behaviourists as 'mentalistic', and were considered to be scientifically unrespectable in the positivist intellectual climate of the early twentieth century. The difficulty of agreeing acceptable definitions of processes invisibly (and hypothetically) lodged in the privacy of the working brain led to them being set aside from scientific consideration. It was partly in reaction to inappropriate restrictions on what could be studied scientifically that so-called mentalistic concepts were dusted off in the 1960s and 1970s, and have returned to full favour today.

Their reinstatement was also partly motivated by the pressure to deal with practical problems that were manifestly best characterized in terms of mental constructs like attention. Thus the performance of radar operators on lengthy watches regularly showed a decline in terms of the number of signals detected that was consistent with the operators suffering lapses of attention increasing in frequency as the watch proceeded, with the most marked increase in the early stages of the watch. While this may not be the only explanation of the so-called 'vigilance decrement', it is a possible one, so long as we allow ourselves to use the term attention and agree what it is and how it works. But what is it, then?

Taking everyday experience as a starting point, everyone knows what it is like to find attention wandering during a lecture or sermon, and to be sharply told to 'pay attention', or to be enjoined to 'turn your attention to the top of the page'. It is also a familiar experience to try to attend to more than one thing at a time – the milk in the saucepan and the ironing, the conversation and the road ahead, the passage of time and the examination essay. Or to have one's attention caught by a newspaper headline. From these examples it can be seen that attention may be focused, divided, shifted, or even involuntarily captured. But it does not follow that these familiar uses of the term are what is intended by psychologists when they talk about attention in a technical way.

It certainly was when the information-processing approach was in its early days. As well as the vigilance problem, there was great interest in the conditions under which an operator (such as an air-traffic controller) could divide attention between two or more simultaneous auditory messages, and the characteristics of an auditory message which would enable the individual to lock attention on to it to the exclusion of other distracting messages (Broadbent 1958). The early studies made extensive use of methods in which two auditory messages served as sources of information presented one to each ear. This was known as the dichotic listening paradigm, and subjects were typically required to give priority to one of the messages (the primary source or channel) over the other (the secondary source or channel). In one particular version of the task, attention was strongly focused on the primary channel by requiring the subject to repeat, or 'shadow', every word of the message. The evidence suggested that subjects were unable to pick up very much information from the secondary source/channel. They could not, for example, do much more than identify the gender of the speaker on the unattended ear when shadowing, and they might not even know what language was being used. This kind of evidence was consistent with the idea of a filter placed early in the information flow which selected information in an all-or-nothing fashion for further processing on the basis of physical properties like ear of arrival, intensity, pitch, location in space. This was the conclusion reached by Broadbent (1958) in the first information-processing analysis of attention. This raises the possibility of inserting 'attention' as a component in the existing model sequence of Figure 2.3 as a distinct processing 'stage'. But to do this the model would have to be elaborated in another way because it presently deals with only a single source (or stream) of information. The model needs to accommodate the competing streams in some way, possibly by incorporating parallel components for the alternative inputs, up to but not beyond the 'attention stage'. This in turn raises another problem, namely where in the sequence to place the attention stage.

In addition, the nature of its mode of operation would need to be clarified. Evidence on this point was obtained when it was found that information was occasionally reported from the unattended channel that implied that it had been subject to semantic processing. Moray (1959), for example, found that subjects would sometimes respond to the occurrence of their own name in the unattended channel. And Treisman (1960) found that subjects would incorporate into the shadowed message words from the other message if they were contextually sensible. It thus became apparent that the filter must be more subtle in operation, not simply shutting out certain input characteristics, and selection was achieved by a process of 'attenuation' of the unwanted information (Treisman, 1960). Thus aspects of the unattended source would pass through the filter in a reduced form, and occasionally evoke a response, particularly if they were highly pertinent to the individual. At the same time the 'filter' mechanism is not tuned purely to arbitrate about the acceptability of events on physical criteria, but it is also sensitive to quite complex attributes of the input, including their meaning to the receiver.

As to the locus of selection, and hence the point in the processing sequence where attention should be inserted in Figure 2.3, nothing in the evidence described so far forces the conclusion that selection occurs at an early stage of processing. Indeed an alternative account was developed by Deutsch and Deutsch (1963) and Norman (1968) which held that the initial treatment of information on the attended and unattended channels is the same. According to these theorists selection is delayed until a response has to be selected, or information must be stored in memory. Only at this relatively late stage of processing are the assigned priorities of the messages put into effect. Empirical tests of the early and late theories have been reported (Treisman and Geffen 1967; Treisman and Riley 1969; Moray *et al.* 1976). Some of the evidence supports an early locus for attentional selection and some supports both an early and a late locus. Neither position is unequivocally supported and this is recognized in the present account by allowing attention to be focused at any processing stage.

Although the locus of selection has continued to be of interest, a climate of opinion (as opposed to contrary evidence) has built up against the idea that attention should be thought of as a processing stage, or as a characteristic of a unique processing stage. Instead attention has come to be considered as a matter of the allocation of processing resources, with information sources and processing operations attracting more or less resources as the task demands require. This is reflected in Figure 2.4, showing a graphic representation of attention as a potential moderating influence on information-processing operations. The assumption of parallel processing of different inputs is widely accepted, with attentional selection among them corresponding to the balance of the resources allocated. Hence the input which is allocated the lion's share of the attentional resources is processed the most efficiently. Since it would only clutter the figure, the possibility of parallel processes is not shown in Figure 2.4. Attention and performance are discussed further in Chapter 5.

Memory

We have admitted our fallibility as information processors by accepting that we cannot deal with all of the inputs we are confronted with at any given instant, and by postulating some arrangement for attentional selection. Another way of dealing with this flood of information, to enable us to check whether something significant has taken place on an unselected 'channel', is to retain a momentary copy of other inputs to be assessed as soon as the main processing activity allows. This would require a buffering system, acting as a brief memory of recent events which have yet to be processed centrally. Such a system would provide an extended opportunity for processing inputs effectively, and also for regulating the rate of flow of information. It remains unclear which processing stage(s) – in the terms of the model – would be likely to receive this kind of supportive treatment.

Aside from the involvement of memory in the attentional control of performance, we need to examine the role of memory in our basic model because at each of its processing stages the storage of information seems to be implicated. For example, Stage 2 has such a requirement for the memorized set of alternative stimuli, and Stage 3 has a similar requirement regarding the alternative responses. Stage 4 may be thought of as drawing on stored specifications of motor responses, possibly in the form of procedures for coordinating and sequencing the muscular actions called for (Legge and Barber 1976). It is less intuitively obvious that Stage 1 may also involve special memory demands, although it is the most obvious candidate for the kind of informational support discussed in the previous paragraph. The assumption is that there is an early memory store which involves a very brief form of storage of the information in a fairly direct and unprocessed state. Indeed information models generally include an array of sensory memories or 'buffers' specialized to deal with visual, auditory, olfactory, kinaesthetic, and other types of input. And a distinction is usually made between peripheral memory, as implicated in the operation of Stage 1, and central memory, as drawn on by Stages 2 and 3. The former is highly transient, and the latter relatively long-lived.

Some practical illustrations of the relative degrees of permanence of different kinds of stored information are helpful at this point. Information presented in the form of a succession of manufactured components to the worker in the quality-control section of a production assembly line must be examined while available; the components themselves contribute an external referent so that the memory of their form and characteristics is a trivial and exceedingly transient aspect of the task. On the other hand what constitutes a faulty component must be a matter of more or less permanent record. The command to a military helicopter pilot to change radio frequency must be acted on promptly to ensure continuous radio contact, but until it is acted on, the specification of the new frequency must be remembered. Similarly the address to which a taxi driver is heading has to be memorized for the duration of the journey. (Of course such trivial and transiently needed facts can often be remembered for some time afterwards, as everyone can verify, but this is an incidental and by no means a guaranteed outcome). Other data do call more positively for permanent storage, such as the names and faces of one's friends and colleagues.

Although it is a view that is not without its critics (see Crowder 1982), it is almost conventional – and certainly convenient for us – to distinguish between a short-term active form of central memory, and a more permanent or long-term form. The former provides a kind of working area, in which information can be held for a short period. Such an activity is considered to require effort, and the storage of only a limited amount of information can be handled by this *working memory*, usually found to be about seven or so items for most kinds of materials like digits, names, and so on (Miller 1956). It is thought that the active rehearsal of information (like a telephone number while dialling, or just acquired directions on how to find your way in a strange city) implicates working memory. If information is not maintained by rehearsal then it is rapidly lost, as if subject to spontaneous decay over time. Indeed in the classical experiment by Peterson and Peterson (1959) the subjects tended to forget something as simple as a single string of three letters (e.g., TFK) in less than twenty seconds, if they were prevented from saying it to themselves (by having to count backwards in threes from a given number) in the interval between presentation and testing.

As the term also suggests, working memory is considered to be involved in the work done in transforming, reducing, and elaborating information for the purposes of more economical storage, the combination of information from other sources, and the solving of problems. According to Baddeley and Hitch (1974), working memory is best thought of as a system for the short-term retention of information *and* certain executive operations relating to decision-making and control. The latter function of working memory is poorly specified at present (Gregg 1986) but may be involved in the control of activities like rehearsal (Baddeley 1983). There is no doubt that the organization and temporal coordination of the component processes associated with any activity has to be accounted for, though whether or not this is intimately connected with working memory is not clear.

In short, working memory is a kind of desktop, a workspace for holding information needed temporarily for the purpose of some other processing activity (Anderson 1980), and its holding capacity is limited in amount and time. In contrast permanent memory or long-term memory is considered to have a capacity that is effectively unlimited, not in the sense that one can remember all that one wishes, but that the size of this store is capable for all practical purposes of being extended indefinitely. It is the repository of our knowledge of the world. It includes verbal knowledge (our internal dictionaries, associations between the entries therein, knowledge of grammatical rules, how words are spelled, and so on); knowledge relevant to skills we have learned like how to utter words, play games, ride a bicycle, read a book, and how to get from home to work; our plans and goals; our beliefs and opinions. One final consideration is that information reaching permanent memory is considered in most accounts to arrive via the working memory, so the latter also serves as an information-transfer system.

Although research on memory is somewhat outside the scope of this book, an information-processing model would be incomplete without peripheral and central forms of information storage. Moreover many of the activities we discuss involve the contribution of permanent memory (e.g., remembering faces, reading text, and using items of domestic equipment, etc.). Full treatments of the issues and evidence bearing on central memory are provided in Anderson (1980), Dodd and White (1982), and Gregg (1986). Greene (1987) discusses memory with particular reference to applications and practical problems.

To make full allowance for memory factors within the information processing model (Figure 2.3), we should need to have a detailed view about the structures and processes involved. What has been reviewed in this section makes it clear that commitment to a position at a detailed level is not appropriate for present purposes, nor is it feasible across the range of topics to be discussed because theoretical convergence on such a position has not yet taken place. An attempt is made to capture the general essence of the requirement for information storage and retrieval by adding a general undifferentiated

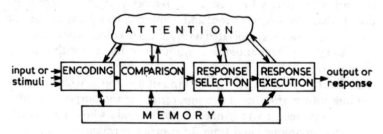

Figure 2.4 Extended-stages model of information processing

'memory' component to the model. This does not explicitly allow for the theoretical refinements and distinctions referred to above, because they remain in most respects a matter of controversy. The general position represented in Figure 2.4 is that memory facilities are available at all stages of information processing, with the activities of storage and retrieval indicated by the two-way flow of information in the diagram.

Methodological considerations

One of the most striking characteristics of the information-processing approach, which is brought out clearly by our 'basic model' is the assumption of the modularity of the processing system. Processing stages are components or modules contributing to the functioning of the overall system. It would be a mistake to be tempted to suppose that the modularity assumption commits us to the strong view that the modules are impregnable islands of processing activity, responsive only to the direct inputs to them and insensitive to the processing operations around them. Whether this is so to a significant extent is part and parcel of what is at issue. It is, after all, perfectly possible to describe a business organization as a collection of departments having a modular form without making the assumption that their operations do not exert mutual influences. The full characterization of the organization will consist of clarifying the functions of the departments, and the nature of the mutual influences. It is true, however, that there is at least one methodological technique in common use in psychology which is geared to the strong assumption of independence of processing stages. It is particularly useful early in an investigation when the outline of the structure of the information-processing sequence is being established. It can also serve to test how far the independence assumption may be pressed.

The 'discovery' of processing stages

The method, known as additive factors logic (sometimes subtractive logic is the term used), is a relatively recent extension of an analytical technique invented over a century ago by Donders, a Dutch physiologist, whose pioneering work on reaction time was published in translation on the occasion of the centenary of his most influential paper (Donders 1969). The notion was that a stage in the information-processing sequence might be added (or deleted) by a well-chosen variation in the task demands. The resulting change in the time taken would indicate the time occupied by the additional (or missing) stage. Consider the basic model in Figure 2.3. Perhaps we could devise a task in which Stage 2 was omitted. The time taken by the new task would, on the assumption that Stages 1, 3, and 4 worked as before, be abbreviated by the amount of time occupied by the central 'classification' stage.

The technique worked well in the hands of Donders, who devised three simple tasks, referred to as the a-, b-, and c-reaction tasks, designed to involve different mixtures of the processes of stimulus detection and discrimination, response choice, and motor responding. All of the tasks involve the detection of the stimulus and the production of the relevant response. The a-reaction task, with the same signal and the same response on each trial, involves only these basic components; no stimulus discrimination is needed and the response has only to be executed not selected. For the b-reaction task there are two possible visual signals, and the subject responds as fast as possible via the appropriate one of a pair of response keys to each of a series of the signals; so there is discrimination between signals, and the selection of one of two responses. The c-reaction task involves the presentation of either of the two signals but only one of them calls for an explicit response; so, according to Donders, there is stimulus discrimination and no response selection. The difference between c and b therefore gives a measure of the time to select the response, and that between c and a gives a measure of the time to discriminate between the stimuli.

The method fell into disuse for various reasons including uncertainty about the nature of the processes involved in the different tasks. For example, it was argued that in the c-reaction, although the response choice is not the same as that for the b-reaction, the subject does nevertheless have to decide whether or not to respond. Hence on this reasoning the differences between b and c, and between c and a, are not those assumed by Donders (for further discussion see Legge and Barber 1976; Pachella 1974; Sternberg 1969). A development of this general line of thinking is due to Sternberg (1969, 1975). According to Sternberg, however, the addition and deletion of stages is not the only means whereby changes in processing times may be brought about. Instead experimental variables can be manipulated that lead to an extension or contraction of the durations of one or more stages.

Sternberg's additive-factors logic, a method for 'discovering' the underlying stages of processing, is widely used, and has become a basic tool of the information processing approach. The rationale of the method of additive factors is that variables (or factors as they are called), with effects on separate independent stages, will be found to influence reaction time in an additive fashion. If the joint effect of two or more factors when applied in combination is the simple sum of the separate effects of the factors considered in isolation, then they are said to be additive. For example, Sternberg (1967) varied stimulus degradation (by presenting the stimulus alone or super-imposed by a checkerboard pattern to decrease its legibility) and memory load (by varying the number of digits to be remembered). He found that the two variables combined additively, and inferred that they influence separate stages. This approach has been applied on a wide scale by Sternberg (1969, 1975) with a notable degree of success (for a recent collation of the results of research analysable in this way, see Wickens 1984).

But while the search for additive factors is accepted as a useful research strategy by stages theorists, it can be argued that it is unsatisfactory on logical grounds because the researcher has to look for factors that do not interact statistically. This requires the acceptance of a statistical null hypothesis, something which is considered to be theoretically suspect. The problem is that it only takes a bad experiment, with crude measurement or poor experi-mental control, to produce evidence consistent with the null hypothesis. Some researchers for this reason feel more comfortable looking for evidence leading to the rejection of a null hypothesis not its acceptance (as suggested by Taylor 1976), and this entails doing experiments in which interactions occur. Although there are alternative explanations a possible inference from evidence of an interaction effect between two factors is that they affect the same processing stage. The method is increasingly hedged about with various technical qualifications and refinements, but continues to be used as a means of probing a problem (Wickens 1984). The additive factors approach is illustrated later in the book.

Summary

In this chapter a general-purpose theoretical framework has been developed in the form of a basic information-processing model of performance. The background of the information-processing approach, in information theory and computing, was traced. A basic model of the processing stages intervening between stimulus and response (input and action) was outlined, and some of its short-comings noted. The nature of information-processing operations was explored, and the need for attentional and memory components in the model was established and a modified working model proposed. Methodological considerations relevant to practical and theoretical developments and applications of the information-processing approach were discussed. This focused on the subtractive and factorial logical methods used in the 'discovery' of processing stages, a set of methods which assume that information processing is of a discoverable modular nature. The outline model developed in this chapter will not be tested to destruction since its role is to provide a means by which the reader may find it convenient to orientate relative to the topics discussed. The next four chapters range over topics combining practical and theoretical issues. More details of the mode of operation of the hypothetical stages and components of the outline model are described.

3 FACES: THEIR PERCEPTION AND MEMORY

In this chapter we examine some of the practical aspects of perceiving and remembering faces, and illustrate why, aside from the intrinsic interest in understanding how we deal with facial information, this is a topic of broad theoretical relevance. We begin with practical questions, such as the possibility of improving face recognition on the part of those for whom it is an important professional skill, some aspects of the procedures used in connection with evidence of face recognition given by eye witnesses, and a discussion of the systems used to help witnesses reconstruct facial images. The inevitably restricted data base that this leads to is supplemented by experimental studies of face recognition taking a closer look at some theoretical issues.

Face recognition may be an element in the evidence given by eye witnesses in legal and similar proceedings, and there is a natural fascination in the question of misidentification because of the unnerving possibility of a prosecution being instigated on the basis of mistaken face identification. In fact a variety of checks and balances are applied in different judiciaries to the admissibility and status of identification evidence, and law enforcement agencies use well-defined procedures to obtain such evidence. In general faces are important social stimuli because they provide one means whereby one individual can recognize or identify another. Furthermore the face may convey information about its owner's age, race, gender, state of health, and emotional state. In some circumstances to fail to be recognized by someone may be a social signal about one's status or attractiveness, and to fail to recognize an acquaintance or friend may be a cause of social embarrassment. Moreover there are some jobs where unsuccessful facial recognition may be a source of professional difficulty, and this includes security attendants and police personnel, and may extend to teachers and social workers and the like. Indeed as we shall see in the next section, the practical importance of quick and reliable recognition of faces has increased to the point where a need has been identified for training courses to teach and improve face recognition skills.

Practical matters: training in face recognition

An existing training course designed to enable the participants to improve their recognition of people was chosen for study by Woodhead, Baddeley, and Simmonds (1979). Various aspects of recognition were incorporated into the training programme, but the main one was face recognition, emphasizing in particular the need to consider the specific features of a face. Training, using the Photofit kit (see p. 43) as the principal demonstration aid, was intensive and lasted for three days. Woodhead, Baddeley, and Simmonds tested the recognition memory of trained and untrained subjects for a set of twenty-four photographs of faces. Relative to their own pre-training scores, the trained subjects showed no improvement in recognition due to training, and they were at no advantage relative to the control subjects. All subjects performed less well on faces that were shown with a change in pose (full-face vs. three-quarter turn) or expression (smiling vs. unsmiling), and could only manage a chance level of performance when the faces were disguised by means of glasses, change of hairstyle, beard, and so forth. Because recognition was affected in this way, it follows that the experimental method was sensitive enough to detect changes in performance that have routinely been obtained in other studies. Any advantage supplied by the training method would have to be subtle indeed to escape detection, and it can at least be concluded that the method did not help trainees to penetrate quite simple variations and disguises.

In two further experiments, Woodhead, Baddeley, and Simmonds used a matching task, with the subject comparing a set of full-face photographs with a longer series of slides including the target faces always in a different pose and with a different expression. So now the observers had the target faces available for reference during the ten-second exposure of each slide, and they had to indicate whether or not the face on the slide matched one of the target faces. Again there was no advantage attributable to training, and if anything the trainees' performance declined slightly.

Woodhead and her colleagues were taken by surprise by the outcome of the investigation because they had been impressed by how the course was put into effect, and were convinced by its rationale. Their preferred explanation as to why the course failed to improve performance (as they measured it) was that it placed undue emphasis on the importance of individual facial features. There is indeed increasing agreement that, while the constituent individual features of a face can be processed in a piecemeal analytic fashion, a complete model of face recognition needs to allow for the possibility that the information in a facial pattern is processed holistically. In this way structural characteristics and relations between features become important, and this is discussed further below.

An alternative explanation for the failure of face recognition to be much influenced by special training is that face recognition levels off in adulthood some way below perfection but is nevertheless not improvable in practice. Why this might be so is not obvious but it should be noted that we do receive exposure to faces on a massive scale, and go on successfully learning to recognize and identify new faces throughout our life spans, at least those faces that are socially significant to us. Face recognition may be unusual in being a perceptual skill, dealing with a 'vocabulary' of thousands of unique but highly similar stimuli, that is more or less universally acquired without special training and seems effortlessly to reach a very high level of proficiency (perhaps in these respects resembling speech recognition). There are of course highly specialized perceptual discriminations, such as are involved in distinguishing between wines, and classifying X-rays, which do improve with extensive practice and training. Others, such as identifying the members of a closed set of stimuli like the letters of the alphabet, reach a level of perfection well before adulthood. Possibly the limiting factors in the case of faces are the high average similarity among them and the sheer size of the set of known faces.

How well are faces remembered?: laboratory studies

Memory for pictures and for words can supply benchmarks against which to compare memory for faces. Picture (and face) memory is most commonly tested in psychological experiments by recognition methods. For example, the task may be to state whether or not the members of a series of stimuli have been seen before, or in a more elaborate variation to indicate which of a pair of stimuli has been seen previously. The subject may in addition meet a more demanding requirement – identifying the stimulus, naming the face or stating what object or scene is depicted. Recall of verbal material is straightforwardly testable by asking the subject to reproduce the to-be-remembered material in oral or written form, but face and picture recall are more problematical because it is difficult to design a satisfactory method for reproducing the stimuli.

Performance levels in picture recognition tasks are usually very high. Following the presentation of a series of stimuli, it is common for recognition to be tested with the use of a sample of the original set of stimuli, the assumption being that the performance on the sample is representative of the subject's memory for the whole set. One typical method of testing recognition is for the subject to be shown on each trial one of the 'old' stimuli from the original presentation along with a new one, and to be asked to indicate which of each old–new pair has been seen before. The subject has to choose one of them and this is called a 'forced-choice' procedure. It was used, for instance, by Shepard (1967) who reported his subjects as achieving 97 per cent accuracy, testing them on sixty-eight old–new pairs to sample a series of 612 pictures; performance was still above chance level 120 days later (57 per cent correct). Standing, Conezio and Haber (1969) reported better than 90 per cent accuracy on a series of 2,560 pictures each shown for ten seconds and tested by 280 forced-choice old vs new trials. Face memory may also be most impressive, as demonstrated by Hochberg and Galper (1967) whose subjects' recognition performance was about 90 per cent correct, on a task procedurally similar to that of Shepard (1967) with a forced-choice test sampling memory for some sixty face photographs by means of fifteen old–new pairs.

Standing (1973) compared memory performance for various kinds of material, including faces, pictures, and words. Picture memory seems to be rather better than face memory when tested on comparable tasks and procedures, and face memory in turn seems rather better than memory for lists of words. Although it makes little practical or theoretical sense to compare levels of performance in this way it is instructive to consider the comparability of the task requirements in order to understand more clearly what is involved in different memory tasks, and possibly what is distinctive about the memory representations involved. Pictures frequently supply a rich variety of visual information and their distinctiveness in this respect may be what marks them out as specially memorable. Clearly pictures may vary in minor details from one occasion or aspect to another, and no doubt the similarity of old and new items in a recognition test could be increased to a point at which performance declined. Investigators have to resort to this kind of manoeuvre to cause a marked drop in picture recognition memory (e.g., Goldstein and Chance 1971).

Although there must be infinitely many ways in which faces may vary physically, the perceptually significant variations among them are surely less than those among pictures, and the intrinsically greater similarity among faces probably accounts for the poorer performance in face recognition tasks. Indeed it testifies to our great sensitivity to the fine differences between faces that performance can be maintained at the high level that it is. Nevertheless it is not difficult to create conditions in which face memory is poor, for example as we have seen, by making quite small changes to the face by the addition or deletion of a feature like a moustache, beard or spectacles, or by a change of hairstyle.

An intriguing and offbeat illustration of what can be achieved in the sphere of identification is provided by the description by Bateson (1977) of a student of his (DKS) who could identify several hundred wild swans at a nature reserve in East Anglia. She claimed that she could remember 450 of them by names she had given them. To test her ability, each of a sample of 100 of some 850 of the swans was photographed, and named by DKS as it was photographed. Presented with a sub-sample of thirty of the clearest photographs, prepared so that incidental background cues were eliminated, she correctly identified twenty-nine of them. The one on which she failed was the only unfamiliar swan in the total of 100 and had not yet been named by her. Her performance was also most impressive on more obscure photographs, and extrapolating from her performance on these photographic samples, it seems that her claim was justified, and was indeed on the conservative side. Aside from illustrating the extraordinary capacity for identification that humans can achieve, this is suggestive of a method that might be used to supply a conservative estimate of how many faces people exposed to a 'closed' community can identify.

In practice faces constitute an open set of stimuli, like many other natural classes of objects like trees, cats, and so on, but unlike them frequently having to be remembered for being unique. In ordinary circumstances therefore we can seem not to be pressed to a limit that becomes apparent, unless we measure performance by some quite rigorous means, such as insisting that the face is associated with the owner's name and other verbal attributes. Although it seems likely that we can each identify hundreds and possibly thousands of faces, this is a matter about which there appears to be no reliable evidence and the actual limitations on real-life face-identification performance, whether for open or closed sets, are simply not known.

Eye-witness testimony: face recognition evidence and procedures

Memory for a face may often be tested in everyday circumstances that are far from ideal and it would not be surprising that performance outside the laboratory fell some way short of the levels that are routinely achieved in experiments. We need to be circumspect about generalizing from laboratory studies of face recognition, although studies like that of Woodhead, Baddeley, and Simmonds (1979; see also Patterson and Baddeley 1977) showing how easily faces may be disguised do seem to have external validity. Face identification by eye witnesses to a crime may be subject to a number of influences not normally operative in laboratory studies, including the very high levels of arousal that may accompany the experience of a criminal act. In general the circumstances in which the face was first seen by an eye witness will differ markedly from those applying when its memory is tested. Indeed if the situational context in which a particular item of information originally occurs needs to be reinstated for memory to be successful, faces present in criminal acts will be hard to recognize or recall (without a realistic mock-up of the crime).

Psychological studies on the matter of face identification range over many other aspects of procedures and circumstances, and there is an increasing amount of specially designed research into the issues surrounding this kind of evidence. Much of the research leads to findings which are noncontroversial and intuitively predictable. Thus face recognition declines with an increasing lapse of time between the initial presentation and the recognition test. Egan, Pittner, and Goldstein (1977) have demonstrated this in a realistic context, confirming the findings of laboratory studies such as that of Shepherd and Ellis (1973). Egan, Pittner, and Goldstein found that performance remained above a chance level until some eight weeks had elapsed. Shepherd and Ellis's evidence includes the finding that distinctive faces, designated as such by perceptual judgements, were forgotten less rapidly than undistinctive ones. Egan, Pittner, and Goldstein also reported a significantly higher correct identification rate for a live lineup than a photographic recognition procedure, with the same chance of making false identifications.

Precautions are necessary to avoid witnesses identifying a suspect while confusing the circumstances of the original encounter, for example, whether at the scene of the crime or when viewing police files of photographs ('mugshots', as they are known). In a study by Brown, Deffenbacher, and Sturgill (1977) a large class of students were asked without warning to pick a so-called criminal from a range of mugshots. The 'criminals' were people who had earlier distributed examination materials to the class, some of whom were seen and some not. Some days later each member of the class picked the 'criminals' from a live lineup. The proportion of criminals 'indicted' if their faces were seen at the mugshot phase as well as on the original occasion of the 'crime' was 0.45. The proportion of indictments for those not seen at the crime or mugshot phases was 0.18. Undoubtedly the participants of this study did not treat it with the seriousness that a genuine crime would merit, and this high false indictment rate may be unrealistic. What is perhaps more important for practical purposes is that the indictment rate was 0.29 if the target face had been seen first at the mugshot phase (and not at the crime). This is reliably higher than the value of 0.18 obtained when the criminal was first and only met at the lineup. Thus an encounter at the mugshot phase served to increase the chance of false indictment. It is possible that subjects simply confused the circumstances of the encounter with the face in question. This is consistent with the findings of another experiment by Brown, Deffenbacher, and Sturgill (1977) in which they showed photographs of faces to subjects in two rooms and later asked them to select the previously seen faces from a series of old-new pairs, and to indicate for each choice in which room it had been seen. While face recognition was very good (96 per cent correct), subjects indicated the correct room at a rate only a little above a chance level (58 per cent).

A further illustration of the practical problems of identification procedures which bears on face recognition, particularly from a methodological point of view, is the effect of similarity on the chance of being picked out from a lineup or identity parade. Davies, Shepherd, and Ellis (1979) found that successful identification of a target face among a set of alternatives (also known as distractors, decoys or foils) was not affected whether the alternatives (including the target) were similar or dissimilar, but the number of false identifications was markedly higher when the set of alternatives was highly similar. In an earlier study, by Buckhout, Figueroa, and Hoff (1975), the target face was emphasized by being printed at an angle and with a distinctive expression, and subjects nominated this face as the suspect more often than when it was not emphasized in this way. This effect was enhanced by suggesting that the suspect was definitely in the display, signifying an even greater readiness by the subject to rely on the misleading cue. How similar the alternatives should be is not a matter that psychologists can decide, of course, though their evidence is a source of information about the likely consequences in terms of false identification rates.

An interesting suggestion about how to assess inter-item similarity among the alternatives for live lineup or photographic procedures has been made by Wells, Leippe, and Ostrom (1979). This is to measure the effective size of the set of alternatives by employing subjects who have not seen the suspect but are given the witness's verbal description of him/her and are asked to identify the suspect on this basis. Clearly if the verbal description refers to the suspect being bearded, for example, and the suspect is the only bearded member of the lineup, then even non-witnesses could infallibly pick the suspect, and the effective size of the lineup would be only one. In general a non-witness should have only a chance probability of selecting the suspect, and so the effective size of the lineup can be estimated from the number of successful non-witnesses. Wells employed this method to assess the lineup procedure in an actual bank robbery case in which a suspect was identified from a lineup of six people, so one-sixth of the non-witnesses should have been successful by chance. In the event the suspect was successfully identified by twenty-five out of forty-one individuals who were not witnesses, and the effective size of the lineup was considered by Wells, Leippe, and Ostrom to be $41/25 = 1.64$ instead of the nominal value of 6. This is near to the point at which the non-suspects could have been omitted!

Further discussion of the specifically 'psycho-legal' considerations to do with face identification is to be found in Deffenbacher and Horney (1981). Relevant evidence is also to be found in the next section on face-recall systems, which are normally employed to help witnesses provide descriptions of suspects.

Recalling a facial image: face-recall systems

Experimental evidence

Drawing a sketch seems the natural and obvious way of recalling a face and communicating it to others, but too few of us are good enough at drawing for this to be a generally useful method, and the police certainly cannot reply on a lightning sketch-artist being on hand among the witnesses to a crime. These considerations, coupled with the apparent difficulty that people have in giving verbal descriptions of faces, account for why face-recall systems like Photofit and Identikit have been in such wide use. These systems are designed principally to help witnesses construct a facial likeness of a person wanted for questioning by the police, and pictures of faces produced by these means are regularly published in newspapers and on television. The Photofit system (Figure 3.1) consists of numerous instances of each of five facial features (forehead–hairline, eyes, nose, mouth and chin). Each feature is a black-and-white photograph taken from a real face, and the whole set of alternatives are arranged as a booklet, with similar features (e.g. thick lips, close-set eyes) grouped together. Witnesses pick out an instance of each feature that is most like the feature of the face being reconstructed, and the selected features are placed together to form a face. This can be revised by replacing features, or by moving forehead and chin, until the witness is satisfied that a good likeness has been produced.

The Photofit system has been experimentally assessed and the conclusion from these experiments is that it has shortcomings as a system for recalling faces (Ellis, Shepherd, and Davies 1975; Ellis, Davies, and Shepherd, 1978). In the first of these studies, subjects asked to reconstruct a pair of Photofit faces had difficulties in selecting the correct set of features from memory, and this was true even when the target face was continuously present. The latter finding is particularly disarming though it could be argued that witnesses have to remember actual not Photofit faces in real life. Hence, in a second experiment, Ellis, Shepherd, and Davies (1975) used photographs of real faces each of which was to be reconstructed from memory using

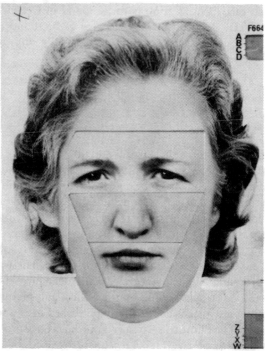

Figure 3.1   A famous face constructed by a skilled Photofit operator with a photograph in front of him. The photograph was that of Margaret Thatcher, the British Prime Minister. Would you have recognized her from the Photofit? See also Figure 3.2

Photofit features, immediately after ten seconds' viewing. The reconstructions were later presented to another independent group of subjects who were asked to compare them with a set of thirty-six photographs including the six original faces. The measure of interest was the success rate of the subjects judging the reconstructions, in selecting the correct original photograph. On a chance basis this would be one in thirty-six, about 3 per cent, whereas in practice it was about 12.5 per cent. This, although better than the chance level, does – as the experimenters comment – leave room for improvement.

The second study by these researchers (Ellis, Davies, and Shepherd 1978) examined some more factors bearing on the quality of Photofit constructions. A short videotaped sequence lasting fifteen seconds or a rather longer one of 2.5 minutes of a man reading a passage was viewed by subjects instructed to pay attention either to the passage itself (with the expectation of receiving a test of comprehension) or to the man's face (with the expectation of making a Photofit construction of it). This difference between conditions relates to the theoretically and practically important distinction between incidental and intentional learning. In this case, the practical significance is of course that witnesses sometimes realize that a crime is being committed and will make a conscious effort to remember details of the event, including the face of anyone involved in it. On other occasions a crime may be viewed by a witness or even experienced at first hand, for example by the victim of a confidence trick, without any awareness that anything untoward has taken place. The results of the experiment, however, while revealing a clear advantage of intention to remember the passage on memory for the passage, showed no advantage in terms of the quality of the Photofit constructions as a consequence of paying attention to the face. And there was no benefit from viewing the recording for longer intervals. Nor in a further experiment was there any improvement by using a trained police operator to administer the Photofit material.

The quality of the reconstructed faces was in all cases assessed by other subjects independently making their judgements on the basis of the similarity of the likeness to the original face. A variety of judgement procedures were used, but the general tenor of the results was that the reconstructions gave only poor impressions of the target faces.

Finally, Ellis, Davies, and Shepherd (1978) compared the Photofit method of producing a facial composite with the use of freehand sketching as a means of recall. While sketches were better than Photofits when the target was present, the results suggested that the Photofit method was rather better as a means of recalling the target from memory. However, the sketches from memory were 'child-like in their simplicity and bore only a vague approximation to the original target faces', and the Photofits were rated only slightly better representations than the sketches.

A comparison of a sketch procedure with the Identikit system was reported by Laughery and Fowler (1980). In the Identikit method numerous alternatives of facial features are supplied in the form of line drawings as transparent sheets, and a composite is prepared by making up an overlay of the selected features. The outcome of this investigation, in which sketch artists worked in collaboration with the subjects, was in considerable agreement with the work of Ellis and his associates. In particular, Laughery and Fowler commented that it was common for subjects who judged the adequacy of the Identikit composites and sketches to comment on how poor the overall quality was.

Why are face-recall systems limited?

The evidence clearly reveals some of the shortcomings of the face-recall systems used in these investigations. It is possible that these inadequacies are attributable to the ways in which they were administered but the research was sponsored by law-enforcement agencies either in Britain or the USA and there seems no basis for assuming that the procedural guidelines of the Photofit and Identikit systems were applied in a damaging or counterproductive way. Nevertheless we can identify some possible reasons why their limitations have been exposed.

One possibility, which is intrinsic to the conduct of the experiments, is that the way in which the composite pictures were judged was inadequate and insensitive, and essentially unfair to the systems being investigated. But this seems effectively ruled out by the fact that Ellis, Davies, and Shepherd (1978), impressed at an early stage of the research by the uniformly low assessments made by the judges of the quality of the reconstructed faces produced by experimental 'witnesses', were careful to use instructions and procedures designed to lead the judges to make quite fine discriminations between the composites produced at the face-recall stage. It was concluded, however, that the judgement procedure was not responsible for the poor showing of the face-recall system.

A second possibility is that the range of features available, although quite extensive, is not wide enough. Certainly subjects sometimes complain of the unavailability among the alternatives of the precise hairstyle, eyes, nose, mouth, or whatever they are looking for. Against this is the finding that there was little gain in having apparently unlimited flexibility in the choice of features, as offered by the sketch procedures. It is not really suprising that most people prove to have extremely limited prowess at sketching faces (Ellis, Davies, and Shepherd 1978). However, the failure of proficient portrait artists to mediate the production of good likenesses (Laughery and Fowler 1980) suggests that it is not merely a matter of the alternative features being restricted that accounts for the poor performance of Photofit and Identikit methods (but see Figure 3.2).

A third factor could be that having to attend to the alternative

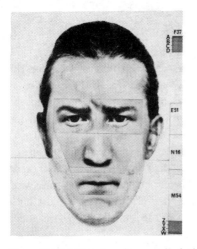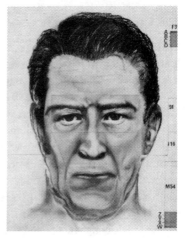

Figure 3.2 (left) Another photograph of a famous face was used for the Photofit by a skilled operator. *(right)* The result was then 'enhanced' by free-hand drawing, among other things, to create a more natural and better likeness. The original photograph was of Ronald Reagan, President of the United States. Would you have recognized him from the constructed image? An experienced operator noted that 'there are times when the basic Photofit is a close likeness, but more often than not we need to enhance them'.

features in relative isolation actually interferes with the memory of the face being constructed. A version of this hypothesis was tested by Davies and Christie (1982). Subjects were shown a target face and were then required to judge the similarity to one feature of the target face of a series of Photofit facial features. Finally they had to select a particular feature on the original face from a set of alternatives. A control group saw no intervening faces and simply made the final selection. Recognition of the target feature was not impaired by making the intervening judgements about features, whether these were seen in isolation, or in the context of a Photofit face. This is suggestive that memory for facial information is not subject to interference from viewing facial features, but it does not constitute a strong test of the hypothesis, which does after all apply to face recall not feature recognition.

Another possibility addressed by the same researchers is that faces are not in fact remembered as collections of isolated features. The point is that if memory for a face principally involves an *integrated* representation of the face, then methods heavily dependent on an analytical consideration of features in isolation will be dubious for the purpose of mediating face recall. Davies and Christie (1982) addressed this question, somewhat indirectly, using their experimental paradigm in which similarity judgements of a series of facial features are made relative to a given feature of a target face. The pattern of similarity scores agreed very well whether or not the features were seen in isolation or as part of a Photofit face so long as the original target face was continuously present. But when the target face was absent, there was good agreement only when the features being judged were themselves presented in a facial (Photofit) context, and not when they were presented in isolation. It appears that the overall perceptual context of a facial pattern makes its individual features more salient. The conclusions of this study were that faces are stored in an integrated form, from which it is difficult to extract feature information, and that face-recall systems may need to be developed which reflect this.

One way would be to start with one of a limited set of alternative *prototype* faces whose feature components may be changed, but which supply an integrated external representation of a face as a baseline. This and other possibilities will no doubt become increasingly feasible with the rapid development of information technology, using computer graphics to supply the repertoire of alternative features, facial frameworks and perhaps ways of varying spatial relations between features. The use of computers to help in the construction of a facial image is in early stages though there are already some interesting approaches (Laughery, Rhodes and Batten 1981). Prototype theory is discussed on pp. 58–62.

One remaining consideration that may bear on the effectiveness of Photofit and Identikit systems is that the initial stage of the procedure entails the verbal description of the target face being elicited by an operator, prior to the construction of the composite image. The composite is also constructed with the operator's help. Thus subject and operator are in verbal interaction prior to and during the construction of the composite, and in particular verbal information about the face is demanded of the subject. This may be in part responsible for the poor fidelity of constructed faces relative to the originals. This could be due either to the limited ability of subjects to give accurate verbal descriptions of a face, or because verbalization interferes with the visualization processes that face recall may depend upon. On the other hand, it is possible, as Christie and Ellis (1981) have observed, that the common assumption that verbal descriptions of faces are inaccurate is itself false, and that face-recall systems fail to tap this source of information efficiently.

Verbal description of faces

Indeed, the evidence relating to methods of verbal description tends to bely this assumption. For example, Goldstein, Harmon, and Lesk (1971) developed an extensive set of features (e.g. face shape – square/round/oval/long; eyebrows – thin/medium/bushy; cheeks – sunken/average/full; hair – short/average/long; etc.) for the classification of photographed faces. The average descriptions by a group of 'jurors' of a collection of target faces were given to a further group of subjects for them to identify the faces. Each subject was given a set of statements of the feature values assigned by the jurors to a particular face. With a population of 255 targets, an identification was achieved in just over seven steps (features) with an identification accuracy of 53 per cent. As a starting point this is not unimpressive but clearly can be bettered. Later work by these authors (Goldstein, Harmon, and Lesk 1972) achieved considerable improvement by placing the human subject in tandem with a computer.

It has to be remembered that face memory is not being tapped by this research on verbal descriptions, since the judges were working with photographs of the target face continuously present. It does show, however, that verbal descriptions of faces can with suitable procedural refinements be highly informative (as no doubt generations of poets and novelists have confidently believed). A correspondingly sophisticated approach to the verbal description of memorized faces seems to be needed. Christie and Ellis (1981) have done some preliminary work here, comparing the accuracy of Photofit constructions and verbal descriptions of faces. Subjects made an initial free verbal description of a face which they had just seen for sixty seconds, and a Photofit likeness was then compiled. Both descriptions and Photofits were then assessed by how well judges could match them to the targets, and verbal descriptions were markedly better than the Photofit constructions. Interestingly there was no correlation between the accuracy of the two methods of recall. Thus a subject who was good at making a verbal description was not necessarily good at using the Photofit to reconstruct the target face, and in the light of this result it seems that the Photofit may not be limited by the subject's ability to make verbal descriptions. The results of this investigation suggest that it may be worth examining methods involving verbal description, at least as a major and systematic component, for their potential as methods of face recall. Questions that remain, for instance, include whether recall by one method helps or hinders recall by another, and whether faces that are hard for someone to describe verbally are also hard to reconstruct.

Applied research and theoretical issues

Before leaving the more practically orientated discussion of face perception and memory, it should be noted that a wide range of quite general issues of a theoretical kind have been touched on. Aside from the questions specifically about faces (like what psychological processes are involved in recognizing faces, and what form the internal representations of faces take), we have had occasion to refer to the effects of arousal, attention, and context on memory, and the biases that influence the decisions that people make about uncertain perceptual evidence. There is unfortunately no scope in this book to follow up all of the issues raised to a satisfactory level of analysis. Further discussion of general issues will be found elsewhere (e.g. in Eysenck 1984; Gregg 1986).

In centring the discussion on practical aspects of face recognition and recall, it is apparent that theoretical issues have not been the driving force behind the applications research. This research has understandably been motivated by practical problems and issues, inevitably raising matters of theoretical interest in an incidental and haphazard fashion. So it is appropriate to review the theoretical analysis of face perception and memory to provide a more co-ordinated framework for discussion, and to illustrate explicitly the links between theory and practice.

Theoretical issues

In the remainder of the chapter we consider some of the theoretical accounts of face perception and memory that have been advanced, and raise issues about the nature of the information-processing operations involved in the perception and memory of visual stimuli. We consider, too, whether face perception may be influenced by verbal, conceptual, and contextual information, and what this may imply about how faces are represented internally. And we ask whether the special significance of faces requires us to postulate processing mechanisms specialized to deal with them. We begin by considering the nature of the information conveyed by a face that allows us to recognize it as a face, and as one we have seen before.

Features in perceiving and judging faces

Theoretical discussions of face recognition frequently refer to facial features, and aids for reconstructing faces from memory (e.g. Photofit and Identikit) often present the options to the subject in the form of building blocks based on features like eyes, mouth, nose, and chin. There may be more to face recognition than this, including the spatial relationships between features, and the overall shape of the face. How important these different aspects are is theoretically of interest; they may for example be weighted differentially, and scrutiny of a face may be ordered in particular ways (top to bottom, for example). This section asks what aspects of faces are perceptually important, and considers ways of assessing their relative standing in face recognition.

A frequency count of the number of spontaneous mentions of features used by a group of subjects in describing a series of monochrome face photographs was reported by Shepherd, Davies, and Ellis (1981). The 'features' most commonly mentioned (in order of decreasing frequency) were hair, eyes, nose, eyebrows, face shape, chin, lips, mouth, ears, face lines, complexion, forehead, and cheeks. Hair was referred to about twice as often as eyes, the next most common feature (0.27 vs 0.13). References to the last items in the list were quite uncommon (0.01 for cheeks, for instance). Aspects of the upper face seem to be drawn to subjects' attention more than the lower face. The relative importance of the upper face region is also suggested by evidence that faces are harder to recognize if the upper part of the face is concealed (Fisher and Cox 1975). The recognition of individual features of a face in isolation is quite difficult, although there is some evidence that the eyes are more informative than the mouth (e.g. McKelvie 1976).

Technically more sophisticated methods for assessing the relative informational status of different parts of the face include the use of eye-movement recording and techniques such as multidimensional scaling. What an observer looks at when viewing a picture may be discovered by recording his or her eye movements by various photographic techniques, or other means such as monitoring the electrical changes that occur on the surface of the skin around the eyes as their muscle systems point them in different directions. The assumption may be made that what is looked at is what is processed, and hence highly informative regions will tend to be fixated more often and for longer periods than areas low in information value.

Mackworth and Morandi (1967) recorded the eye movements of one group of subjects as they examined a picture and asked a second independent group to indicate the most informative regions of the picture. The regions concentrated on by the viewing and the information-judging groups tended to agree. Although the parallel experiment for faces does not seem to have been done, the eye movements of observers looking at photographs of faces were recorded by Walker-Smith, Gale, and Findlay (1977). They found that fixations tended to be aimed at the central area of the face, mainly around the eyes, nose, and mouth. Fixation patterns were subject otherwise to marked individual differences, and the sequence (though not the overall distribution) of fixations varied with task demands. It is not surprising that individuals vary in the emphasis which they place on different facial attributes, and hence in their fixation patterns when gazing at a face. Moreover for task differences (comparison of faces presented successively vs simultaneously) to be associated with differences in scanning patterns is suggestive of their different informational priorities. The subjects took little more than a second or so to decide about each face they saw so the picture emerging from this study is understandably limited. In the light of these findings the pessimistic appraisal of such methods by Shepherd, Davies, and Ellis (1981), who concluded that they are unreliable and their findings equivocal, seems premature.

Shepherd, Davies, and Ellis (1981) have described some promising developments for discovering which attributes of faces are perceptually salient. The methods in question are based on the use of multidimensional scaling techniques. These are statistical techniques that are used to reveal the dimensions and relationships among them underlying subjective judgements of a collection of stimuli. Such techniques are considered to be particularly useful when the physical dimensions on which subjects base their judgements are obscure, or when these dimensions are psychological ones (e.g. attractiveness). The similarities (and differences) among a set of faces, for instance, may be judged by asking subjects to sort them into categories containing like items. Another method of assembling the basic data is to ask subjects to rate the similarity of each pair of faces, or to indicate the least similar of a triad of faces. No rules for making the judgements are otherwise imposed, but any systematic tendency for subjects to refer to common attributes of the stimuli should be apparent on the application of an appropriate multidimensional scaling technique. This is signalled in the output of the scaling process as one or more dimensions around which the similarity data are organized. The labelling of the dimensions may be achieved by referring the data so obtained to independent measures of the stimuli. The investigator may do this, for example, by asking a separate group of subjects to assess the stimuli in terms of a set of scales, named on the basis of other independent considerations and sources of evidence.

This quite elaborate procedure has been used in a number of investigations reviewed by Shepherd, Davies, and Ellis (1981). It is clear that the relative homogeneity of the faces being judged influences the pattern of the findings that emerges, and seems to indicate a moving frame of reference in terms of which the faces are judged. This is reasonable since if, for instance, the faces are all hairless as opposed to including a mixture of faces with and without beards and moustaches, then comparisons in terms of facial hair are precluded, and subjects have to look elsewhere for points of similarity and difference. Homogeneity regarding race and to a lesser extent gender also influences the choice of dimensions on which faces are judged. Shepherd, Davies, and Ellis concluded that hair (length, colour, texture) and face shape seem to be the most salient features according to the multidimensional scaling studies. Interestingly, shape is an aspect of a face that is not so easy to manipulate in experimental studies, and it is not an aspect that is readily available for variation in recall systems like Identikit and Photofit, though this should be within the bounds of possibility with computer-driven graphic facilities. It is also of considerable theoretical significance that the overall shape of the face, a configural property which is difficult to conceptualize as a compound of elementary components, is important in perceptual judgements of faces.

The differential importance of different aspects of facial patterns thus provides one source of evidence about the nature of the representations of faces in memory. By the same token the data from these studies may help to indicate the kind of perceptual processes involved in recognizing and identifying faces.

Are there face-specific analysing mechanisms?

Faces constitute a class of visual stimuli that do seem rather special in several respects, partly because of their everyday significance in conveying visual information about personal attributes (e.g. age and gender), and emotional state. And there are other indications that have led some theorists (e.g. Yin 1969) to consider that special face-analysing mechanisms need to be postulated. The evidence that led Yin to this conclusion included the experimental demonstration that face recognition is particularly affected by certain trans-formations. Photographic negatives of faces are, for example, hard to recognize (Galper 1970). Moreover as Yin (1969) himself showed, faces are harder to recognize when presented upside-down, even though the basic form of the face is not affected by such transformations. The stimuli used by Yin for comparison purposes, as 'mono-oriented' stimuli, included pictures of houses, normally never seen upside-down; although also worse recognized when inverted, these were affected much less than faces. The evidence is subject to different interpretations, however. For example, it is objected that the enormous prior experience that people have of discriminating upright faces makes it difficult to make a proper comparison (Goldstein and Chance 1981).

There are two other strands of evidence bearing on the special stimuli/mechanisms suggestion. First there is a body of research on the developmental course of face recognition (Carey 1980). It seems that the development of face recognition is paralleled by few other perceptual abilities. Of particular interest is the finding that although the rudiments of face perception are established in very young children (by about 6–7 months according to Carey 1981), there is a protracted developmental improvement up to the age of about 10, and during adolescence a temporary *decline* in face recognition skills (Flin 1980) appears to occur. Nonetheless this may simply reflect the unique combination of component skills on which adult face recognition depends rather than a reliance on a single special mechanism.

The second area of research which is relevant is concerned with the neuropsychological condition known as *prosopagnosia*. This is a rare condition observed in some brain-damaged patients and involves an inability to identify faces, even those of the most familiar persons. The patient continues to be able to name the parts of individual faces, and can even distinguish between faces, but appears to be unable to identify what makes a face individual (Hécaen 1981). It is often associated with other disorders of visual-object recognition but it does occasionally occur in a relatively 'pure' form. It is consistent with the idea that we are equipped with a special face-processing mechanism (Yin 1970; Whiteley and Warrington 1977), though this is a matter of dispute (e.g. Ellis 1975, 1981).

In any event the affected site in the prosopagnosic patient's brain seems to be in the right hemisphere according to clincial and anatomical findings (Benton 1980; Hécaen 1981). This is consistent with the view that psychological functions are lateralized in the cortex, and in particular that the right cerebral hemisphere is associated with visuospatial tasks (while the left is concerned with verbal behaviour). The particular involvement of the right hemisphere in processing facial stimuli is supported by studies with normal subjects (Patterson and Bradshaw 1975; Rizzolatti, Umilta, and Berlucchi 1971). These show faster or more accurate processing in face-recognition tests when the stimuli are projected to the right hemisphere than when stimuli are projected to the left hemisphere (this is achieved by presenting the stimuli to the left and right visual fields respectively). Of course this evidence does not force one to the conclusion that face processing entails special mechanisms. It has been noted by Bradshaw and Nettleton (1981) that superior face-recognition performance when stimuli are presented to the right hemisphere is consistent with that hemisphere's special capability for dealing with holistic properties of stimuli. Indeed they advance the general proposition that the verbal vs spatial distinction traditionally made in relation to the left and right hemisphere should be replaced by one in terms of analytic vs holistic processing, a distinction suggestive relative to face recognition as we see in the next section.

Some of the strongest evidence in support of the special-mechanism hypothesis was presented by Whiteley and Warrington (1977) who discussed three clinical cases with relatively clearcut symptomatology, suggesting a selective deficit in processing faces in company with a variety of other perceptual difficulties. Thus the three patients varied in their performance on tasks involving object and letter recognition and only showed a consistent impairment on a face-matching task.

Critics of the special mechanism hypothesis contend that although faces should be considered as special stimuli, there is nothing unique about the information-processing mechanisms that are used in recognizing and memorizing faces. One argument, for example, is that face perception samples the processes normally available to deal with visual stimuli, but because of their complex (indeed dynamic) composition, it is just the particular configuration of processes used in face processing that is unique, and no special mechanism needs to be invoked. Hence although a low correlation is found between face recognition and performance on various elementary perceptual tests of ability, it might need to be a wide-ranging battery of tests that would adequately capture the set of abilities tapped by face perception. Moreover, the battery would need to incorporate complex abilities that relied on integrating attributes of a stimulus and assessing relations between them. The special mechanism hypothesis seems to have little merit *per se*, but does make the point that different classes of visual stimuli may draw upon a range of processes currently little understood. Recognition of letters and digits may depend on a restricted subset of the processes available for pattern recognition at large, and a wider subset be called on for the perception of faces. Some of the accounts of simple pattern recognition, and the terms they routinely use, are difficult to apply in the explanation of face recognition, and this is illustrated in the following section.

Feature analysis and face recognition

Faces are one class of 'patterns' that can be recognized by humans, and theoretical discussion of face perception owes a great deal to the wider theoretical and experimental literature dealing with pattern recognition (including patterns such as letters, digits, and other symbols). A treatment of the basic issues and theoretical alternatives is to be found in Neisser (1967; see also Dodd and White 1982). Neisser's (1967) own theoretical model of pattern recognition has been highly influential, and assumes that recognition involves the analysis of patterns as combinations of elementary features (for letters and digits, these features are thought to be straight lines and curves). The internal representation of a given pattern may consist of a list of these features (Neisser 1967), and a structural description of their interconnections (Sutherland, 1973). Further questions arise concerning the mode of operation of the model, for instance whether features are processed in sequential or parallel fashion.

This is known as the serial vs parallel processing issue. Research by Bradshaw and Wallace (1971) serves to illustrate what may be involved. In this study the investigators presented pairs of faces about which subjects had to make same–different judgements. The stimuli were composed of Identikit features, and the number of 'features' that differed was systematically varied. The number of features should not, according to Bradshaw and Wallace, affect reaction time if they are processed in parallel. Since there was a systematic decrease in reaction time as the number of discrepant features increased, Bradshaw and Wallace concluded that there was no evidence of parallel processing. They likewise concluded on the basis of this effect on reaction time that the faces were not being processed as 'gestalten' or wholes, as opposed to being treated as a collection of independent features. It could, however, be argued that the task heavily predisposed the subjects to use an analytical perceptual strategy, focusing on individual features in a serial fashion. It may not therefore be representative of how faces are normally handled by the perceptual system. An experiment by Matthews (1978) is therefore of interest, because in what was more or less a replication of the Bradshaw and Wallace study, he examined the detail of subjects' performance again in a same–different task, using police Identikit line-drawings of pairs of faces (differing on between one and six features). He also found that subjects were quicker to decide the fewer the features there were in common. But, looking more closely at the results, it was found that if the differences involved the hairline/forehead region of the faces, the eyes, or the chin, then subjects made uniformly fast responses. The detailed effects on speed of responding suggested a serial top-to-bottom scan and comparison of the two faces. There therefore seem to be a limited set of 'primary', possibly structurally definitive, features which are helpful in the development and specification of a gestalt into which the remaining 'secondary' features can be fitted. The primary features resemble what others refer to as 'configural' properties.

Another relevant study is that of Homa, Haver, and Schwartz (1976), who were concerned to pursue in the context of face recognition the analogy with the word-superiority effect – that is, the superior performance subjects show at identifying individual letters when embedded in a word than in a non-word. Accordingly their subjects were asked to indicate which feature (eyes/nose/mouth, each chosen from among five variations) had been presented on a face which they had just seen. The feature in question was not known to them until the face had been removed (masked by 'noise') from view. The faces were seen in a normal intact form (analogous to the 'word' format) or in a scrambled version (analogous to the 'non-word' format). In the event the scrambled faces led to poorer recognition of the features than the intact version, and to this extent the parallel with the word-recognition literature was upheld. Homa, Haver, and Schwarz contended on this basis that a face can act as a perceptual gestalt in facilitating the processing of its parts. How this might work is not clear, but it could be that the intact faces are at an advantage because the spatial predictability of the features of an intact face would enable the use of ingrained order for encoding the individual facial features.

Walker-Smith, Gale, and Findlay (1977), on the basis of eye-movement patterns recorded while subjects viewed faces, proposed that a 'general gestalt' is registered during the initial fixation. This enables a face 'framework' to be established, and the relative locations of the features are found via peripheral vision, without directly viewing them. The individual features typically are directly fixated, and the information derived thereby is fitted into the facial framework, which supplies a configural specification of the face. The framework appears to have perceptual precedence over the fine-grained featural information. Hence there seem to be two types of information in faces; subjects can be viewed as utilizing a simple list specifying the appearance of individual features, together with configural information specifying the spatial relations between them. The face as a whole may therefore serve as a framework – a configural context – that supports detailed visual analysis, possibly by enabling the details to be processed according to a routine order.

Facial prototypes

It is not uncommon to hear a person's face being described as Churchillian, or someone being thought to be the spitting image of Paul Newman, or in a less complimentary way being considered to have the look of a spaniel. The degree of resemblance does not have to be very great to be commented on (and challenged by others), though it is very striking in the case of identical twins, and in general people often spontaneously remark on the likeness of one face to another. It seems that the judgement of perceptual similarity poses no particular problem for most of us, and is the basis of investigations such as the study of Shepherd, Davies, and Ellis (1981) discussed above (p. 53).

Indeed some theorists have begun to ask if the recognition of faces is mediated by their resemblance to one of a limited set of prototype faces. The key idea in prototype theory (which has general application to a number of areas of cognition and perception) is that the resemblance between stimuli is important in their recognition, and many stimuli may be linked with one prototype. Each stimulus belongs to a class and each member of the class has some attributes in common with other members of the class. The representative member of the class is its prototype and members of the class not only share some attributes with one another (and of course with the prototype), but also deviate in various degrees from the prototype. The prototypes could be thought of as anchors for judgement and recognition.

The representation of a face would on this reasoning take the form of a record of the relevant prototype along with a note of any discrepancies at the level of the individual features. This would inject into the theoretical treatment of face recognition a mechanism that would seem to be geared to accommodate the evidence of configural, holistic, effects that are presently hard to interpret as featural effects. Prototypes could exist for other types of stimuli like letters and so this is not a way of resurrecting the special-mechanism hypothesis. Recognition could then be assumed to involve a two-stage process, in which the face to be recognized is first classified as an instance of one of the prototypes, followed by detailed analysis of featural deviations. The judgement of the perceptual similarity of two faces could be mediated by the prototype or the feature level of representation. Further elaboration of the basic assumptions, regarding the independence and relative timing of the two stages, for example, would be necessary for a predictive account of face perception and memory to be developed.

There is little evidence on the prototype theory of face recognition, and somewhat surprisingly it has only recently begun to be experimentally investigated. Moreover the evidence at first sight is not promising. Ellis (1981) described a version of prototype theory in which the prototypes are composites formed by a kind of averaging process across a set of similar faces. In one experiment subjects briefly viewed each of a series of faces taken from groups of similar faces (their similarity was established in advance by a multidimensional scaling method). Recognition of these target faces was tested with an old–new procedure with accompanying 'distractors', none of which had been seen before. These included photographic composites of the groups of faces from which the targets had been drawn. The other distractors were normal photographs selected from groups of faces unrelated to the targets. If a prototype was formed during the initial viewing, the composite distractors would be expected to have a high prototypical value, being more similar to the prototype for the original faces than to the unrelated faces. The ease of classifying the composite distractors was no poorer than for normal distractors, despite the presumably high prototypical value of the former. This suggests that prototypes may not be readily formed by brief experience of the sort entailed in this experiment, and in any case it is not really clear what function they would serve. It is possible also that the appearance of the photographic composite faces was sufficiently unusual to offset any disadvantage arising from their manufactured similarity to the targets.

On account of these kinds of unpromising signs, Ellis (1981) was inclined to favour an alternative version of prototype theory, advanced by Light, Kayra-Stuart, and Hollander (1979) on the basis of a study of people's judgements of the 'typicality' of faces. Its basic assumption is that there is a single facial prototype which 'typical' faces tend to resemble and which distinctive or unusual faces tend not to resemble. A face may differ from the prototype on any facial dimension and its similarity to the prototype will decide whether or not it is easy to recognize. A face resembling the prototype will be harder to recognize than a distinctive one.

Another variant on the prototype idea which seems not to have been explored is that we have a prototype for each face that we know, from a particular standard or a preferred aspect, together with a set of transformations by which to recover any view of it. In the light of our varying ability to recognize faces, it would need to be assumed that the quality of the prototype (or some other aspect of the representation process) varies for different faces. The storage requirements of such a system, which is an important consideration according to some theorists (Neisser 1967) would be defined by the number of faces that can be efficiently recognized, and although this appears to be impressive (see p. 38) it does not seem absurdly high relative to the capacity of the nervous system.

The notion that a face may be remembered in terms of a preferred perspective is consistent with the more general proposition that the perception of objects involves a 'privileged' or 'canonical' perspective (Palmer, Rosch, and Chase 1981). These investigators introduced the idea of an object's canonical perspective to convey the idea that there is an aspect of an object that is best for the purpose of imagining it, and from which it is considered subjectively best represented. Subjects were shown a collection of objects (shoe, telephone, horse, etc.) photographed from twelve different perspectives (front, back, top, side, side-top, back-top, etc.) and were asked to judge how good each picture was an example of the object in question. Another task was to imagine each object in turn and to report how much of the various surfaces of the object (top, side, back, front) could be seen in the imaged version. A further task was to take a photograph of each object to depict it optimally. The results for the different tasks agreed very well and provided strong evidence for a variable which the investigators described as canonicalness of perspective. This variable appears to be closely related to the visibility of aspects of the target objects. It was further found that objects presented in their canonical perspective were recognized faster and more accurately than in other perspectives. The time to recognize a non-canonical representation of an object may indicate the nature of the transformation process needed to map that view onto the canonical form (cf. Shepard and Metzler 1971). Of course this does not tell us what a prototype – if this is what a canonical perspective amounts to – consists of. It could be a 'template', a more or less holistic graphic copy of the object, optimized for perceptual purposes. But the canonical form could just as easily be a description in terms of a collection of features (which have as a collection been optimally represented).

It will be noticed that no evidence has been given that directly supports or even tests prototype theory. There is some, though it mainly involves the use of specially designed and rather artificial stimuli like patterns of dots (Posner and Keele 1968). Stimuli of a more natural kind were studied by Rosch et al. (1976). Subjects were asked to name a variety of objects, each of which could be labelled by a term at different levels of the hierarchy to which it belonged. Thus a tulip may be called a plant at the most general (superordinate) level, a flower at the intermediate level, and a tulip at the most specific (subordinate) level. Responses were most commonly at the intermediate level, using what Rosch et al. termed the basic-level name (flower in the present case), and such responses were given faster than the superordinate or subordinate category names. It is arguable from this that the basic-level name relates to the prototype of the category.

Whether the prototype concept will prove useful in the context of face perception remains to be seen. It is clear that a more refined theoretical account, and some direct experimental analysis, will be needed – and no doubt is forthcoming. Three possible and largely speculative variations on the prototype concept pertinent to face-perception theory have been identified, and their varying practical ramifications should be considered. There may be a single prototype for the human face (as suggested by Ellis 1981), and variations from it perhaps along feature-specific dimensions would constitute the variations among faces. The prototype could thus serve as an encoding framework, but the account of face perception would otherwise be given in terms of feature processing. A second possibility is for there to be a number of basic face prototypes, standing as reference points in a perceptual domain representing the dimensions on which faces may be perceptually distinguished. They could be sited in the domain to make memorizing and remembering faces efficient, and might at the same time be optimally distinctive in perceptual terms. A third alternative (suggested by the work on canonical perspectives) is that each face is remembered in unique prototypical form, as a characteristic view of the individual. In the second two cases, the possibility has to be admitted of an individual-differences factor; there is no reason at present to suppose that prototypes are shared. Practical consequences flow from these different possibilities, for instance as to the appropriateness of supplying prototype faces as face-recognition aids.

Influence of conceptual and contextual information

Visual perception is not achieved as an island of independent-processing activity, and the final issue to be discussed relates to some of the non-perceptual factors that may influence the perception and memory of faces. The research includes work complementing the studies on the direct verbal description of faces (p. 99), and is concerned with the contribution of indirect verbal factors. The first indications, however, are that the verbal mediation of face recognition is ineffective. Thus Chance and Goldstein (1976) found that subjects asked to describe faces verbally, or to associate verbally to them, were one week later at no advantage relative to a group asked merely to remember the faces; and the 'verbal coding' group were unable to recall what they had said about the faces. Furthermore, Cohen and Nodine (1978) found that an intervening verbal task interfered less with face-recognition performance than did a visual task. On the other hand, Kerr and Winograd (1982) found that faces were recognized better if the subject was supplied with a verbal context (e.g. he smokes cigars, she's a psychiatrist, etc.) to accompany the presentation of the faces to be memorized. Recognition was improved most when the initial encoding context was reinstated at the time of face recognition. The discrepancy between these sources of evidence is apparent. The greater sensitivity of the Kerr and Winograd method of assessing the influence of verbal information on face recognition is one possible reason but it is clear that further work needs to be done.

Another important development in research on face perception concerns the role of familiarity. There are several lines of work (including neuropsychological and developmental studies) where the distinction between familiar and unfamiliar faces has been commented upon. Ellis (1981), for example, argues that we first have to recognize a face as a face, and then check it for evidence of familiarity. An experimental study by Bruce (1979) has also examined this question and has made an interesting additional contribution relating to the influence of conceptual information on face recognition. Bruce used distractors in a visual-search task with faces as the stimuli that were similar or dissimiliar to the target face, one of four well-known politicians. The distractors were otherwise the faces of other famous or unfamiliar people, and the familiar distractors were either also of politicians, or actors and media people. Naturally the configural differences (i.e. arising from the dissimilar distractors) were quickly spotted. Also unfamiliar faces were as a whole rejected as non-targets more quickly than familiar ones. Most interestingly it was also found that among the familiar distractors, responses were faster if the faces belonged to people from a different profession (i.e. non-politicians).

It appears from Bruce's study that visual and categorical analyses proceed in parallel, both (according to Bruce) supplying positive and negative evidence to a decision process, a response being issued when a threshold amount of information is accumulated. The conceptual analysis assesses both familiarity and occupation-related information and generates the greatest amount of positive information in the case of a familiar and same-occupation distractor. Rather than information about the visual and conceptual aspects of a stimulus being acquired in a strictly parallel but independent fashion, the two processes may work interactively. The familiarity of a face seems to be established very quickly, and may serve to narrow the range of alternatives which are being considered. What 'occupation-related' information consists of is not clear, since it is not obvious that politicians or 'media personalities' possess unique visual characteristics, though they may belong to more fundamental classes defined in terms of physical attractiveness. In any event the plainest implication of this research is that the perceptual processes underlying the recognition of faces are not simply driven by the information given by the face as a stimulus. The contrast here is a generally relevant one between 'bottom-up' and 'top-down' processing. The former refers to processing which is driven by the data in the stimulus array, and the latter to a range of higher-order influences including the familiarity and categorical properties of the stimulus.

Recent theoretical developments have focused on how familiar faces are recognized, and parallels with how words are recognized have been mooted (Hay and Young 1982; Bruce 1983). Experimental results from the word-recognition literature (such as the priming effects discussed in Chapter 6) have been replicated using faces as stimuli for recognition. The similarities and differences in the complex patterns of findings are used, together with the analogy with word-recognition models such as that of Morton (1979), to throw light on the nature of face recognition. In Morton's model, for instance, an account of the effect of context on word recognition is given, and Bruce and Valentine (1986) have tested predictions for a parallel account of the effect of context on face recognition. How far such analogies can be taken is not clear, but one of the benefits may be that we shall learn more about the 'semantics' of faces, a theoretical advance that should also be of practical value.

Another important development is the acknowledgement that an expanded theoretical framework is needed for a successful account of face perception and memory. It is not much of an imaginative leap to see that what we have considered in this chapter is a limited part of the overall process of perceiving and remembering *people*. We concentrated on the contribution of facial information – indeed we characterized the issues in terms of the perception and memory of faces. We even excluded the matter of how other visual information (regarding posture, gait, body shape, clothing, and so forth) enters the process. However, in the present section it was hinted that information which is not given in the facial pattern, and is merely associated with it (like verbal context), may serve to facilitate the perceptual process (and perhaps sometimes to impede it). What may be termed the significance or meaning of a face (the owner's name, relationship with the perceiver, and other personal information) seem likely to be bound up with the processing of the face. Indeed there is a complex parcel of information associated with any individual, and an array of non-verbal signals that a face may deliberately or inadvertently convey. Moreover the use of facial and related information normally occurs in the course of everyday social interactions, another potential source of influence on the processing of facial pattern information. So a comprehensive account of the latter may need to recognize its component status in the larger endeavour of understanding the perception and memory of persons. Facial information can give access to other personal information, and the reverse may also be true as is suggested by evidence of verbal-context effects (e.g. Kerr and Winograd 1982). The former is acknowledged in recent theoretical developments which expand the framework within which the perception of faces is considered (e.g. Bruce and Young 1986). There is no space to examine these larger perspectives, but they can be expected to be an increasingly prominent part of future basic and applied research.

Summary

A framework for understanding the psychological processes underlying face perception and memory has been presented in this chapter. Some implications of applied and basic research for such a framework have been considered, and it should be noted that there is mutual support in these different enterprises. According to both approaches, a conventional account in terms of feature analysis is effective within limits, but it needs to be supplemented perhaps by recognizing the importance of some holistic form of influence. The latter may be thought of as some configural information, which is descriptive of the relational qualities of the assembly of individual features. It may be related to the proposed concept of a facial prototype, some support for which is apparent in both applied and basic research. Different facial features contribute differently to face recognition, and their relative importance for certain perceptual judgement tasks has been studied.

The applied research on face recognition and recall includes the question of the improvability of face recognition, which in adults may be hard to effect. The major theoretical point, concerning the explanatory shortfall of feature analysis, is also made by the research on face recall aids. The widely used systems like Identikit and Photofit fare poorly in experimental evaluations, and a range of explanations of their weaknesses were considered, including their reliance on individual features. These studies raised the question of the contribution of verbal information in memory for faces. This was also illustrated by a discussion of the possibility of producing a reliable verbal description of a face by the systematic application of an adjective checklist. Studies bearing on a related question, of the co-ordination of visual information about a face and verbal information about its owner, suggest that face recognition is improved if a verbal context is available.

Basic findings on face recognition were reviewed. Memory for faces is affected by many of the factors that influence performance in many other memory tasks, including the interval between presentation and memory testing, arousal, context, and judgemental bias.

General questions to do with pattern recognition, including those concerning feature analysis, were raised. The ambit of the discussion was limited mainly to the nature of the operations of early processes, Stages 1 and 2 in the basic model, for the particular class of visual information contained in the human face. The need for an important qualification of the model is implied by findings interpreted in terms of a top-down influence in the information-processing sequence. The need was also noted for a wider perspective, expanding the terms of reference of theory to accommodate the contribution to the processing of faces of related perceptual and non-perceptual information.

4 DESIGN FOR ACTION

Much of what is of practical interest in this chapter involves the choice of simple actions. For a more comprehensive account a wider range of human activities would need to be examined, ranging from the quite lowly ones which we shall in fact concentrate on, to the complex ones like chess and computer programming dealt with elsewhere (Anderson 1980) which depend on comparatively high-order cognitive processes. The former are mainly quite simple motor actions and often relate to questions to do with the design of equipment: like what should be the relative positions in the cockpit of an aircraft of the various instruments and controls used by the flight crew; or, more mundanely, where should the burners of a cooker be situated in relation to the controls to activate them. The interest lies in how to design and deploy the displays and controls which mediate people's actions on the world, and particularly their actions on machines and complex systems like computers. The psychological theory and conceptual analysis underlying the practical conclusions that may be reached are comparatively undeveloped, although there have been some very useful insights in the last few years. Interpretations which refer to 'procedural knowledge'

(Anderson 1980), and to 'mental models' (Aitkenhead and Slack 1985) are feasible in an information-processing framework, but we shall have more basic theoretical questions in view. The applications context of this chapter is one in which some unusually well-defined and concrete questions may be posed. What is unusual is that the tangible context for the application of psychology is readily apparent, as can be seen from the cockpit and cooker examples just mentioned.

Control–display relationships: practical circumstances

Actions may, as when we push, pull, rotate, turn, or release a held object, be more or less direct and their likely consequences readily apparent. The object is variously liable to move away from or towards us, to turn, tilt, fall, and so forth. Such action–effect sequences are natural primitive instances of *compatible* relationships. The effect may, however, be mediated by a tool, as when a hunter releases the string of his bow to fire an arrow. Here a fine degree of skill is involved for the action to be executed with success, but the action–effect sequence is itself quite obvious. In other cases the physical linkage between the action and the outcome may be obscure, having perhaps been engineered or manufactured.

The nature of the linkage may be unknown to the individual responsible for the action, but there may be some expectation on his or her part as to what the outcome associated with a particular action is likely to be. For example, we understand that a doorknob has to be turned to gain entry to a room, even though we may have only a crude impression of the quite simple mechanical operations that are involved. Similarly drivers may have a clear understanding of the consequence of turning the steering wheel of a car without having (or needing) the least idea of how this is physically achieved. There is nevertheless a practical advantage in the direct relationship between the direction of turn of the steering wheel and the direction of movement of the vehicle, a relationship that may be thought of as compatible. It is instructive to contrast this with the incompatible relationship (certainly for novices) between the control action and the effect on direction of movement for a tiller-steered vessel. It is as if the driver of a car operates on the assumption that the control system (steering wheel) and the driving wheels have a direct linkage. The same assumption seems to be made by the beginner steering by tiller for the first time. This supplies a hint as to why some theorists have supposed that the individual possesses a 'mental model' of the system being operated in terms of which actions are mediated (Welford 1968). In fact the physical connection between the steering mechanism and the driving wheels of a car is much less direct than the connection between the tiller and the rudder of a boat. The difficulty arises because the tiller has to be held in the opposite direction to that in which the boat is to travel. It usually does not take long for the beginner to correct the inappropriate tendency to turn the tiller the wrong way, though it is alarmingly prone to return when at panic stations. Perhaps in learning to steer a boat the beginner has to acquire an appropriate mental model of the tiller-rudder system, having at first applied an unsuitable one.

Today's electronic technology enables the linkage between action and effect for many complex systems to be effectively arbitrary, and although its actual details may be totally obscure to the operator, this is irrelevant because the action–effect connection can be tailored to more or less any demands. The action–effect relationship may therefore be functionally well-chosen in the sense that the operator's expectations as to the effect are confirmed, and the required action can be chosen on the basis of them. For example, when you want to print a letter that has been entered and corrected using a word-processing program, it is of no interest to you how the program achieves this, and your concern will be to produce the letter in a printed form with a minimum of fuss. In particular the designer of the system in question is today given such flexibility of choice that the linkage may be programmed to fit well with the preferences and expectations of the user. (This talk of preferences and expectations is not to beg the question of their causal status. In a more traditional language they come about because of 'reinforcement', the pattern of rewards and punishments that shaped their behavioural precedents.) It would on the face of it seem to be sensible to arrange for the way the user issues the command to the computer to 'print my letter' to be reminiscent of this familiar and well-understood verbal sequence. Thus allowing for the fact that computer-talk is normally on the cryptic side, and so abbreviations tend to abound, most people would be at home with a command sequence like <PRINT: PB.LET> and would be less comfortable with <PB.LET: PRINT>. Here it is assumed that the term PB.LET was chosen by the producer of the letter (initials PB) as an effective reminder of the document being produced. However, in such matters it may be safer to rely on empirical evidence, and we shall defer a conclusion until we have considered a relevant study (see p. 97).

As the performance and level of equipment of aircraft has increased, an increasing number of displays and controls have needed to be installed in the limited space of the cockpit. The modern aircrew are surrounded by an extraordinary array of monitoring instruments, clocks, dials, and controls, and this presents a context of action possibilities that may influence the operator's performance regarding individual components of the system. The placement of these devices has to be carefully planned, to optimize the operator's performance in terms of attention, speed, and accuracy of response. There is a need for the whole system context to be taken into account; it could, for instance, be inappropriate to optimize the design of a particular piece of equipment on the basis of tests using it in a central visual location if the practical reality is that, because of its comparative infrequency of use, it will be situated well to the side of the operator. In fact the proliferation of displays and controls and the associated instrumentation has become a sufficiently serious problem in the helicopter cockpit that the use of direct voice input is under review to attempt to save space. The idea is to provide the pilot with an on-board voice recognition system that can recognize and respond to a limited set of basic commands, such as changing radio frequency. Consequently a number of control devices may be removed and the related hardware be moved to a less cluttered part of the aircraft. In addition the pilot would be spared the need to operate at least some manual devices. This example of how developing technologies will affect the cockpit of the future has begged the question of whether pilot performance will be affected. It begs the question in particular of the relative compatibilities of the alternative action–effect sequences, and the display–action sequences that voice and manual controls entail. There is one *a priori* advantage of the voice system which is that there is no risk of the pilot having to look away from any displays being monitored. This is a useful illustration because it draws attention to what we may think of as the response mode or modality (manual vs vocal in this case), a distinction that is more familiar in the context of sensory processes.

The relationships between displays and controls, and between controls and their effects on the environment, vary in what we have loosely termed their 'compatibility'. To clarify this idea, we shall explore some situations in some detail where the effects of compatibility are demonstrated. It will turn out that this apparently simple concept is quite elusive and hard to define, although a body of evidence will be described which has given rise to clearcut design recommendations, certainly applicable to a limited set of situations. Some ideas have been introduced that may aid the understanding of actions and of compatibility, and it can be seen that today's technological options enable systems and equipment to be constructed so that displays, actions and outcomes are deliberately matched in terms of the user's preferences and expectations if this is desirable.

Compatibility: population stereotypes

If you wake in the middle of the night in a strange room, and want to put on the room light, you will not have to think twice about whether to push the switch up or down. Your expectation is so strong, and it is shared by so many people from your national community, that it can be described as a 'population stereotype'. On the other hand, if you are from the United States, you will expect the movement to be 'up' for ON, whereas it will be 'down' for ON if you are British. The existence of opposite conventions shows us that there is nothing 'natural' about this particular stereotype. It is presumably as strong as it is in any one country because it is based on innumerable encounters with light switches in the past. The exceptions to the rule are those multiway switches which are found on landings, stairways, and in corridors, which have to work in both directions and are capable of inducing a moment's puzzlement because half the time they confound the stereotype.

A movement which is a population stereotype is said to be 'compatible'. The example of the light switch is an instance where conventional arrangements may be said to have a high degree of compatibility between the control and its effect. Compatibility is a characteristic too of configurations of displays and controls as we shall see. It is a concept which may be broadened to include a more general range of tasks and activities where actions and their outcomes, messages and the consequences they signal, may be considered to be more or less well matched. And people's expectations as to how things will turn out, or what they should do to produce a particular outcome, can serve as the basis for assessing the compatibility of a particular arrangement.

The 'on' stereotype

A very common arrangement is the use of rotary knobs to control the on–off state of a device. This is found on radios, televisions, dimmer switches, and sundry other pieces of domestic equipment. Such devices are commonly expected to be switched on by a clockwise turn of the control knob, and this is in fact the engineering convention that has been widely (but by no means universally) adopted. Indeed 'clockwise-for-on' seems to be a population stereotype, recently confirmed in an investigation in which 73 per cent of the 200 subjects made a clockwise movement to turn on a lamp (Barber and Rogers, unpublished report). The majority of people are right-handed and it seems that clockwise rotations of the hand are rather easier to perform than anticlockwise ones; certainly from an unsupported resting position there is greater scope for moving the wrist rightwards than leftwards (Pheasant 1986). This relative ease of making clockwise movements with the right hand may be in some way responsible for the tendency for people to expect a clockwise turn to produce more or less *any* effect. Most of us have had the irritating experience when attempting to turn off a radio whose on–off control also serves as the volume control, of finding the volume increasing because we have opted to turn the control clockwise for off. We also obtained evidence of a clockwise-for-anything tendency when we asked people to turn a light off using a rotary control. Older people (over 60) were as prone as younger people (under 50) to make a clockwise turn for 'on' (72 vs 74 per cent respectively). The latter group showed an equally marked tendency to make an anticlockwise-for-off turn (72 per cent). However, the older people were as a group unsure about what to do; indeed a small majority of them (58 per cent) made a clockwise turn of the control to turn the light off. Hence although the stereotype for the 'on' action was reversible for the younger group, this was not the case for the older group. Their performance seems to have been overlaid with the tendency to respond 'clockwise-for-anything'.

There is of course a whole class of actions which conflict with the 'clockwise-for-on' stereotype and convention. Taps and valves that control the flow of a liquid or gas are typically constructed with an anticlockwise-for-on action (largely because of engineering considerations). We have all had extensive experience at least with water taps, and the corresponding anticlockwise-for-on stereotype is quite strong. We found that 80 per cent of our subjects made an anticlockwise movement to operate a tap, and 72 per cent a clockwise movement to turn it off. This stereotype was therefore more reversible than the previous example, and there was no sign of a change in the strength of these tendencies with age. Observing children in a nursery school, Ballantine (1983) found that 3-year-old children almost universally showed the anticlockwise-for-on stereotype for a water tap.

It is intriguing from a practical point of view that these conflicting stereotypes seem to coexist comfortably in our domestic worlds, though it is possible that accidents are sometimes precipitated because of the incorrect selection of a stereotype, for example increasing the gas flow under a boiling pan of milk by the mistaken application of the clockwise-for-anything tendency. It is of interest too that the foot controls on motor vehicles to increase speed (accelerator pedal) and decrease it (brake pedal) are adjacent and are activated by the same action, a downward pressure of the foot. It is not apparent from the existing evidence whether the confusion about which action to apply (e.g. clockwise vs anticlockwise rotation to turn off a gas burner on an unfamilar hob) is exacerbated when the individual is also uncertain about which control to operate. Opposing psychological accounts about the likelihood of uncertainty of one aspect of an action affecting some other could be formulated; for example, uncertainties might not multiply if the actions were independently represented internally, or if the criteria involved in the choice of separate actions were independent. Aside from the interesting psychological issues this raises, it seems an important practical question, since it could be a factor in accident causation.

Direction-of-motion stereotypes

Much of the research into stereotypes has focused on direction-of-movement relationships with a detectable industrial-applications slant in the sense that the control is linked with a display indicator, the task for the subject or operator being to make some desired change in the setting of the display by manipulating the control. The display may, for example, depict the amount of current flowing in an electrical circuit, or it may be the pressure gauge on a component in a manufacturing process.

Ergonomists have studied control-display relationships very intensively, the most thorough investigations being of situations like those illustrated in Figures 4.1 and 4.2 (Loveless 1962). The control

(a)   (b)

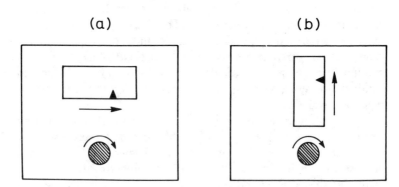

Figure 4.1   Linear display indicator with a rotary control. Expected direction of pointer movement on a horizontal indicator (a) and a vertical indicator (b) for a clockwise movement of the control

mechanism may be a slider, joystick, lever, or knob, while the display indicator may be linear (horizontal or vertical), or circular. In addition to these analogue types of displays, contemporary technology makes it a relatively straightforward matter to offer the option of having a digital representation of the information. Many other complications have to be taken into account like the position of the operator, which way the scale markings should run, and so on, so clearcut principles that work for all situations cannot be expected to be found. Moreover the kind of conflict between movement tendencies or expectations, as discussed in the previous section, not surprisingly is found to be rife in these more complicated circumstances.

A fairly clear expectation is found for a clockwise movement of a knob control to be associated with a rightward movement of a horizontal linear indicator (Figure 4.1a) or an upward movement of a vertical one (Figure 4.1b). In addition there is a general expectation that a knob used to control a circular display should operate in a clockwise-for-clockwise fashion. That is to say, a clockwise action of the control produces a clockwise movement of the display pointer. But the force of this expectation is compromised by the simultaneous influence of the clockwise-for-right and clockwise-for-up tendencies which are found to apply to linear displays. It is as if the operator sees the movement of the indicator as having a momentary linear component as well as its more global rotary movement. The local global components then seem to combine as shown in Figure 4.2.

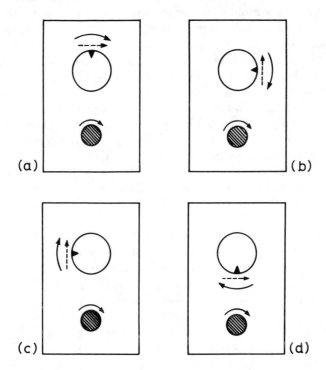

Figure 4.2 Circular display indicator with rotary control. Components of expected movement of pointer for clockwise movement of the control at four positions of the pointer

When the pointer is at the top (Figure 4.2a) and on the left (Figure 4.2c) the clockwise rotary stereotype is supplemented by the clockwise-for-right and clockwise-for-up tendencies respectively. But it is correspondingly weakened when the pointer is at the right (Figure 4.2b) and at the bottom (Figure 4.2d), because these same tendencies are in opposition to the clockwise-for-clockwise tendency. The latter is evidently more potent in this situation so the outcome is a variation in the strength of the stereotype (rather than a reversal in its direction), depending on the initial position of the pointer. The evidence across a considerable variety of situations, illustrating the profusion of direction-of-movement tendencies and the interplay between them, was reviewed by Loveless (1962) and has been extended by Petropolous and Brebner (1981).

The possibility of two uncertain expectations about different aspects of a single task acting in consort or in conflict was raised in the previous section. In that case there were two distinct subtasks involved (selecting the correct burner, and selecting the correct action to operate it). The two actions themselves may be combined in a more or less smooth joint action. In the example discussed in this section the aspects of the overall task shown to be influential are components of the display considered as a visual configuration. There are no subtasks to combine, but the display does contain two stimulus properties, separately capable of influencing the operator's course of action. Moreover these stimulus properties are given in an integrated form in the display in the sense that the occurrence of one necessarily entails the other, and it is difficult to attend to or process information about only one at a time. It is possible, however, that in both cases the sources of influence on the person's action are integrated as a single expectation underlying the conduct of the overall task. Further research is needed to establish whether this analogy between action-related and stimulus-related expectations is valid and helpful in the understanding of performance.

Theoretical issues that may be relevant to the display-control stereotypes discussed here include that of the relative strengths of global and local factors on the perception of complex visual displays (Navon 1977), and the distinction between integral and separable stimulus dimensions (Garner 1974).

Spatial compatibility

It is often the case that a piece of equipment has several controls and displays (e.g. the controls and dashboard display of a car) and the linkage between them is spatially extended, so there is a degree of latitude about where they may be situated relative to one another. All else being equal, a designer is well advised to opt for an arrangement with spatial compatibility. This is one where the positional association between the controls and their displays is 'obvious', 'direct', or 'natural', at least in the sense of being the connection expected by a majority of potential users.

The practical importance of spatial compatibility should not be underestimated. It was first documented in dramatic form by Fitts and Jones in 1947 (see Fitts and Jones 1961) who made a survey of 'pilot error' incidents during the Second World War, many of which were found to be due to inappropriate positioning of controls or actual incompatibility of the control-display arrangement. This is illustrated by the following quotations:

> We were on the final approach at about 600 feet when we noticed an unusual sound in the engines. What had happened was that the pilot had taken hold of the prop controls and was using them for throttles. They were next to the pilot while the throttles were in the centre. This was a bad installation also, because the gauge for the props was on the right of the manifold-pressure gauge while the prop controls were on the left of the throttle controls.

Despite the slightly impenetrable technicalities of this description, it is possible to imagine the alarm that must have been experienced so close to ground level because of the pilot's error. It is remarkable, however, in the light of the warning sounded by these early investigations that a military helicopter still in service with the US armed forces in the 1980s has a blatantly incompatible relationship between a pair of crucial displays and the associated controls (Hartzell et al. 1982).

The domestic cooker provides a good if mundane example of the problem of spatial compatibility. Frequently the control panel of a typical four-burner hob is positioned in front of the burners. The question of whether people have strong expectations or preferences as to how the displays (i.e. the burners) and the controls are organized, and of whether there are performance differences resulting from different arrangements, has been studied in a number of investigations. Chapanis and Lindenbaum (1959) found that errors in operating the appropriate control could be avoided by placing the burners in a staggered sequence as shown in Figure 4.3a. Although safer arrangements can be envisaged (try mentally reaching out for a pan on burner B when A and C are also in action), this design appears to have a considerable degree of spatial compatibility. This is not so with the arrangement in Figure 4.3b which gave rise to errors in performance, as did a variety of other designs. Preferred and actual designs do show a great deal of variation and it seems that there is little consensus in people's expectations (Ray and Ray 1979; Shinar and Acton 1978), so stereotypes seem not to have developed here. Although it might be expected that an individual's experience would play a part in determining his or her expectations, Smith (1981) found in a paper-and-pencil test that the two commonest designs in the US (in which the left pair of controls operate two of the front burners) were not among the four most popular patterns chosen by his subjects.

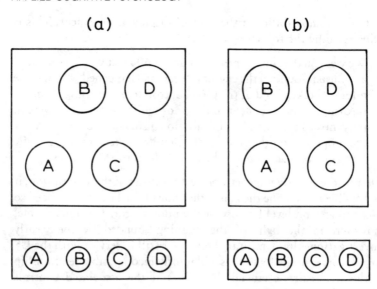

Figure 4.3   Schematic arrangements of cooker-hob controls (shown as a horizontal strip) and the associated burners

As a way of signalling the spatial relationship between burners and controls it would be possible to use a colour coding system applied to both. But this has limited application since the burners are obscured as soon as pans are placed on them. Since many people express some uncertainty about which control operates which burner on the cooker at home, a major problem with cooker hob design may be the users' incomplete mental models of the connection between the spatial layout of the controls and that of the burners. It would surely be helpful, at least in the long run, for manufacturers to agree on a standard arrangement, even if it is one without inherent spatial compatibility. It is arguable that if compatibility cannot be easily engineered into the design then at least one should aim for consistency regarding the spatial disposition of the controls and displays.

The failure to adopt a standard layout for the controls of a car is another example where the potential benefits of design consistency seem to have been ignored. Once a driver has become accustomed to a particular car, some adjustment is understandably necessary when the time comes to drive a different model. If it is indeed a new model its dimensions and performance will differ, and the driver expects to have to make corresponding allowances for these variations. What is distinctly unwelcome is the necessity of having to learn a new set of controls and rules for operating traffic indicators, windscreen washers, and the other necessary paraphernalia of motoring. Most disconcertingly perhaps, traffic indicators are sometimes located to the left of the steering column and sometimes to the right. It is easy to scoff at the driver of an unfamiliar car, who grasps the wrong set of controls, squirting soapy liquid over the windscreen in an abortive attempt to warn other road users of an intention to turn left. And I know one individual who in the fading evening light has had to drive a hire car some thirty miles with its hazard lights flashing because he could not find how to operate the headlights. He later shamefacedly discovered that the headlight control stick was operated by rotating it, not by lifting, lowering, pulling, pushing, or even threatening it with extreme violence. Whenever a driver uses an unfamiliar car, he or she may have to countermand an engrained set of expectations and stereotypes, which at the most trivial level is a recipe for annoyance, and surely cannot be a recipe for safety.

In short, the implication is that consistency in the design conventions for commonplace equipment would be beneficial to the users of such equipment. It would be premature to pronounce on the relative weights to be attached to the properties of compatibility and consistency. Only the former has been subjected to extensive experimental analysis, and we next examine some of the evidence and its theoretical implications.

Spatial compatibility: Experimental studies

Laboratory-based investigations of spatial compatibility have focused on display-control (display–action) relationships not on the control-display (action–effect) relationships, and much of the research consequently refers to stimulus–response or S–R compatibility. In the first study we consider, Morin and Grant (1955) used a single display of ten lamps set out in a horizontal row with ten keys arranged also in a row directly below them. The 'mapping' of stimuli (lamps) onto responses (keys) was varied, and it was the effect of this S–R mapping that was of interest. For one group, the mapping was direct, the response on any trial being made via the key immediately below the illuminated lamp. The second group had a reverse mapping, the leftmost key for the rightmost lamp, the next leftmost key for the next rightmost lamp, and so on. For the third group the assignment of keys to lamps was random, and their performance was comfortably the slowest and most error-prone of the three conditions. The direct-mapping condition gave the best performance and the reverse mapping was between the other two, though quite close to the direct condition. The mapping for the direct condition is inherent in the display, and that for the reverse condition is – with the use of a simple translation code – also straightforward. The difficulty in the random condition presumably arose because each mapping from stimulus to response was arbitrary and had to be individually memorized.

Fitts and Seeger (1953), with a considerably more complex study involving the manipulation of both stimulus and response arrangements, showed that performance was best, in terms of speed and error-rate, when the spatial mapping of stimuli and responses corresponded to the population stereotype (as defined by the experimenters' best guess). Figures 4.4 shows the results for four of the nine conditions used. For stimulus arrangement S1 one of the lamps was illuminated on each trial, and for S2 either one or two of the lamps were displayed. The response in R1 was the appropriate movement of a single stylus, while in R2 a pair of styli were used, one or both being moved as necessary. To illustrate how the indirect (incompatible) mapping worked, consider the combination S1–R2 with the 'north-west' light on. In this case the subject had to respond by moving the left stylus to the left and the right stylus upwards. Similarly with the 'north' light on, only the right-hand stylus was needed, with an upward movement. The mapping between stimuli and responses was specified in a similar way for S2–R1. Subjects in these conditions performed best in S1–R1 as shown in Figure 4.4, and across the whole experiment the best performance for a given stimulus configuration depended on the arrangement of the responses. From the evidence it seems reasonable to conclude that performance was optimized when the stimulus-response mapping was most direct.

Findings such as these have a clear relevance for the layout of displays and controls, for instance for control panels in complex industrial systems. The practical significance of the results concerning speed of response would be small if responses were only made occasionally, but the cumulative cost of making incompatible responses could be serious if they were made frequently. More important in many practical circumstances is the indication from the experimental work that errors are more likely to be precipitated by incompatible display-control layouts, since erroneous responses may

	Response arrangement	
	R1	R2
Stimulus arrangement		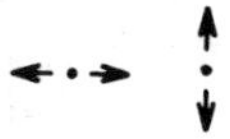
S1 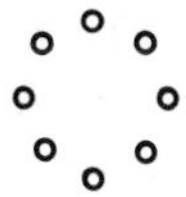	RT = 0.39 Errors = 4.4%	RT = 0.58 Errors = 11.6%
S2 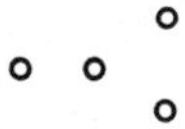	RT = 0.77 Errors = 16.3%	RT = 0.48 Errors = 8.44%

Figure 4.4   Reaction times (in seconds) and errors for a subset of the conditions used by Fitts and Seeger (1953) to examine spatial compatibility

be costly or dangerous. Incompatible arrangements of this sort may generally be avoided at the design stage, which is when expert advice is best sought but seldom is.

Practice with incompatible stimulus–response mappings may bring performance closer to the level achieved with compatible mappings, as shown in Fitts and Seeger (1953). Indeed other investigators have given their subjects sufficient training or experience under the incompatible conditions for their performance to be equalized with that of subjects working with a compatible arrangement. But this equivalence may be more apparent than real, especially if it is demonstrated under ideal conditions. Suppose the performance of two groups of workers is equalized in this way, and they are then tested under more demanding circumstances, such as doing the task in tandem with some other, secondary, task. Alternatively they could be tested in distracting conditions, or in a state of fatigue or stress. Under such conditions performance on both compatible and incompatible arrangements is liable to be impaired, but the incompatible version of the task is likely to be the more drastically affected. A collection of studies illustrating this is discussed by Loveless (1962).

One of the difficulties of using an incompatible arrangement is that outside the working environment the operator may get experience with the normally more dominant way of responding. This inevitably undermines the effect of practice with the incompatible arrangement. Furthermore the disadvantage of an incompatible arrangement may be overcome when the performance has to be sustained over a period of operation, but show up when an isolated discrete action has to be made. Thus a moving target may be followed using a joystick control in the opposite, incompatible, direction with a high degree of accuracy, changes in direction of the target being tracked or compensated for with accuracy. Yet the *initial* movement when starting up the performance may be faulty, and this may be exacerbated if the initial movement is impulsive or made in response to an emergency.

Compatibility and choice

Performance in a task is generally slower if there are more alternative courses of action. Compatibility between stimuli and responses may be implicated in this relationship. In Chapter 2 the relationship was characterized as an effect of uncertainty in the process of decision-making, and it was noted that a direct relationship has been found to obtain between reaction time and a formal measure of information. In particular when it is arranged for the stimuli to occur equally often though in an otherwise random sequence, the average reaction time increases in direct relation to the logarithm of n (see Figure 2.1). One construction placed on this finding referred to the increased time taken to decide among the stimuli (see p. 19). The argument was that the rate of increase in reaction time may be thought of as an index of the rate of information processing, of deciding which stimulus has been presented.

It was later found that the rate measure (which can be estimated by the slope of the linear function between reaction time and log n) varied from experiment to experiment. One factor that influenced the slope was the amount of practice that the subjects had in the task. For example, Mowbray and Rhoades (1959) found that the difference between a two-choice and a four-choice reaction time task was effectively eliminated by two months of practice (entailing some 30,000 reaction times). A second factor was the compatibility between the stimuli and responses. A particularly striking finding was reported by Leonard (1959) who designed a task with a very high degree of compatibility, due to the directness of the stimulus–response connections. This involved the use of vibratory stimuli delivered to the fingertips of the subject, the task simply being to remove the finger stimulated from the vibrator as quickly as possible. Reaction time with no uncertainty ($n=1$) was faster than any other condition, but reaction time for larger values of n did not follow the usual increasing relationship.

Other researchers added evidence showing that the slope of the reaction time vs information relationship depended on the degree of S–R compatibility (Fitts and Posner 1967). In doing so investigators increased the range of tasks used, and compared what seemed to be natural and what seemed arbitrary mappings of stimuli onto responses. In the course of these studies the concept of S–R compatibility was considerably broadened. As well as visual stimuli like lamps which may be spatially separated, there is an interest in how people deal with visual stimuli such as digits and letters. These types of stimuli may be presented on a display without spatial compatibility being an issue either because successive stimuli appear at the same location, or their spatial location though uncertain may be irrelevant (as in many search tasks). Thus within the visual modality there are various stimulus types to be investigated. In addition certain kinds of stimuli, like digits and letters, have both visual and auditory representations, and may be presented to a subject in either modality. Here is a difference in input modality, and the consequences for performance are naturally of practical as well as theoretical interest. For example, reaction times might be compared for digits displayed on a screen as opposed to being presented via headphones. Another distinction concerns the response modality used for the task. For the digit identification task, the subject could be asked to respond vocally, naming each stimulus as it is presented. Alternatively a manual response could be required, such as pressing the appropriate one of a set of keys. The different degrees of compatibility characterizing the various combinations of stimulus type, input modality and response modality have been studied experimentally, though there are many factors (like the number of stimuli) that serve to qualify the conclusions that may be drawn.

Of some practical interest are those instances where performance is very fast and accurate, and some special combinations have been identified. We have already mentioned tasks with a very high degree of visual spatial S–R compatibility (Morin and Grant 1955) and vibrotactile stimuli (Leonard 1959). Because of its high degree of compatibility, the latter arrangement has been identified by Dodds, Clark-Carter, and Howarth (1986) as of potential use in a guidance device for blind people. Auditory devices have been developed for this purpose giving a tonal signal to indicate the proximity of objects in the pathway ahead, but these make the user conspicuous and a silent alternative would be preferred by at least some users. The vibrotactile version might, for instance, code the distance to collision in two-foot zones via four different vibratory signals, one to each finger of the hand carrying the signalling device.

For alphabetical and numerical stimuli, a highly compatible arrangement is one in which the stimuli are presented to the ear and the response is vocal. Instances of very high degrees of compatibility seem to involve a close matching between the input and output modality, to the extent perhaps that the stimulus bears a near-resemblance to the feedback produced by the response. This is nicely captured by Greenwald (1972) in his term 'ideomotor compatibility'. Reaction times for ideomotor compatible tasks are fast, and increase by only a small amount as the number of alternative stimuli increases (i.e. the slope of the reaction time vs information function is small).

An important account of compatibility is given by Wickens (1984), who noted that S–R compatibility not only depends on input and output modality relations, but also on the central-processing code used in the task. The processing demands of the task may entail information being held and processed in a memory/processing system, and the code used at this stage may, for instance, be spatial or verbal. Accordingly it is best to use an auditory/vocal modality combination for a task that requires verbal mediation, and a visuo-spatial/manual combination for a spatial task. It has been suggested by some theorists (including Wickens 1984) that tasks with a sufficiently high degree of S–R compatibility demand so few central-processing resources, and require so little monitoring during execution, that they may be thought of as 'automatic'.

Compatibility: theoretical considerations

We have by this time clearly established that performance is affected by compatibility, though what is meant by compatibility is possibly less clear. Some clarification of the concept, and a theoretical framework into which it can be fitted, are needed. To summarize the earlier discussion, compatible arrangements of displays and controls, of controls relative to their effects, are compatible by virtue of being congruent with population stereotypes. They are what people expect. The compatible response from a set of alternatives, relative to a given stimulus, is the dominant or preferred response, that whose associative connection with the target is the strongest. The compatible arrangement will generally produce the best performance (usually assessed in terms of speed and accuracy, though qualitative aspects could be taken into account). But there is a sense of circularity in much of this, and we seem to be more engaged in the business of redescription than definition, let alone the more distant prospect of explanation.

Compatibility can be considered in terms of information-processing ideas, and it has been discussed as a matter of the recoding operations intervening between the registration of the stimulus and the production of the appropriate response (Fitts and Seeger 1953). The extent of this recoding activity is less for a compatible mapping than an incompatible one. Moreover fewer recodings will require less time and so a compatible response will be a fast one. It follows that population stereotypes are those which entail the least amount of recoding, and what people are reflecting in their choice of a preferred response is one requiring the least recoding effort. The difficulty, as ever, is to know independently of the expression of a preference, or the time taken to produce a response, which is a compatible and which an incompatible response. The recoding operations, if they exist, are themselves not directly open to inspection. Nevertheless this approach, even if it is found wanting, is useful because it invites us to consider what the hypothetical activity intervening between stimulus and response may consist of. In line with this approach it could be assumed, following Welford (1960), that the central information-processing sequence includes a 'translation' stage, whose business it is to select the appropriate course of action, given the stimulus identified by the first stages of input/encoding and comparison/identification (see Figure 2.3). Indeed Figure 2.3 incorporated a 'response-selection' stage, and the evidence discussed in this chapter suggests that the notion of code translation is a useful way of thinking about what at a more detailed level that stage does. What is fed to the response-selection/translation mechanism is assumed to be a coded version of the original stimulus. A coded representation of the response is needed for the output stage to work with and the translation mechanism has to form this response code. The recoding operations between stimulus and response codes may be more or less involved as we have seen. It may in some circumstances be necessary for computational effort to be undertaken before the response code is available. For instance, suppose you are given a string of digits each of which you have first to double, and then add 3 to the result. The arithmetical steps will take time and will constitute some of the recoding operations the task calls for at the translation stage. The mapping of stimulus onto response (e.g. 2 onto 7) is an incompatible one. (Research on compatibility has not usually employed such a contrived mapping of stimuli onto responses as in this illustration, and most studies have used direct, reversed, and random mappings as in the research of Morin and Grant (1955) discussed on p. 79. Although the recoding operations of these tasks seem intuitively quite straightforward, they remain psychologically obscure.) In contrast the task of simply repeating back whichever digit is presented would seem to require no recoding by the translation stage, and uses a compatible mapping. On this account the stimulus code is the same for both tasks, and the effect of compatibility is located at the response-selection/translation stage. In the next section some evidence will be reviewed bearing on this possibility.

To be surer about what stage is affected we can apply the additive-factors logic of Sternberg (1969, 1975), a method for 'discovering' the underlying stages of processing (introduced in Chapter 2, p. 33). There are many factors apart from compatibility that may influence performance, and one should be alert to the possibility of mis-construing differences in the time taken to do a task as necessarily indicative of differences in compatibility. Plainly the digits in the task described in the previous paragraph could be made very difficult to hear (or see), and reaction time would no doubt be affected. However this would seem likely (accepting the stages theory) to affect the time to produce the stimulus code (input stage) and would not influence the recoding operations of the translation stage.

It will be recalled from Chapter 2 that the rationale of the method of additive factors is that factors that have effects on separate independent stages will be found to influence reaction time in an additive fashion, and those that affect the same stage will interact statistically. In a previous section it was noted that there is abundant evidence that the effect of the number of choices is influenced by (i.e. interacts with) the effect of S–R compatibility. Hence these two factors, the latter being considerably better specified than the former, may be presumed to affect one stage in common. Which stage may act as the shared locus of effect is considered in the next section.

Locus of compatibility effects

The underlying assumption of much of the research using reaction-time paradigms to investigate the effects of compatibility seems to be that they exert their influence principally at the translation (response–selection) stage. We look now at some evidence that bears on this question. An enduring difficulty of the additive-factors method is that identification of which stage of processing a given factor affects has to be achieved by manipulating another factor, or factors, whose locus of influence is also likely to be uncertain.

For example, the repetition effect in choice–reaction time is equivocal in just this way. This phenomenon was reported by Bertelson (1961) in an experiment in which he found that when the stimulus was a repetition of that on the immediately preceding trial, reaction time was quicker than when the stimulus was changed. But in this experiment whatever could be said about the stimulus, whether it repeated or changed, could be also be said about the response. This was because there was a one-to-one mapping of stimuli onto responses. So the repetition effect could be due to the processing of the stimulus, the response, or both. Bertelson (1963) went on to show that the size of the repetition effect was greater when the S–R mapping was incompatible than when it was compatible. That is, there was an interaction between the repetition factor and compatibility. It follows on the additive-factors logic that the two factors affect a common processing stage, though the locus of this stage remains as uncertain as that of the repetition effect.

In fact Bertelson (1965) cleverly disentangled the stimulus and response contributions of the repetition effect in his task using a procedure in which one pair of stimuli was mapped onto one response, and a second pair onto a second response (this is known as a many-to-one mapping). This enabled him to repeat a stimulus and the response, to change the stimulus but repeat the response, or to change them both. There was some evidence of a small and independent stimulus effect (when the response repeated it was rather slower when the stimulus changed than when it too was repeated). But the overall repetition effect was mainly due to a repetition of the response. As for the effect of compatibility, it should be emphasized that it was not manipulated in this experiment. Although the evidence supports the view that compatibility is response-based, the position would be clearer if the last experiment were to be repeated with compatibility as one of the experimental variables. On the reasoning of the additive-factors logic, the response-repetition effect should be different for compatible and incompatible mappings.

Possibly the most clearcut evidence about the locus of spatial S–R compatibility is provided by a study by Shulman and McConkie (1973). The evidence can be given a relatively straightforward interpretation because of the relatively circumscribed nature of the experiment. Shulman and McConkie used a two-choice reaction time task to look at compatibility effects under two different response arrangements that can be thought of as producing a difference in 'response discriminability'. The stimulus on any trial was simply the letter X presented some four degrees to the left or the right of the centre of a display panel, and the task was to indicate the position of the X, left or right. The subject signalled the response in one of two ways, either using the index fingers on the left and right hand, or using the index and middle fingers of the right hand. Compatibility was varied by requiring a direct (compatible) or a crossover (incompatible) mapping of stimulus position on to response position. The condition in which different hands were used for responding is assumed to have the higher response discriminability (i.e. the ease of distinguishing between the responses is greater) than that in which the fingers on the same hand were used. This assumption is supported by the finding that reaction time for the different hands condition was less than that for the same hand condition. Stimulus presentation factors were the same for all response conditions and the response discriminability variable seems to have been well-chosen to have an effect localized on the part of the information-processing system responsible for output.

The result of the experiment was that there was a significant interaction effect between compatibility and response discriminability. Moreover the compatibility effect was bigger when the responses were more difficult to discriminate. This kind of interaction effect is called 'overadditivity', the larger effect of the interacting factor (response discriminability in this case) being obtained for the slower of the base conditions (S–R compatibility). Accepting that the response discriminability factor is limited in its influence to output processes, then even if compatibility has a diffuse locus of influence, the interaction effect in Shulman and McConkie's experiment seems convincingly to point to the joint effect of these two factors on a common, response-related, stage of processing. Perhaps this is connected with response selection, but we cannot rule out on the evidence that this stage might be responsible for some very late process such as response monitoring or response execution (Welford 1968).

Implications for stages models

Aside from the problem of demonstrating in a satisfactory way that compatibility – or any other factor – affects a specific stage of processing, there are other difficulties in the interpretation of the evidence. For example, it is assumed in the additive-factors method that successive stages are independent, and this assumption may not be valid. Independence, in this context, refers to the durations of the separate processing stages; thus the time taken by a later stage is not affected by that of an earlier stage. Even though a stimulus takes a long time to encode, this should not affect the time to select a response once the stimulus code is available. But it is possible that the difficulty of generating a stimulus code may be reflected at later stages of processing. For example, stages could be operated relative to some criterion of adequacy, which might then serve as a link between the activity of different stages. If a code is hard to produce at the input stage, because the stimulus is degraded or otherwise hard to discriminate, then the adequacy criterion may take a long time to achieve. This could in turn lead to an adjustment of the criterion applied at some other stage or stages, and they could also be delayed. In particular, if the criterion at the response-selection stage were to be made more stringent when, for example, the input stage has taken a long time because of poor stimulus quality, then we would expect a non-additive outcome when a factor affecting the response-selection stage (like compatibility) is applied. This is not an argument that is advanced with any force, but to illustrate how the non-additivity of two factors may reflect the non-independence of processing stages. It is of interest, however, that Rabbitt (1967) reported a small but statistically significant interaction between compatibility and *stimulus* discriminability, an effect that presumably influences a stage prior to response selection. Stanovich and Pachella (1977) also found an interaction between an early-stage factor (stimulus contrast) and compatibility.

There are two other possibilities. One is that the actual representation formed at any stage is not of an all-or-none character, but may vary in strength or quality, and may consequently affect the time taken in succeeding stages. A second possibility, discussed by McClelland (1979), is for later processes to be triggered before the completion of earlier ones. This is known as 'cascading' and may also be reflected by interactions between factors. The latter possibility, of temporal overlap, was favoured by Stanovich and Pachella (1977) as a way of accounting for the 'underadditivity' of the interaction between contrast and compatibility: that is, the effect of contrast was greater for the high compatibility version of their task (naming digits) than for the low compatibility version (button-pressing in response to digits). In any event it is plain that the problem of localizing the effect of compatibility, or any other factor, is less straightforward than was apparent at the beginning of this section. Nevertheless, the accumulation of evidence makes it reasonable for us to proceed with the working hypothesis that compatibility is mainly effective at the response-selection stage.

Interference effects and compatibility

When a task involves stimuli with more than one dimension of variation (e.g. colour, size, location, shape, etc.), processing one dimension may be affected by incidental variation on the other dimensions. This is demonstrated very clearly with 'multidimensional' visual and auditory stimuli. The evidence suggests that when two dimensions vary in a co-ordinated way, so that one of them is 'redundant' (i.e. it supplies no independent information), then performance in classifying the stimulus may be speeded up. On the other hand if the two dimensions vary independently, and classification is based on only one of them, then performance may be slowed down. These outcomes are not inevitable, and the conditions under which facilitation and interference effects for perceptual classification tasks are obtained are discussed by Garner (1974). In practice one dimension of a stimulus may be dominant in a perceptual sense, and processing of less salient aspects of the stimulus may be affected by incidental variations on the dominant dimension.

Another aspect of a task that may be problematical if it varies incidentally is the compatibility between secondary properties of the stimuli and the response alternatives. Consider, for example, the string of letters GREEN written in red ink. If the task is to name the ink colour, performance is slowed down relative to a reference condition in which the letter string is not a word (e.g. XXXXX) or is a 'neutral' word. The delay in colour-naming is an interference effect. Little or no facilitation is obtained if the ink colour and the word name are congruent (e.g. RED in red ink). This task, introduced by Stroop (1935), has been extensively studied (Dyer 1973), and there are many variations of it. Green and Barber (1983) reported an auditory version in which the subject heard the words 'man' and 'girl' spoken in both male and female voices. (The apparently sexist language in this study was justified by the fact that the use of 'woman' as a stimulus instead of 'girl' was ruled out because of its bisyllabic nature, and the use of a boy's voice – with 'boy' instead of 'man' – was likely to cause difficulty in discriminating voice gender.) The task was to classify the stimuli in terms of the speaker's gender, and when gender of the voice was incongruent with the word spoken (e.g. 'girl' spoken in a male voice), there was an interference effect.

In both the visual and auditory versions of the Stroop task, the incidental or irrelevant property of the stimulus (word name in the visual case, word spoken in the auditory case) can be thought of as specifying an alternative response, which for incongruent stimuli conflicts with the correct response. The level of S–R compatibility between the irrelevant 'stimulus' and its 'response' may help explain why interference occurs. For the colour task, for instance, the S–R compatibility for word-naming is perhaps much higher than that for colour-naming. Indeed it seems almost obligatory to read the word when presented. Conflicting codes for the stimulus appear to be produced, and an analysis in terms of compatibility would be consistent with a response-based explanation, although this would be disputed by some authorities (e.g. Seymour 1977).

One of the dimensions of variation within a task that could incidentally introduce an irrelevant and possibly competing compatibility effect is stimulus location. As noted earlier the effect of spatial compatibility is quite marked, and it is of interest to enquire whether it can exert an incidental interference (or facilitation) effect. Consider, for example, a task in which a red or a green visual stimulus may appear at one of two locations on a display screen, the subject having to decide on each trial which colour has been presented. The positions the stimuli may occupy is entirely irrelevant to the performance, but in fact they appear at one of two positions, left or right, relative to a central point on a display screen. Suppose now that the responses are made via a pair of keys arranged one to the left (for red, say), and one to the right (for green). Consequently there is an opportunity for a left-sided stimulus to be responded to by a keypress on the left (if the stimulus is red) or by a keypress on the right (if it is green), and these may be thought of as incidental S–R mappings which are compatible and incompatible respectively. In general such task arrangements will sometimes involve the stimulus being on the same side as the response, and sometimes on the opposite side.

In the event, responses are faster and more accurate when the stimulus and response are in spatial correspondence than when they are not. Although it is difficult to establish a neutral baseline condition, there is some evidence that both facilitation and inhibition effects are involved (corresponding to when spatial compatibility is respectively aiding and hindering the mapping of the relevant stimulus characteristic onto the response). The phenomenon occurs for auditory and for visual stimuli (Simon and Small 1969; Craft and Simon 1970). A variety of stimulus dimensions have served as the task-relevant attributes, including colour and pitch. The phenomenon has been thoroughly investigated by Simon and his associates, and has been characterized in some of their work as the 'source of stimulation' effect (Simon 1969), meaning that there is a tendency to respond in the direction of the stimulus. There is, however, some debate as to this form of explanation (Wallace 1971), and as to which stage or stages of processing are implicated in the mediation of the effect (Hammond and Barber 1978).

An interpretation of the Simon effect in terms of incidental S–R compatibility seems plausible, and has the attraction of drawing on an explanatory framework advanced to deal with the compatibility literature in general and other interference effects such as the Stroop and related effects (e.g. performance differences between global and local aspects of a stimulus: Navon 1977). This is by no means the only way of accounting for the effects of incidental variations in the attributes of a stimulus on the processing of a task-relevant attribute, but has the advantage of offering the basis for a unified account of several phenomena. Moreover it supplies a useful general warning to task designers to be alert to the possibility of performance being incidentally driven by irrelevant task features. One possible way of assessing their strength would be to measure users' preferences relative to the alternative responses allowed in or required by the task.

Practical example: effect of irrelevant directional information

Whitaker and Sommer (1986) reported a study in which the effect of an irrelevant feature of the stimuli used in the task affected the performance of the task. They noted that there are some traffic signs which supply directional information at the same time as carrying contrary directional information within the structure of the 'logo' portrayed on the sign (e.g., the implicit left-to-right direction of the aircraft on the airport sign illustrated in Figure 4.5(a)). Each of the signs in Figure 4.5 (which are North American in origin) relates to a destination, and the task for the driver intending to reach one of these destinations is to follow the direction given by the sign. The question addressed by Whitaker and Sommer was whether or not the presence of conflicting irrelevant directional information would affect the perception of and speed of response to the sign. They looked at two aspects of subjects' performance in laboratory settings, having prepared versions of the signs in which the irrelevant direction cue was sometimes congruent and sometimes incongruent with the intended direction. First, they asked whether perceptual judgements of the signs (for instance, as to their clarity) were affected by the irrelevant directional cue. Next they asked whether speeded responses (i.e., responses made under the instruction to respond as fast as possible) would be influenced by this form of perceptual conflict. The data from both parts of the investigation clearly demonstrated an interference effect, with perceptual ratings and reaction times adversely affected when there was conflicting directional information. This did not apply, however, when the conflicting cue was small compared to the intended directional cue (e.g., Figure 4.5(d)). It should be added that the tasks were not done with the kind of competition for attention that characterizes a real-world driving environment. One useful extension therefore would be to replicate this study with a suitable 'dual-task' version (see Chapter 5) to stimulate the appropriate kind of constraint.

Complex actions, choice and compatibility

This chapter began with some general instances of action–effect and display–action sequences, the compatibility of the paired components being identified as a possible contributing influence to the efficiency of the action in a given case. In the event the discussion has deliberately been limited to simple situations. Nevertheless

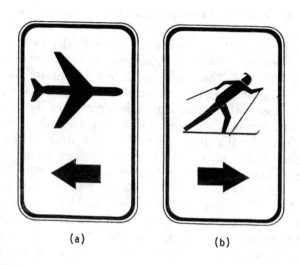

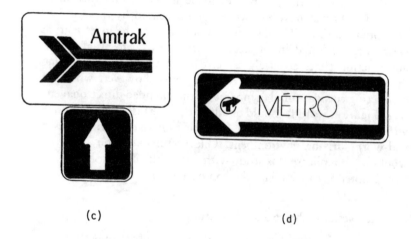

Figure 4.5 Examples of directional signs bearing irrelevant directional information: (a) airport – conflicting; (b) skier – concordant; (c) Amtrak – orthogonal; (d) Metro – conflicting. (From Whitaker and Sommer 1986)

compatibility may be an important factor in complex tasks too. Certainly it is possible to use the concept in a more general way, as suggested by McCormick and Sanders (1982) and Smith (1981). This is illustrated by references to conceptual or symbolic compatibility, in which an arbitrarily assigned state of a display (e.g. green traffic light) signals a particular action (driving past the light). Similarly red is used in a general way in western cultures to signify danger, or the desirability of cautious behaviour at least. Most people agree on the symbolic meaning, and the symbol and the indicated action are thus compatible.

Smith's (1981) investigation using a paper-and-pencil method of enquiring about people's expectations and preferences regarding displays, actions, and effects, covered a wide range of everyday situations and is a useful source of illustrations of compatible and incompatible action-related arrangements. Whether compatibility is a concept that can do service in a wider variety of circumstances is not clear. It is arguable that it may be little more than a way of alluding to the degree of correspondence between two (or more) aspects of performance and task arrangement (including the display, the action, its effect, and their internal representations). Nevertheless it is important from a practical point of view to know which of these elements of performance may be affected one way or the other. Theoretically it remains to be seen how these concepts, and that of compatibility, may be developed.

Recent studies hold promise of such a development within the framework of the information-processing approach, illustrated by John, Rosenbloom, and Newell (1985). They applied a model based on the concepts of goals, objectives, methods, and selection rules (known as GOMS) to study memory for abbreviations of computer command names. The command names referred to (like 'delete', 'print', 'copy', and 'replace') may be issued by the user via a keyboard to initiate computer operations, and it is often convenient to allow users to employ abbreviated versions of them. This raises the question of how to generate such abbreviations. The 'delete' command might, for instance, be abbreviated by removing all the vowels to produce 'dlt'. An alternative would be to use a special keyboard character reserved for command use, in conjunction with a single additional letter to specify the command (e.g. its first letter); for 'delete' the user would then type the key sequence 'command character' followed by 'd'. As John, Rosenbloom, and Newell observed, such abbreviation techniques are alternative specifications of a mapping between stimuli and responses, and so an analysis in terms of S–R compatibility might be profitable. As to the GOMS analysis (Card, Moran, and Newell, 1983), this is an applied information-processing model in which it is assumed that the performance of a reaction-time task is based on the execution of an algorithm, consisting of a program-like sequence of basic cognitive operations (mapping, retrieval from memory, and motor execution for the present task). Different algorithms will be called for by different tasks and, in the present case, will be needed for different abbreviation conditions. One possible algorithm when dealing with an abbreviation formed by vowel-deletion is to work it out from scratch by considering the command syllable by syllable, typing only the consonants. An alternative is to have learned the abbreviation well enough to be able to type it in one burst. John, Rosenbloom, and Newell found that subjects were quicker to begin entering the abbreviations when they had been produced by vowel-deletion than when they were formed by the initial letter preceded by a special character, but they took less time to type the abbreviation in the special-character condition. The slow initial responses in the special-character condition are probably attributable to the fact that there were two classes of commands, each member of a class having a co-member in the other class with the same initial letter, a different special character being assigned to each class. Hence the subject had first to decide which class the command belonged to, and therefore which special character was needed, before stripping off the initial letter of the command. This arbitrary memory load seems to have been reflected in the performance, and the estimated memory retrieval time (1,200 msec) was at least ten times as long as the times for the other hypothesized mental operations (60 msec for mapping, 120 msec for a keystroke).

The interest here lies in the extension of the concept of S–R compatibility to a more complex cognitive task than many we have considered, and of the application of a model that is a sophisticated and better specified member of the family of information-processing models introduced in Chapter 2. The GOMS analysis (Card, Moran, and Newell 1983) has been applied to the performance of expert computer users of text editors (word-processing programs), and is an impressive example of the application of the information-processing approach. The work of John, Rosenbloom, and Newell is also of interest in applying the concept of compatibility to an area, human–computer interaction, in which (as these workers point out) S–R compatibility could be expected to be an important consideration, but has yet to receive much attention.

This is apparent without delving into the complexities of 'user-friendliness' of software and the human–computer interface. It is striking, for example, that there is no accepted convention regarding the layout of quite basic aspects of computer keyboards; the first five keyboards I found within 100 feet of my office had the control keys which move the display 'cursor' up, down and across the screen positioned in five different ways. Users may be forgiven for supposing that this kind of thing reflects a special form of bloody-mindedness somewhere along the way. Unfortunately the basic research does not seem to have been done, although much is known about normal alphabetic and numerical keys and their layout, and the skill of typing in general (Cooper 1983). Latterly with the introduction of electronic technology, changes to keyboard design have become more common, easier to implement and to evaluate. For example, users' preferences and performance using calculator and digital telephone keyboards have been examined (Conrad and Hull 1968). This early interest has been followed by extensive research into the design and selection of keyboards and other input devices for interaction with computer-based systems, but little convergence on common design standards is apparent.

As to studies at the level of the interaction between the user and the computer system itself, there is an increasing body of research, and the question of compatibility has been raised. This includes the question of whether it is advantageous for there to be 'compatibility' between a computer command language and natural language. A simple example was cited at the beginning of the chapter, as to whether users would find it easier to learn and use a system in which the command to print a letter had the form PRINT: MYLETTER rather than MYLETTER:PRINT. But computer commands commonly entail more involved sequences than this, often calling for several terms strung together according to a special syntax. The possibility that compatibility with the syntax of natural language might be advantageous was investigated by Barnard *et al.* (1981). They found that command sequences in the natural order of verb/direct object/indirect object were *learned* no faster than sequences in the somewhat more unusual order formed by placing the indirect object before the direct object (the verb always going first). The results did, however, indicate that the speed with which command sequences were issued was faster when there was positional compatibility between the three elements of a sequence as displayed on the computer screen and the order in which they had to be entered via the keyboard. This kind of research suggests that it may be helpful to think about the performance of quite complex tasks in terms of 'compatibility', for instance as it may apply to the ordering of mental operations and actions. Whether such examples would readily yield to the GOMS analysis, and how useful it is to press the concept of compatibility, remains to be seen.

Summary

Factors influencing the selection of certain simple actions have been discussed, with particular reference to the relation between actions and their effects, and between signals and the ensuing actions. They may vary in what is described as their compatibility, and knowledge of this topic is pertinent to task design. In terms of the basic information-processing model the interest has principally focused on Stage 3. There is some theoretical importance in understanding Stage 3 and its mode of operation, and this chapter illustrates something of the complexities of response selection, and the associated internal representation of actions. Population stereotypes in the movements associated in particular situations, like turning on a light, demonstrate the uniformity of people's expectations and preferences, and hence presumably of the associated mental substrate. This was illustrated by a range of action–effect stereotypes, and investigations of them. Display–action relationships, also having a stereotypical aspect, have also been studied experimentally, in particular by research on spatial compatibility. Various other types of stimulus–response compatibility (display–action) relationships were also discussed, and practical examples were given.

The theoretical analysis of simple actions examined the effect of the degree of choice (number of alternatives), and how this is influenced by the compatibility factor. The difficulty of pinpointing the locus of effect of compatibility was illustrated, though there is clear evidence in support of the widely accepted assumption that this includes the response selection stage. The possibility of incidental compatibility effects was also underlined. This refers to performance being affected by task-irrelevant variables that may have a strong degree of compatibility with a possible (though not necessarily expected) response in the task. The application of compatibility in a wider context, to more complex actions and tasks, was also considered.

5 MENTAL WORKLOAD, ATTENTION, AND PERFORMANCE

It is ironical in an age when unemployment is the bane of industrial societies that certain jobs may place excessive demands on the worker. However, the overloading that an operator may be subject to is of a mental kind, not physical as would be the case a generation or two ago. Indeed we are told that with the age of information technology we are at the threshold of yet more dramatic changes in the nature of work.

In this chapter we consider some aspects of human performance at its margins. Some ways by which the mental load of the work to be done can be assessed will be examined, to see what implications there may be about the nature of performance. Excessive workload may arise from the worker having to do too many things at a time. This is not inevitable, however, and we also review research on 'multiple-task performance' which has examined the circumstances under which the performance of more than one task can be effectively co-ordinated. There may be practical lessons here for task design and the organization of work. A related question is whether there are differences between individuals in terms of this co-ordinative – or time-sharing – ability. It may be possible to identify people who have a high level of this ability, or to devise training procedures to develop it. This may have implications for personnel selection and training relative to complex tasks. These are practical questions, but sensible approaches to them depend on sound theoretical analysis.

Mental workload

Operator overload: when resources fail

The task of the operator in a complex modern system, who may for example be responsible for the control of an aircraft, a power station, or a production line, may require him or her to keep track of many sources of information, and to act on them in a decision-making role. The rate at which information is presented may be very low, and this brings special problems because of the need to maintain the worker's interest and alertness. The problems we are concerned with here, however, are those which arise when the operator is working at the upper margins of his or her ability, when there may simply be too much to do. When mental workload is very high, the operator's performance may merely deteriorate with nothing more catastrophic than a loss in productivity. But on other occasions the consequences may be fatal.

One such incident took place in Yugoslavia in the area of Zagreb in September 1976, when a British Airways Trident was in collision with a DC–9 of Inex Adria Airways. All 176 passengers and crew were killed. The circumstances leading up to the collision were complex and the official accident report reached some conclusions about the causes that have been criticized in certain quarters (British Airways Air Safety Review, 7, July 1983). However, one of the contributory factors to the accident was clearly considered to be the overloading of the air-traffic controller responsible for the air sector in which the two aircraft were flying at the time of impact.

The DC–9 was flying from Split to Cologne with 108 West German tourists and it climbed, during the time it was in contact with the Zagreb Area Control Centre, from 13,000 to 33,000 feet. Radio contact was established with the air-traffic controller responsible for the upper sector (31,000 feet and above) a mere thirty-seven seconds before the collision. During this brief time it was only possible for the controller to establish the flight level of the DC–9, and, realizing the danger, to warn the DC–9 crew of their proximity to another aircraft. The passage of an aircraft across sectors is by no means an adventitious matter and the procedure for handing an aircraft from one sector to another involves co-ordinated action on the part of the air-traffic controllers. There is some dispute as to how well this was effected on this particular occasion but it is clear that the upper-sector controller received scant notice of the DC-9's arrival in his sector. On leaving the middle sector the DC-9 was instructed to make the routine change of radio frequency to enable communication to take place with the upper-sector controller. Meanwhile the Trident, on its way from London to Istanbul, was in level flight at 33,000 feet having first made contact on the upper-sector radio frequency some ten minutes before the collision.

It was nearly two minutes before the DC-9 first communicated with the upper-sector controller, following the instruction to change to the upper-sector radio frequency. Meanwhile the controller for that sector had been working without his assistant, having in effect been responsible for two jobs for some minutes. Moreover there were eleven aircraft in his sector, he was in radio communication with four other overflying aircraft, and he took part in a telephone conversation with Belgrade regarding two others. In that short interval he transmitted eight messages and received eleven. The task facing him seems to a lay observer to have been an unenviable one, and it is apparent from the working practices for air-traffic control (cf. Sperandio 1978) that this is not a mistaken impression. Indeed the enquiry board were clear in their view that he had been subject to overloading. (He was subsequently prosecuted, held partly responsible for the accident, and was jailed.)

Nature of mental workload

By definition, overload occurs when an operator is called to perform beyond the limits of his or her resources. This can be viewed as one extreme of a continuum of states of mental workload. Questions then arise about avoiding overload, and about the definition and methods of measuring mental workload. Questions arise more generally as to the nature of the mental and processing 'resources' at the operator's disposal, how they vary and what work-related and other factors influence them. The practical significance is considerable; as Moray (1982) has observed, mental workload assessment is important 'for reasons of safety, efficiency, wage setting, and health'. Theoretical interest lies in the views of the nature of human performance that implicitly inform the study of mental workload.

There is in fact an extensive literature on mental workload although a great deal of the research and discussion has been published in relatively inaccessible journals and reports. Much of this work originated in the investigation of the complex skills entailed in flying an aircraft. Particularly in the case of high performance aircraft, the pilot is engaging in a continuous manual control task which itself may be extremely demanding, but has often to be done in tandem with other tasks requiring control and monitoring activities. A range of instruments in the cockpit has to be monitored and appropriate actions taken, and communications with ground control and other aircraft may take place.

Recent technological developments, however, have meant that the pilot's task has changed, with the introduction of more automatic aids into the cockpit or the flight deck. This shift in how functions are allocated between operators and machines is not limited to flying, and many contemporary jobs are affected by similar developments. Engineers have seen to it that the need for manual control of complex systems like aircraft and manufacturing plant is diminishing, and the role and responsibilities of the worker are being redefined as a result. In parallel with these changes, which involve a shift from manual control to monitoring activities, there is a widespread and increasing need to measure mental workload, and to understand human performance of complex tasks. Moray (1982) observed that human operators may appear to do less now that automatic control of machine systems is increasingly common, and the type of work has often changed from the physical control of a machine to monitoring the activity of an automatic system. Nevertheless while physical exertion may itself be much reduced, considerably greater *mental* load may be placed on the operator. Although there is widespread agreement about the importance of measuring mental workload, there is little consensus about how to do this, and there is not much agreement about how to define the concept. This is partly a result of the variety of disciplines that have been involved in the study of workload. We shall look at some of the available methods to provide a broad and practical view of performance.

Measuring mental workload

Researchers from different backgrounds are likely to have different priorities and purposes and hence will adopt methods of measurement that suit their objectives. There is no primacy of one set of methods over another, though it remains of interest to ask about which is best suited for which purpose, and what interrelations exist between different measures, and to provide a rounded picture of performance.

Primary-task measures

Perhaps the most obvious index of mental workload is the performance on the task in hand, and we therefore begin with the primary-task measures. It seems natural to expect that as the mental load imposed by the task increases so performance will suffer. Unfortunately matters are rarely as simple as this, and the task may indeed become harder and impose greater demands (in terms of the number or complexity of the operations to be carried out per unit of time) without performance changing. This may be possible because the operator is working within his or her limits, or because a change in how the task is handled may take place to accommodate the increased demands. Indeed such strategic changes in how the task is conducted are likely to be of particular interest in the context of mental workload estimation. They are, however, unlikely to be clearly signalled by simple measures of performance such as time per task operation, and it may be necessary to have recourse to quite subtle indices of performance, such as measures of the patterning of component actions. Clearly care is needed to devise measures that are sufficiently sensitive for practical purposes, and most importantly that give due warning of when conditions of overloading are approached.

Primary-task measures tend to be specific in the sense that each new task produces its own crop of possible measurements. And while time to carry out the whole task (or its subcomponents), and the frequency with which errors are made and corrective steps taken, can often be measured from situation to situation, it is not easy to compare tasks in terms of mental workload on this basis. It makes little sense to compare the mental demands of doing a crossword and completing a tax return on the basis of the time taken. Similarly in some industrial and military situations it is vital that errors are not made so it would not make sense to set out to use them as a performance measure.

Formal measures

System and control engineers have been more interested in definitions and measures that focus on the formal properties of the task. Since a great deal of their efforts have been directed at an understanding of the workload imposed by manual control tasks, measures that reflect the nature of such tasks have been developed. For our purposes we can think of manual control as requiring the operator to follow a 'track' defined by a moving target. Car drivers, aircraft pilots, lathe operators, and the players of many video games, all have to engage in forms of tracking at various stages of their activity. Measures of their workload have been devised, using mathematical concepts outside the scope of this book, that take account of the different kinds of control that are possible with different kinds of linkage between the operator and the action of the machine being controlled. The operator typically will have a device, such as the steering wheel or the 'accelerator' pedal of a car, whose positional setting controls some aspect of the machine's activity. The steering wheel controls the car's position and is known as a zero order control, while the accelerator (despite its name) controls the car's velocity and is a first order control. These are the simplest and much the commonest forms of control. Workload increases with an increase in the order of control, and with an increase in the 'lead' time elapsing between the operator's action and the movement or other response of the machine. Unfortunately not many tasks are open to a mathematical characterization (in terms of control theory or queueing theory, for instance), and until such time as they are formal approaches will be limited in application.

Secondary-task measures

The next collection of measures of workload are due mainly to psychologists and ergonomists. Their backgrounds and interests have led them to emphasize the spare mental capacity that an operator has available, as an objective measure of mental workload. The method is to require the operator to engage in an extra, secondary, task while carrying out the principal (or primary) activity. A pilot may for instance be asked to do a tapping task while flying the aircraft. The regularity of the tapping response, measured as the variability of the times between successive taps, is taken as an index of the pilot's spare mental capacity. Variability is expected to increase as mental workload increases, and there is some evidence that this is so (Casali and Wierwille 1984). Brown (1978) has reviewed the use of the secondary-task method for workload measurement.

The decision to use secondary-task measures requires that a number of assumptions be made, for example that the execution of the tapping task entails no interference with the primary task of flying, an assumption that can relatively easily be checked. More important from a theoretical perspective, in using a particular secondary task it is assumed that it draws on the same resources as the primary task. This may be justified if there is a general stock of processing resources which can be shared out to any task regardless of its composition and operating requirements, in which case resources may be straightforwardly reassigned from one task to another. On the other hand, resources may be more specific than this and two tasks may be capable of being performed simultaneously because they draw on separate resources. If the second of these possibilities applies then the secondary task under consideration would not be an appropriate measure of spare capacity (of the resource being used for the primary task), and not a valid measure of the workload imposed by the primary task. In such a case we might find that performance on the secondary task would be unchanged as workload (on the primary task) increased, even to the point where the performance on the primary task actually broke down. Theoretical analyses of attention and performance are relevant here and the matter is taken up on p. 130.

Physiological measures

Measures of physiological activity have recommended themselves to some researchers as indicators of mental workload. This includes measures such as heart rate and its variability, blood pressure, rate of breathing, levels of certain hormones in the urine, electroencephalogram (EEG), and pupil diameter. They are not interchangeable and their suitability for different purposes varies, partly as a function of their relation to underlying psychological processes, and partly due to the differing amounts of time they take to respond and recover after responding (Hamilton *et al.* 1979).

The assumption is that a generalized pool of resources for information processing is available, varying not in its composition but in its size – the possibility of an upper limit is explicitly admitted in some accounts. As the amount of resources demanded by a task increases, physiological activation mechanisms are called into play to increase the size of this resource pool. Thus as more mental resources need to be recruited, this will be reflected in increased central nervous system activity, and evidence of this is considered to be provided by appropriate physiological measures.

Physiological measures are commonly used as indices of the activation or arousal of the central nervous system, and consequently of the degree of stress to which the individual is exposed. This may reflect the presence in the environment of factors like extremes of sensory stimulation (heat, noise, vibration) which arguably do not intrinsically impose a mental load. Variation in physiological arousal may also occur with time of day, the incentives available, drugs taken, and anxiety (Hockey 1983). In addition, physical exercise brings about systematic changes in a variety of physiological measures. Indeed the rationale for the use of physiological measures of mental workload partly follows the analogy between physical workload and a mental counterpart thereof. Given the accompaniment of other arousal-related factors (emotional and environmental stressors) that are endemic to the performance of any task, it can be seen that changes in physiological variables might be hard to associate unambiguously with variations in the cognitive demands of a task.

Moreover some measures are particularly associated with the autonomic nervous system (e.g. pupil diameter) and might be of limited use for the study of mental workload. On the other hand, the case may be made that despite the difficulty of distinguishing between emotional and information processing, they both pose a mental load for the operator (Hamilton et al. 1979). It is possible that heavy mental demands will be more difficult to deal with if the individual is in a state of high anxiety or general arousal, and so it seems reasonable to insist that a full account of mental workload should routinely accommodate such factors. This is not in sight at present, although it is clear that emotional state (and other arousal factors) cannot be treated merely as a nuisance variable.

A set of physiological measures (heart rate, respiration rate, pupil diameter, number of eyeblinks) was used in a series of studies, summarized by Casali and Wierwille (1984), as measures of mental workload for various tasks in an aircraft simulator. The tasks were chosen to tap perceptual, motor, mediational (problem-solving, computational), and communication processes. The outcome was patchy with no measure reflecting workload level consistently, and

Casali and Wierwille concluded that the physiological measures 'did not fare well as indicators of mental workload level'.

It is possible, however, that the search for a general universal indicator of workload is inappropriate. The point was made earlier that any two physiological measures may reflect different psychological processes contributing to different aspects of mental workload. There are some fairly obvious connections to be made here, such as the relationship between motor activity and the electromyogram, a measure of the electrical changes on the skin which accompany muscle activity and tension. But not many physiological measures can be as well aimed as this, and it is not a straightforward matter to choose a measure that will reveal a particular aspect of mental information loading. This would be to assume that specific kinds of mental effort make calls on specific resources. An alternative is that the resources in question are undifferentiated. This contrast may also be made relative to the use of secondary-task measures. As to the research discussed by Casali and Wierwille (1984), no obvious pattern of associations that might be diagnostic of specialized resources is apparent from the results. For example, they found that heart rate increased with an increase in perceptual load, and respiration rate increased with psychomotor load. It is not apparent why these particular physiological/psychological pairings should have emerged.

Some promising advances in the study of the psychophysiological correlates of mental workload have been made recently, using the method of recording the changes in electrical activity of the brain via electrodes placed on the scalp. This is related to the traditional EEG method but seeks to identify instantaneous changes in certain components of brain activity that are produced when a stimulus is presented. This electrical activity is called the evoked cortical potential (EP), and much interest has been expressed in the component of the EP wave occurring about 300 msec after the evoking stimulus. This is called the P300 component (P because it is a positive potential) and its sensitivity to changes in the accompanying mental load has been studied. It is of interest because it seems to be affected by perceptual and cognitive factors not by response demands. The amplitude of the P300 component was found by Isreal et al. (1980) to decrease as the display monitored by the subjects increased in complexity. The evoking stimuli were provided by a tone sequence which accompanied the monitoring task and which the subjects had to keep a mental tally of. This kind of well-aimed psychophysiological measure seems to be of considerable promise because it appears to tap cognitive load more convincingly than most physiological techniques, although in the version just described it entails some intrusion in the main task.

Subjective measures of mental workload

Psychologists have also contributed techniques for measuring subjective aspects of workload, that is, the workload as experienced by the operator. Moray (1982) noted that this is viewed by many as the only important measure of mental workload. One of the most intriguing approaches to the measurement of subjective mental workload originated in research into the handling qualities of aircraft. The most commonly used is a scale devised by Cooper and Harper (1969). The CH scale, as it is known, is mainly given to test pilots for them to assess the 'flyability' of an aircraft. Its reliability and validity as a test instrument are high. The pilot may for instance make assessements on a ten-point scale of the ease and precision with which the aircraft can be controlled under a variety of conditions. The scale is marked with verbal descriptors that relate to this particular task (e.g., 'very easy to control with good precision', 'controllable, but only very imprecisely', 'nearly uncontrollable', etc.). A decision tree structure is often used (see Skipper, Rieger, and Wierwille 1986), in which the operator is guided to a particular scale point by answering a series of questions which branch out to progressively more detailed aspects of the performance of the task. Leading off at the simplest level, a three-choice question may be posed, for example, concerning whether the task can be done without any errors at all, with an acceptable number of errors, or only with an intolerably high number of errors. It has been observed that such scales may be used to assess how demanding the task is, to provide an index of subjective mental workload (see Casali and Wierwille 1984). Their adaptation for the measurement of subjective mental workload in general, for tasks other than flying aircraft, has been recommended (Moray, 1982; Skipper, Rieger, and Wierwille 1986). What is of particular interest here is that it is the operators themselves who are asked for an assessment of the task demands.

As noted earlier in this section, measures of objective workload have been devised on the basis of control theory. These apply to tasks which may be characterized mathematically in certain ways (Levison 1979). An almost perfect correlation was obtained between subjective mental load measured on an appropriately modified version of the CH scale and control theory measures of objective workload for a tracking task (Wewerinke 1974). But correlations between subjective and objective measures of mental workload are not always as high as this (Hicks and Wierwille 1979).

Strategies, objectives, and workload

One might hope for high intercorrelations between different measures of workload if only for the sake of parsimony. But mental workload is a matter of some complexity and it seems reasonable to anticipate that many factors and variables will contribute in a full account (Moray 1982). It is not just that different resources (general or specialized) may be needed for particular tasks or task components, it is also a question of the strategic deployment of those resources, the operator gearing his or her efforts to objectives that may vary at different levels of mental workload. This is well illustrated by a study by Tulga (cited by Moray 1982), which testifies to the importance of the operator's own assessment of mental workload, and shows the complex relation between subjective and objective load. Tulga's study was concerned with a theoretical model of time stress (in effect the rate of arrival of items for processing), a factor that may intuitively be seen to be related to mental load. An operator was presented with a display depicting queues comprising items of different values, which had to be dealt with so as to maximize the value of the items serviced. Initially as the rate of arrival rose (and, therefore, objective mental workload increased), subjective load also increased, and performance was efficient (that is, value was maximized). But a condition of overload was reached beyond which performance deteriorated, yet subjective load decreased. It appears that this was because the operator no longer sought to maintain perfect performance. Thus subjective mental load may depend not only on objective load, but also on the operator's criterion as to the accuracy, speed, and precision of the performance to be produced.

It is clear from Tulga's study that the operator's objectives – and strategies for achieving them – may influence the experienced degree of workload. It is arguable that the subjective monitoring of performance by the operator contributes in an important way to the setting of achievable task goals. Another study which illustrates this is Sperandio's (1978) discussion of field research into the performance strategies of French civil air-traffic controllers. As is apparent from the illustration at the start of this chapter, one of the objective indices of mental load for an air-traffic controller is the number of aircraft in the sector for which the controller is responsible. This simplifies the matter of workload since the task confronting the controller increases in difficulty, not just because there are more problems to deal with, but also because the complexity of the individual problems also increases as the available airspace decreases. Acceptable solutions to the problem of avoiding collisions become harder to devise. A further complication is that the nature of the work varies from one control station to another, and the problems vary too, depending, for example, on whether aircraft are passing through the controller's sector or whether they are landing. In the light of these problems the number of aircraft is a suitable objective workload measure for practical purposes since it is convenient and reliable.

Sperandio observed three different ways of dealing with the overall task, depending on how many aircraft are in hand. When there were between one and three to be controlled, full details of the aircraft's course, altitude, speed, and other characteristics of the flight were taken into account and optimized flightpaths were calculated. For between four and six aircraft, a change in this strategy was noted as the problem as a whole became more complex. The solution might require all aircraft to adopt uniform speed and stereotyped flightpaths, but although the spacing between them might be optimized, their individual flightpaths could not be. It seems that the collection of aircraft are treated as individuals within a configuration. For seven or more aircraft simultaneously, there is a problem arising from the saturation of the airspace, and aircraft have to wait in 'stacks', each one having flight characteristics (e.g., speed and descent path) very like its neighbours, and having to queue until the controller can deal with it individually.

In practice the separation criterion (ensuring that aircraft are at a safe distance) is the most important consideration. Nevertheless there are other goals for the efficient management of air-traffic control, including fuel consumption and punctuality. It can be appreciated that this exacerbates the difficulty of specifying mental workload in objective terms. Moreover the existence of these multiple goals undoubtedly serves to prompt shifts in the control strategy, as when the number of aircraft controlled falls to a sufficiently low number for flightpaths to be optimized in terms of fuel economy and time of arrival.

One approach to the measurement of performance, and to the effects of workload, is to record those occasions when mistakes or unintended actions are made. 'Slips of action' are common enough in everyday life (Reason 1979), and everyone can tell of such incidents as when the sugar inadvertently ended up in the teapot instead of the cup. The incidence of performance errors was noted by Langan-Fox and Empson (1985) in a study of military air-traffic controllers. Most of the time such mistakes were noted by the individual concerned, or by a colleague, and the great majority of errors recorded in this study were inconsequential. They do, however, constitute a measure of primary-task performance, and it was found that more of them were made as workload increased (workload was indicated by the number of aircraft at a given time in radio contact with the controller in question).

A reasonable general conclusion is that one source of excess workload is having to do more than one thing at a time. People who are good at dealing with such difficulties may perhaps be adept at rapidly switching attention from one task, or aspect of a task, to another. It would therefore be of some practical value to identify such individuals, and to ascertain whether or not they are suitable for tasks involving an element of attentional time-sharing. This also raises the question of how general is this kind of skill. This is addressed in the following section.

Concurrent performance and time sharing

The principal task of the driver of a moving vehicle is to steer the vehicle along an appropriate path. This is as true for the driver of a car or bus as it is for the pilot of an aircraft. The selection of pilots, and their training, naturally places emphasis on the possession of a high degree of the relevant kind of perceptual-motor skill, that is, the ability to guide a controlled object along a chosen trajectory. Nevertheless, although for a few learner drivers the actual business of steering does itself seem to present a serious obstacle, anyone who has learned to drive will recognize that this is likely to be only part of the story. The driver has frequently to deal with several sources of information at once, including the manoeuvres of other road users, traffic signals and road signs, while using road speed and conditions and engine sound to decide when to brake, change gear, and accelerate. Moreover it is not uncommon for drivers to undertake all of this as well as trying to conduct a conversation with a passenger. It is noteworthy that when traffic conditions worsen, and particularly in an emergency, the driver (and the nervous passenger) will allow the conversation to lapse so that all the driver's resources can be devoted to the control of the vehicle. From this we can see that an important aspect of the skill of driving is the co-ordination of a set of actions and subskills. These for a driver may involve the judgement of timing, distances, and speeds, the anticipation of the actions of other road users, the registration and use of symbolic information (road signs), the use of memory relating to the route being followed, and so forth.

Although flying an aircraft is a much more complicated matter (obviously one fundamental difference is that flying involves control in three dimensions), the similarities between driving and flying are informative. The pilot too is faced with the task of controlling a complex system and has to achieve this by the *concurrent performance* of a set of contributing activities needing to be appropriately co-ordinated and programmed. This co-ordinative skill is described as *time-sharing*. It is arguably a skill that is needed by operators of many of today's complex control systems (e.g. in aircraft flight decks, air-traffic-control systems, power-station control rooms). There are a number of instructive ways of characterizing certain key aspects of such tasks. One common consideration is that the operator may have to keep track of several sources of information. The operator may often have to divide attention between two or more sources of information, and sometimes it will be imperative to focus attention on one source, and to avoid distraction from others. Such *a priori* considerations make it clear that there is an intimate connection between *attention* and performance.

Indeed it is reported that flight instructors consider that attention is highly important in learning to fly modern high-performance aircraft. Trainee pilots are said often to fail 'because of a failure to divide attention among concurrent activities or among concurrent signals, or else because they are slow to recognize the significance of crucial signals which arrive on unattended channels' (Gopher and Kahneman 1971). There is no reason to suppose that this is not true of civil aircraft too, in which the perceptual-motor demands of piloting the aircraft are lower, but the co-ordinative activities – although aided in various ways by technical devices which are unavailable in the cramped cockpit of the military aircraft – still place a very high load on the operator on the flight deck.

Selection for time-sharing tasks

In line with their analysis of the difficulties faced by trainee pilots, Gopher and Kahneman (1971) used a dichotic listening test to examine the question of whether performance on a laboratory test of selective attention may be used to predict performance in flight training. In such a test subjects have to respond to a message presented to one ear while ignoring a second message relayed to the other ear. Gopher and Kahneman designed their test to assess subjects' performance firstly in holding their attention on one of a pair of simple messages from which certain target items had to be reported; and, secondly, in switching attention to a specified message, signalled by an orientating cue. One indicator of failure to attend in the first task was the number of omissions (items not reported). Measured in this way for the 100 flight cadets tested, poor attention was significantly and negatively related ($r=-0.26$) to success in flight training (measured on a three-point scale related to the stage reached in training – rejected during training on light aircraft, rejected during training on jets, or achieved advanced training on jets).

A second index of failure to attend was the number of intrusions: items from the wrong message that were mistakenly reported as targets. The correlation between this measure and success in training was low and not statistically significant ($r=-0.10$). Unfortunately intrusions were too rare for a sensible conclusion to be drawn and it is not clear whether the ability to maintain attention in this case is important. The data on omissions suggest on the face of it that this is so, but other evidence indicates that it is chiefly a matter of subjects failing to *listen* rather than a more particular failure to attend selectively to the appropriate message. This is based on the finding that the omission rate in a monitoring task correlates with performance to the same extent whether or not there is a concurrent message to ignore. Nevertheless the low rate of intrusion errors leaves the question unsettled and the fine grain of attentional performance seems to merit further investigation in this context.

As to the attention-switching task, good performance was quite impressively linked with success in training ($r=0.36$). The principal conclusion from this study is that the ability to switch attention rapidly is related to proficiency in pilot training. This has been confirmed by Gopher (1982), and Kahneman, Ben-Ishai, and Lotan (1973) have further shown it to be significantly related to the frequency of accidents on the part of bus-drivers.

At first glance these studies seem to be something of a success story. We should, however, note some reservations about the evidence. The correlation coefficients between performance on the dichotic listening test and the various aspects of performance outside the laboratory were uniformly rather low in absolute terms. The strongest relationship obtained was between the second part of the attention test and success in flying school (Gopher and Kahneman 1971). The correlation coefficient r was 0.36 which indicates that even in this best case there are some 87 per cent $(100 - 100 \times r^2)$ of the variation in flying success left to account for. A cautious assessment of the findings would need to take heed of the impressive regularity with which statistically reliable predictive relationships have occurred in this series of studies, at the same time as noting the relative weakness of the relationships obtained.

While it is entirely reasonable to interpret the findings of this predictive type of research as a useful test of an individual's ability to switch attention in a flexible manner, it is possible that the task depends on the exercise of some other, more general, ability. This problem of causality is of course ever-present with correlational studies. In the present case it is possible that the performance in both the listening test and the real-world tasks depends, at least in part, on the possession of a relatively high degree of cognitive flexibility. But this, it might be objected, is no more than general intelligence, something people in many professions find advantageous! It is of interest that in the Gopher and Kahneman (1971) research a measure of intelligence had a small but significant correlation of 0.21 with both the attention-switching test and the flight criterion. What the attention test is tapping needs further examination, especially in the light of the failure of McKenna, Duncan, and Brown (1986) to obtain a significant correlation between it and measures of accident rate among a sample of 153 bus-drivers (a conclusion which also applied to the measure of intelligence used by these investigators). Indeed as a result of this last study, the situation regarding the prediction of complex performance, seemingly dependent on an ability to switch attention, is quite open. It may transpire that performance in complex tasks is so highly specialized that attempts to predict it using general laboratory procedures, and to use the latter as a basis on which to select individuals, are fruitless and will necessitate the design and development of suitably specialized prediction tasks. It is almost a truism that the best index of future performance on a task is performance during training on the task itself. Hence a solution may be to use trainability tests (small samples of the training procedure) as a selection device (Robertson and Downs 1979).

It does, however, remain a distinct possibility that the real-world task which is the predictive target of the laboratory analogue may itself not have been subjected to a sufficiently close analysis, and it is arguable that, if it were, then better-designed tests could be developed. Indeed the contribution and weight of different elements of a particular performance might be clearer if a more comprehensive task analysis were made. For example, in the driver-accident-rate studies, failure of attention is likely to be only one of many possible causes of a driving accident. Quite apart from anything else, there are all those occasions when the accident is genuinely not the fault of the driver. Moreover drivers have accidents because of poor judgement, recklessness, and so on. Hence the attention test is likely to imply an imperfect general model of what mediates performance in a driving accident. This is one of the reasons why the correlations between attention switching and accident rate are bound to be limited in size (McKenna, Duncan, and Brown 1986).

Time-sharing ability: a general factor in performance?

Other researchers have sought evidence of a general time-sharing ability. Two recent studies illustrate the approaches that have been taken. The first is some research undertaken by Wickens, Mountford, and Schreiner (1981) using a battery of four 'information-processing tasks' in various dual-task arrangements. There was an auditory task (reporting whether or not successive spoken letters in a sequence were in alphabetical order) and three visual tasks; these were a tracking task (preventing a moving target from leaving a central region on the horizontal axis of the display i.e. unidimensional compensatory tracking), classification (making a judgement about the values of a pair of digits), and spatial judgement (assessing the position at which two lines would intersect if extended). Forty subjects did combinations of each task in tandem with others, including the three visual tasks in a dual arrangement with themselves (spatially separated on the display), as well as the basic tasks alone. The subjects each attended for three days, the first of which was devoted to a practice session of one hour, and was followed by two further sessions also one hour long. As can be seen from the number of experimental conditions, there were inevitably frequent changes in the nature of the task demands. In fact each block of trials under a given condition lasted only two minutes with an equal rest interval between blocks.

Following the application of the statistical technique of factor analysis to the single and dual task data, Wickens, Mountford, and Schreiner concluded that there was no evidence for 'a transituational general factor of time-sharing efficiency'. But as the investigators noted, the scope for this was limited by the small number of factors that could emerge in the course of analysis, and those that did so seem to reflect single-task performance in a fairly direct fashion. One other feature of this study that possibly militates against the conclusion that there is no general time-sharing factor is the crowded schedule of conditions that faced the subjects, giving them scarcely any opportunity to develop an effective way of handling the task combinations. In most practical situations the operator does not have to switch between task conditions with such confusing frequency. The importance of allowing the operator to settle on a strategy for handling the task is in fact demonstrated by a study by Damos, Smist, and Bittner (1983) which we shall examine presently.

Experience and strategies in time-sharing

A question of some practical interest related to that of the existence or otherwise of a time-sharing factor is whether experience and training on one time-sharing task are generalizable to another, particularly if the second is from a different class of task. Damos and Wickens (1980) gave subjects practice on a combined task involving classification and sequential memory, and then transferred them to a dual-axis (two-dimensional) tracking task. Their performance was compared with a control group who had been given practice at the separate single-axis components (horizontal and vertical) of the joint tracking task. The latter involved the manipulation of two response levers, one for each dimension of movement. Judged on this basis, prior practice on the combination of discrete tasks yielded positive transfer to the dual-axis tracking task. This suggests that a time-sharing skill may be acquired that is to some extent generalizable. The interesting feature of this study is that the contrast between the training and transfer tasks was quite marked (involving differences in terms of cognitive vs perceptual-motor demands as well as between discrete and continuous pacing).

A second notable aspect of this study is that the investigators, by means of a detailed examination of performance, found that a variety of discernible response strategies were adopted by the subjects, with apparent spontaneity. For example, three strategies were identified in the performances of different subjects when the two discrete tasks (classification and running memory) were undertaken in combination. These were referred to as simultaneous responding (co-ordinated responses issued effectively simultaneously, i.e. within 100 msec), alternating responding (responses alternating between the two tasks), and massed responding (runs of two or more responses made on one task before a response on the other). Simultaneous responding was found to be the most efficient, and massed the least.

In a further study, Damos, Smist, and Bittner (1983) looked at the effect of an instructed strategy change on the joint performance of two discrete tasks. Some of the subjects who naturally adopted one of the two less efficient strategies (massed or alternating) were subsequently instructed to switch to the simultaneous strategy. During the ensuing session, performance for all subjects approached an asymptotic level, but while those changing from the alternating to the simultaneous strategy converged on the level achieved by those who had adopted this strategy at the outset, the performance of those shifting from the massed strategy settled at a level some 25 per cent slower than the other two groups of subjects. The shift to a new strategy also seemed quite difficult for those moving from a massed strategy because after the shift their performance was for some time impaired relative to the best level they had reached with massed responding. It is important to note that the performance of all groups of subjects on the single-task conditions was not significantly different. Because of the limited nature of the tasks used Damos and her colleagues emphasized that their study does not bear on the question of a general time-sharing ability. None the less it is intriguing that the individual differences in response strategy manifested by their subjects should have such strong and pervasive effects on performance. Further developments of this kind of research seem likely to have important theoretical and practical implications. There is clearly more to be done in this developing field of applied research, and although there appear to be shortcomings in many of the published studies, there are some data that are suggestive of a time-sharing ability. Improved experimental methods (including a wider representation of both single and multiple-task arrangements, the use of more subjects, and a more informed use of factor analytic techniques) are among the recommendations of a recent review of this research (Ackerman, Schneider, and Wickens 1984). To this we might add the need to take into account differences between individuals in terms of ability and choice of performance strategy.

Time-sharing and attention switching

The time-sharing concept bridges two broad possibilities. The first is that resources are shared between the component tasks but that otherwise performance on them proceeds in parallel, and more or less continuously (at least no less continuously than when done singly). So the tasks may, because capacity is shared, have to operate at a slower rate, though the temporal structure of the performance is essentially unchanged. The second possibility is that capacity is shared temporally, so that performance is managed by switching from one component task to another, with total capacity allocated to the task in hand at any time. The switch from one task to another may be triggered, according to alternative versions of this hypothesis, at fixed points in time, or at convenient points in the stream of inputs and outputs (and processing operations).

The time to switch from one activity to another is clearly of some significance in the capacity-switching versions of time-sharing (but not in the capacity-sharing account, because of its continuous-processing assumption). In Broadbent's (1958) model of attention, switching between input channels could occur once every one-third of a second (a rate estimated in part from studies then available on dual-task performance). Others have pointed to the possibility of the brain's alpha rhythm (a periodic fluctuation of electrical activity measured at the brain's surface and most apparent when the individual is in a resting state) acting as a time base in terms of which processing operations may be synchronized and co-ordinated. This rhythm, which ranges between about 8 and 13 cycles per second (Hz), could also be used to schedule the opportunities to sample sources of information in different input channels. On this basis a switching time in attention of about one-tenth of a second would be expected (given that the average alpha rhythm is about 10 Hz).

Whether or not the time-sharing concept is valid, and whether or not there is a connection between alpha and the timing of information-processing operations, it is of interest to investigate the consequences for speed of reaction of attending to the wrong 'channel'. Research on visual attention to spatial locations has shown that slower responses are given when the subject is not attending to the point where the stimulus arrives (Posner 1980). Since this has been shown to occur in the absence of (or need for) changes in the position of the eye, it seems to follow that it takes time to switch attention from point to point in the visual field. Moreover there is evidence that this shift in attention is of a continuous kind, rather as if an attentional torch-beam is swung from one location to another (Shulman, Remington, and McLean (1979), though there is some doubt about the replicability of this finding (Remington and Pierce 1984). The time to switch attention intramodally does not seem to have been directly estimated but the paradigm used in the visual-attention studies would seem to be modifiable for this purpose, and is similar to that used to estimate the time to switch attention from one modality to another.

This issue has been investigated quite thoroughly. Laberge, VanGelder, and Yellott (1971) did so by presenting the stimulus for response either auditorily or visually, on each trial giving the subject a cue as to which modality was to be used. On a proportion of trials the cue was correct and there was no need to switch to the other modality, but on a proportion of occasions it was wrong and (assuming the subject was attending to the cued channel) a switch between channels was needed. Reaction times were delayed by about 100 msec when attention switching was necessary, and this was taken as the time to switch between visual and auditory modalities. This is rather longer than the time estimated by Kristofferson (1967) using a variety of methods, always involving the simultaneous presentation of a tone and a light. For one task the subjects had the job of discriminating whether or not the offsets of the light and sound were simultaneous, and in a second they had to respond as fast as possible to the offset of whichever stimulus terminated first. For the reaction-time task the critical channel was sometimes known in advance, but sometimes not. On a proportion of trials in the latter case the subject would have to switch between channels (assuming attention was never anywhere else). The switching time from one channel to the other, which was estimated to be about 50 msec, was very similar on each of the methods used (including alpha measurement, though Kristofferson expressed some scepticism about the significance of this).

There may be few practical applications of this research, though there are some circumstances when it could be important not to be attending to the wrong source of information if the time penalty for doing so is of the order of 50–100 msec. For example, consider the case of the 100-metre sprinter whose performance is today measured electronically accurate to 100ths of a second. If a runner like Carl Lewis, who has a habit of running the distance in just under or very close to ten seconds, is attending other than to the starter's gun then he could be delayed by up to a tenth of a second, which is a metre's headstart to an opponent. As to the connection between attention-switching and time-sharing, no research seems to have been done though it would seem a relationship that would be worthy of investigation.

The studies of attention-switching time have focused closely on the temporal microstructure of performance and there is embodied in them a view that seems to deny the possibility of the concurrent performance of two tasks. The ideas of time-sharing and attention-switching are problematical because there is no final level of temporal analysis that is insisted upon. Nevertheless they present a competing explanation for theorists interested in the idea of continuous-resource allocation to contend with, which they may accommodate by tasks designed to minimize the opportunity for time-sharing as we shall see in the next section. Indeed, how to design tasks so that they can be effectively carried out simultaneously with a minimum of detriment to one another is the main practical issue that remains to be discussed.

Limits in concurrent performance

It is a minor tradition in the world of contemporary/modern jazz to play more than one instrument at a time, and some extraordinary sounds and sights have been achieved, for example by the blind jazz musician Rahsaan Roland Kirk, playing two reed instruments and a nose flute simultaneously. Street musicians have a longer tradition of the 'one-man band', which involves concurrent performance or time-sharing of several activities. This kind of achievement is the product of many hours, even years, of practice, and its acquisition is not straightforwardly amenable to study in the laboratory. None the less psychologists have a longstanding interest in such performances; for instance, Solomons and Stein (1896) reported the introspective fruits of their efforts to learn to do various combined reading and writing tasks, such as reading while writing down dictated words. The objective, which was eventually achieved, was what they termed 'automatism': to perform one of the tasks without being conscious of it. The equation of automaticity, as it is called today, with unconscious processing has echoes in some contemporary accounts of performance. Some recent studies of concurrent performance will be reviewed in this section.

Limitations on the performance of tasks which involve the deployment of attentional resources – focused on one source of information to the exclusion of others, or distributed among several – are clearly demonstrated in the many studies of auditory attention (reviewed by Broadbent 1958). For example, when two streams of auditory signals (passages of text, strings of digits, letters, or unrelated words) are presented together, one for close attention as in the shadowing paradigm (repeating the words of a speaker as they are heard: see p. 25), relatively little information is picked up from the second stream. Although conditions can be contrived that show that the secondary stream of information is not shut out altogether, generally only superficial aspects of the unattended message are noted, such as the gender of the speaker's voice (Broadbent 1958).

Although there has been little research directed at the issue it is clear that the opportunity for extended practice at such tasks is highly beneficial. Experimenters frequently get a great deal of experience in their own research tasks in the course of designing experiments and testing apparatus, and so forth; and with this in mind, Underwood (1974) compared the performance on shadowing tasks of a highly experienced experimenter with a group of his own subjects. The experimenter was Moray, and his existing level of shadowing skill was bolstered by several hours' additional practice. Moray's performance easily exceeded that of the inexperienced subjects who had taken part in his experiments. The advantage was most marked in conditions which caused the inexperienced subjects most difficulty. The task was to shadow one of a pair of auditory streams of words, one to each ear, and to report whenever a digit occurred in either the attended (shadowed) or the unattended stream. This was most difficult if the same voice was used for both components of the task; compared to the 72 per cent of the digits in the attended stream detected by unpractised subjects, even Moray detected only 88 per cent. For the unattended or secondary stream the difference was very marked with Moray's performance strikingly better (67 vs 8 per cent).

Minimizing interference between tasks

The component tasks in Underwood's (1974) study were presented within the same modality and a great deal of practice was necessary for performance to reach the level it did. Nonetheless the possibility of masking one stream of information by the other at a relatively peripheral, perhaps sensory, stage of processing provides a reason for expecting a persisting limitation in performance. This consideration has led to a body of research that has tried to avoid peripheral limitations of this sort, by presenting the messages to be processed via different input modalities. This may remove one set of obstacles to the efficient handling of two activities simultaneously, but there are others. It is of course obvious that the efficiency of doing two tasks at once will be impaired, even if we arrange for the inputs to be separated, if the same response mechanism (e.g. voice) is simultaneously required by both. In fact investigators in the selective attention field have naturally avoided using the same response modality, for example when shadowing (vocal response) is combined with target detection (tapping a key) as in a study by Treisman and Geffen (1967).

The contribution in attention studies of response selection and control has been little studied (although see McLeod 1977; Wickens 1984). This aspect of attention is relatively little understood, and is an important area for future research. A relevant incidental observation was made by Allport, Antonis, and Reynolds (1972) who noted that when their music-student subjects were asked to do shadowing and sight-reading simultaneously, the two performances, although eventually capable of being carried on independently, seemed initially to be driven by a common rhythm (that of the music, as one might expect). In fact two *manual* responses, such as tapping on two separate keys in time with different rhythms, are particularly prone to such difficulties, one response rhythm tending to dominate the organization and performance of the other (Peters 1977; Klapp 1979). Moreover this has been shown to apply too when a manual response is combined with an articulatory response. Although the articulatory response is achieved via the vocal musculature, subjects also making a repetitive manual response have great difficulty in controlling the two independently (Klapp 1981). The separation of two response modalities may not be achieved as easily as it might appear.

Performance without peripheral limitations

Nevertheless it is clear that studies of concurrent performance intended to test for the existence or otherwise of central-processing limitations should avoid bottlenecks due to non-central limitations. This requires, as a minimum for the task, information to be presented via distinct modalities (e.g. visual vs auditory) and the responses to be produced by separate output systems (e.g. manual vs vocal). Performance under such conditions, and with the added impetus of extended practice, has been examined in a number of recent studies. The practical implications for task design are of course of interest, but the main motivation for this research has been theoretical. A common basic assumption in much of the literature on concurrent performance is that it is fundamentally limited as a consequence of the finite general-purpose capacity of central-information processing. The locus of this hypothetical capacity limitation, the central bottleneck, has been the focus of much interest. The basic assumption, in terms of the terminology that has been widely accepted, is that there is a limited supply of processing resources which are undifferentiated and unspecialized in nature, and which can be devoted with more or less total flexibility to one task or another, or to one aspect of a task or another. This, however, has been challenged in recent years (Allport 1980; Neisser 1976) on the basis of a body of experiments which have been duly cautious about inadvertent restrictions on performance due to non-central bottle-necks. The claim has been made that under propitious circumstances, when such restrictions are stripped away, performance of two tasks can proceed without mutual interference. We shall look first at a sample of these experiments and develop their theoretical significance in the context of the generalized resource model of performance.

As noted above, Allport, Antonis, and Reynolds (1972) had their subjects perform the somewhat unlikely combination of shadowing and sight-reading piano music. The subjects were proficient pianists and, as we know, they had some difficulty organizing the response part of the combined task. But the problem was soon overcome and the sight-reading was unaffected by shadowing, the latter also being virtually unharmed by the dual-task context. If the joint demands of the two tasks had been met by time-sharing, this would be likely to have shown up in the fine structure of the performances, with more bursts and pauses when doing the dual condition, but the detail of the data failed to reveal a change of this sort. The evidence was interpreted as supporting a multiprocessor model of performance, with parallel operation of specialized processors responsible for the conduct of the two tasks of shadowing and sight-reading. This is considered possible in such an account because the processing requirements of the two tasks are sufficiently different. Interference occurs if the processor, specialized or not, is called on by both tasks.

The next study in this accumulation of evidence is that of Shaffer (1975), who studied a single highly-skilled typist doing a variety of additional tasks while typing. Her copy-typing was normally in the region of 100 words per minute, and was as quick when shadowing auditory material as when not. She could also maintain her typing speed when reciting nursery rhymes, though she had difficulty when reciting the alphabet when typing (and was worse at the recitation task too). The last of these findings suggests that a difficulty arises when some common central representation (of letters, in this case) is accessed in the course of the tasks. For audio-typing, her performance declined when she was concurrently required to recite a rhyme. There was also evidence in the errors she made of some 'crosstalk' between the two streams of information (occasional words from one stream being incorrectly produced in the other), implying dependence on a common processor. Difficulty was also apparent when shadowing and audiotyping, not surprisingly, since a common input system was in use.

The most striking of these findings was the typist's ability to type from visual copy while shadowing, which has been interpreted to mean that a common linguistic base was simultaneously in use for the two tasks. On the other hand high copy-typing speeds are frequently achieved by using a letter-by-letter transcription strategy, and it is possible that this enabled Shaffer's subject to insulate her typing from the influence of the shadowing task, which may with more confidence be assumed to depend on access to a central linguistic system. This view is consistent with the difficulty that was found in reciting the alphabet when copy-typing. It is also of interest that audiotyping (auditory input plus manual output) was difficult in conjunction with reciting aloud (internal 'input' plus vocal output), a finding that suggests that the subject found it difficult to listen while monitoring (auditorily) her vocal output. Speaking and listening simultaneously is clearly a difficult task combination, though it is not one which necessarily defeats all-comers. Most of us have met the person who talks on through our own feeble efforts to contribute to a conversation, though his or her comprehension of what we are saying may obviously be questionable. The difficulties of this task combination, however, are routinely negotiated by simultaneous translators, sometimes with considerable overlap in the input and output phases of the task (Gerver 1974).

The previous two studies demonstrate first the advantages that may accrue from a judicious selection of the modes of presentation and output. They also show that complex and difficult central information-processing activities may be carried out in tandem, when the individual has an unusually high degree of skill. The evidence so far is broadly consistent with a multiprocessor model, with independent parallel channels allowing the concurrent performance of sufficiently different tasks. Perhaps we should add that the component tasks must be quite routine and undemanding to the performer, and it would be of interest to see how unexpected conditions influence dual task performance. For example, if the typist encounters a sequence in aLtErNaTiNg CaSe, no doubt inter-response times will increase. The question is whether this momentary difficulty would be passed on to the second task. It is not obvious why it should if processing the two tasks is truly independent, and depends on separate mechanisms.

Although reservations have been expressed above, Shaffer's (1975) investigation demonstrates, it has been claimed, that it is possible under the right conditions for the central mental dictionary or lexicon, in which the semantic characteristics of words is represented, to be employed by the demands of two separate tasks. This has sometimes seemed to be the acme of achievement under dual-task conditions (Neisser 1976), because it seems to involve one of the deepest levels of processing and information representation. Presumably to achieve it would be inconsistent with the assumption that only a single thought can enter consciousness at a time, and certainly to have two separate semantically coherent streams of information active in consciousness at once seems an intuitive and introspective impossibility. Whether what Shaffer's typist was doing is tantamount to a contradiction of this depends on whether she was

simultaneous translators, sometimes with considerable overlap in the input and output phases of the task (Gerver 1974).

The previous two studies demonstrate first the advantages that may accrue from a judicious selection of the modes of presentation and output. They also show that complex and difficult central

This issue was also examined in a study by Spelke, Hirst, and Neisser (1976), in which they employed two students over a period of several months in a series of conditions like those of Solomons and Stein (1896). In these tasks the attempt was undertaken to learn to read and write simultaneously. At the outset the subjects' speed and comprehension when reading silently was established. They were then asked to do this when copying down a string of dictated words, an extra demand that led to a considerable disruption of reading in terms of speed and understanding. But with an hour's practice a day for about six weeks, they managed to do both tasks at once and their reading recovered to its initial level of proficiency.

The investigators then introduced various constraints in the dictated material, for example presenting sublists of rhyming words, words from the same category, and words forming sentences, instead of the random strings used at the outset. Only when the rhyming words were introduced was this spontaneously noticed by the subjects, who expressed some disbelief that they had copied the other sublists without becoming aware of it. Next the investigators asked the subjects to try to spot the occasions when a sequence of words from a category or forming a sentence appeared in the dictation. Reading was again impaired to begin with as they came to terms with this new additional demand, but again performance recovered with further extended practice. Finally the requirement was imposed for the category of each dictated word to be written down, still with the silent-reading task. The new task combination led to poorer reading performance, but with a considerable amount of additional practice even this extraordinary pairing was achieved at no cost in terms of reading speed and comprehension. This finally seems to overcome any objection that the component tasks are not linguistic ones.

Massive amounts of practice appear to be a prerequisite for the efficient conduct of two simultaneous tasks (in addition to the caveat regarding the avoidance of peripheral limitations on performance). This is relevant to industrial and commercial applications where extended opportunities for perfecting routine skills are customary, and would favour the development of efficient concurrent performance of two or more skills. Two further studies, however, indicate that people without much special practice can combine two suitably designed tasks which individually place quite high demands on processing resources.

Minimization of interference: functional separation

In the first study, by Rollins and Hendricks (1980), the subjects did an auditory task in tandem with either a visual or a second auditory task. The subject was presented with two streams of information, one for each task. Task 1 always used auditory input, words presented in rapid succession (up to 120 per minute). Different versions of the task were studied in three separate experiments – shadowing numbers, supplying antonyms to words, or categorizing them. In each case this continued until a target word occurred in the Task 2 input stream. The same four versions of Task 2 were used in each experiment: auditory word detection, visual word detection, visual category detection, and visual rhyme detection. These tasks were capable of being done with no errors when performed alone. The findings in the dual-task conditions were that those tasks involving semantic analysis of visually presented words could be done to a high standard concurrently with any one of the auditory tasks (averaging about 90 per cent correct), but monitoring for words presented auditorily at the same time as another auditory task was poorly done (roughly 30 per cent correct). In addition the task of detecting words rhyming with a given target word was also very difficult (averaging about 35 per cent correct). This was interpreted in terms of the convergence of the two inputs on common speech-analysing mechanisms, which evidently cannot be simultaneously accessed by two inputs without a severe penalty. It is often possible for subjects to avoid this limitation by 'buffering' the auditory information in the articulatory component of working memory for a short time, but in these experiments the opportunity for this was reduced by the high input rate and the use of a lengthy string of items exceeding the capacity of this buffer store. In any event it is clear that subjects could only assess the acoustic characteristics of visually presented words with difficulty if engaged in an auditory task which also involved words. On the other hand simultaneous semantic analysis was less of a problem. Although the subjects did not achieve perfect performance on even the most propitious task combination, it should be remembered that they were quite unpractised at the tasks, alone or in combination. One feature of the results that should be noted is that there was some shortfall on Task 2 relative to the error-free performance possible without Task 1 in *all* conditions, even though this was slight in the best conditions.

In an experiment in a similar vein, Shallice, McLeod, and Lewis (1985) found that subjects could monitor a rapid stream of spoken words (150 per minute) for a target name while reading aloud a stream of single words (about 135 per minute) with a mere 10 per cent decrement in performance in both tasks relative to single-task conditions. The investigation was aimed at discovering whether speech-perception and speech-production systems are separable or utilize common resources (involving information relevant to the speech-related properties of words). If the systems are separate then reading aloud may be considered to depend on speech production (phonological output), while name detection depends on speech perception (phonological input).

Of course this assumes that the tasks place sufficiently high demands on the necessary resources for a major performance decrement to result if they were shared. It is possible, however, that the small decrement in performance means that the individual demands of reading aloud and name detection were too low for common resource-sharing to show up. Shallice, McLeod, and Lewis therefore used various control conditions to decide the issue. Shadowing one of a pair of messages (at 100 words per minute) was used as one of the control conditions, as a way of loading the phonological input-system resources. A second task was to monitor the number of syllables in a string of words, stopping when a two-syllable word was heard. This was assumed to depend on the use of the phonological output system, in this case being accessed for information about the segmentation characteristics of words (especially salient for the production of their spoken versions). Task combinations studied by Shallice, McLeod, and Lewis were shadowing plus name detection (both loading the phonological-input system), reading and syllable counting (both loading the phonological output system), and the name detection plus reading aloud combination (each loading a different system) as before. The experiment showed that the two-task combinations, drawing on what were assumed to be common resources, suffered considerably greater impairment (30–40 per cent) than the combination using different resources.

A further possibility is that the large decrements obtained with syllable counting and shadowing were due to them placing much greater demands on general processing resources than name detection, and hence were considerably more difficult than name detection to do in combination with any other task. This was discounted when it was shown that each of the auditory tasks was capable of being combined at a quite high level of performance with a difficult visual choice reaction-time task (with only 4–11 per cent decrements). This task was chosen to have little or no structural resemblance (in terms of modalities used) with the auditory tasks, and was adjusted in difficulty level (by increasing the presentation rate) so that when done alone each subject's performance was on the point of breakdown.

The principal conclusion drawn in this closely reasoned study was that speech perception and production systems are functionally separate because of the relatively small deficit in performance when printed words were read aloud while spoken names were being monitored. It should be noted that this small impairment in performance calls for explanation, possibly in terms of a general resource which may be shared among concurrent activities even if they otherwise call on functionally separate systems. It should also be noted that the subjects in this study coped with the joint demands of the two tasks without special or extended practice.

Theoretical considerations

What is the theoretical significance of the findings on concurrent performance? Allport (1980) cited evidence of 'minimal interference' between tasks to support his critique of the commonly accepted idea of performance being constrained by a general-purpose limited-processing capacity. A similar position was also taken by Neisser (1976). Although Neisser had little to say by way of theoretical explanation of how two complex skills can coexist without detriment, Allport postulated on the basis of the evidence a set of specialized processors dealing with particular well-practised skills which can be simultaneously operative with no interference between them.

Residual cost in organizing concurrent responses

A complete theory of multiple task performance, and of resource allocation, has to accommodate a wide variety of findings as we have seen, including evidence that there is invariably a small deficit in performance of a task when it is done in company of a second task, even in the most propitious of circumstances. Hence the strength of the conclusions that may be drawn from the studies that show minimal interference should not be exaggerated. Broadbent (1982) noted that close inspection of the reported data indicates that a small degree of interference occurs even under the most favourable circumstances. The interference seldom reaches a level at which it is statistically significant, but it is regular enough to suggest that full independence is not achieved.

Broadbent observed in addition that the predictability of the stimulus material (reading stories, shadowing text, sight-reading music, reciting rhymes) is often very high, and the presentation of this material may afford opportunities for a degree of effective time-sharing between the tasks. This seems to have been avoided in recent studies (Rollins and Hendricks 1980; Shallice, McLeod, and Lewis 1985) because stimulus sequences are random strings of words, and the presentation rates are very high or are individually adjusted so that the task is only just manageable.

Apart from these reservations it is clear that sophisticated theoretical accounts are beginning to be given, developing from Allport's suggestion about specialized processors, which make complex assumptions about the 'functional architecture' of the information-processing system (e.g. Wickens 1984; Shallice, McLeod, and Lewis 1985). From a practical point of view the experimental demonstrations give evidence of what people can do concurrently given appropriate conditions. Their full practical value has yet to be realized, but it can be seen that interference between tasks can be minimized by careful design, and extensive practice, though there may be a small residual cost attributable to having to organize two responses.

Resource theory in information processing

It remains to consider one further theoretical aspect of multiple-task performance. We have frequently alluded to the concept of processing resources in this chapter and elsewhere. For example, in the discussion of the secondary-task method of assessing mental workload, it was considered important that the so-called primary task received top priority, and should not be impaired in the company of the secondary task. Whatever spare resources were available could be taken up by the secondary task. It is implicit that matters could be otherwise, and that the joint resources could be shared in a different proportion. In fact most of the research discussed in the present section, while indicating to the subject that both tasks should be engaged in, has left the subject to select an appropriate balance between the two activities. It is apparent that the balance could be swayed more directly by the emphasis of the instructions given to the subject, or perhaps by the incentives associated with the level of performance achieved. It seems reasonable to assume that as one task is emphasized to a greater degree so it will receive a greater share of the available resources, and so its performance may be expected to improve as that on the other task declines. Thus a kind of trading relationship exists between the two tasks and the interference about the biases and efficiency of performance that may be made on the basis of the form of this relationship, known as the performance-resource characteristic, have been thoroughly discussed (Navon and Gopher 1979; Norman and Bobrow 1975; Wickens 1984).

The first comprehensive account of resource theory assumed that processing resources were generally available to all processing stages and all tasks that made a call on them, the actual share received being regulated by an allocation policy (Kahneman 1973). The most recent developments of resource theory – motivated by the sort of evidence reviewed in the previous section – have seen a move away from the assumption that processing resources are undifferentiated in nature. Wickens (1984), for example, postulated that there are resources specialized relative to three aspects of a task: the input modality, the processing stage, and the central-processing code that is used. The model deals in particular with visual and auditory modalities (each associated with a reservoir of resources), and assumes that a distinction may be made between early and late processing stages (input and central decisional operations are pooled, and are contrasted with response-related operations). Finally the mental operations involved in a task may be thought of as taking place in a structure which is specialized to deal with information coded in the appropriate form (verbal vs spatial), and which also has a dedicated resource reservoir. It will be seen that the idea of resources also being associated with the code in terms of which central representations are processed is connected with the working-memory concept of Baddeley and Hitch (1974). Resources are not transferable from one stage to another, nor from one code or modality to another. But when two tasks make simultaneous calls on the same resource reservoir, resource allocation is necessary and this will be decided in terms of task priorities, incentives, and so forth. This comprehensive model accommodates a wide range of findings, though it is not without its shortcomings (for further discussion, see Wickens 1984).

There remain an intriguing collection of observations, strands of evidence, and lines of theoretical analysis that may already threaten the current assumptions and conceptual framework of resource theory. Space remains only to give them the barest mention, but the interested reader will find a stimulating literature continuing to accumulate around the topics discussed in this chapter. For instance, Duncan (1979) has drawn attention to the fact that when two tasks are done together, their joint performance is affected by relationships (perceptual, central, and motor) between them that necessarily do not come into play in single-task conditions. More formal evidence of these 'emergent properties' is given by Duncan, but a simple everyday illustration is provided by the difficulty which most people experience when patting the head with one hand while rubbing the stomach with the other, two activities which on their own give rise to no difficulty at all. This particular example relates to the problem of co-ordinating two dissimilar motor actions (see also Klapp 1979, 1981). A particularly striking finding reported by Klapp *et al.* (1985) that seems to confound most versions of resource theory is that increasing the perceptual distinctiveness of two rhythmic input sequences (hence presumably accessing separate resources) makes it more difficult for them to be tracked by separate tapping responses. It seems that the two rhythmic outputs must be treated by the subject as a unified activity, and this is facilitated by enabling them to be perceived in an integrated fashion.

'Resources', 'capacity', and information processing

Finally we must grasp the nettle and ask what are the 'processing resources' that theoretical accounts refer to. They appear to be the mental stuff that it takes to produce efficient, fast, error-free, unimpeded performance. But if we hope for definitional clarity this really leads nowhere, because we have no independent specification of anything in this definitional circle. Euphemisms such as 'capacity' have also been used and the referents of these terms are not usually defined. It is of interest, however, that Kahneman (1973) linked capacity with the concept of arousal, and this certainly raises intriguing connections, though it does not fill the definitional gap. It is helpful to note the analogy that was intended in the early usage of 'capacity' with the central-processing capacity of a computer (Moray 1967). Even in this connection it will be found that the concept tends to generate controversy despite the obviously more tangible context in which it is relevant. However, measures are agreed by computer scientists which entail a complex of factors including the speed at which the computer's central-processing operations are executed, the size of the memory store, and so on. It is also instructive to note that complications are introduced as soon as the information-processing structure changes, for instance, as when central operations may be carried out in parallel as they are in the most sophisticated machines. It is also noteworthy, relative to the earlier discussion of mental-workload measurement, that the power of a computing system may be measured in terms of a set of 'benchmarks', a collection of standard tasks whose times of execution on the given computer system are used to index the performance of the system. It is arguable that we still know so little of the central-information-processing architecture of the human brain that we cannot expect much greater clarity regarding key concepts such as processing resources, and shall for the present have to accept the existing allusive force of the term.

Practical issue: using a car-phone while driving

Radios and radio-telephones have long been a feature of the driving environment of taxi-drivers, police drivers, and others, but recent technological developments bring these facilities to a much wider public. Cell-phone networks now enable communication by mobile telephone to take place within and even beyond national boundaries, instead of being limited to the relatively small neighbourhoods previously covered by radio transmission systems. An increasingly wide population of users now have access to car-phones, and these individuals are mainly business people, who need ready access to a telephone for professional purposes. But they are not professional drivers whose use of a mobile telephone is integral to their work as is the case in taxi-driving or traffic-police work.

Suppliers of car-phones clearly recognize the potential problems associated with phoning while driving. One of the problems that they have allowed for is the possible interference between the manual task of dialling a number and manipulating the steering wheel, by the provision of a 'hands-free' facility. This facility is described in the brochure of one manufacturer as a recommended option, which 'allows conversation whilst maintaining your normal driving position, including both hands on the steering wheel'. It is plainly seen as a component in a dual-task arrangement since it provides 'ease of operation whilst driving'. Thus the driver is not expected to restrict the use of the mobile phone to when the vehicle is stationary. Furthermore an interesting assumption is brought out by the remark that 'when in use, conversation can be continued with both hands on the wheel, *just like talking with a passenger in the vehicle*' (italics added). In fact traditional users of mobile telephones, like taxi-drivers and traffic police, communicate with a control room or base where the personnel are familiar with the circumstances under which the telephone is used on the road. Moreover the communication with such drivers tends to be relatively simple, and certainly stereotyped in nature. In contrast, the business executive may call or be called by someone quite unused to this form of communication, who will be unfamiliar with any allowance that may be needed in the manner of communicating – callers may even be unaware of the fact that they are speaking to someone driving a car. And the communication with the driver may vary from the trivial to the momentous, and certainly may cast the driver in a demanding decision-making role. It is most doubtful that this kind of car-phone use is 'just like talking with a passenger in the vehicle'. It is possible that using a car-phone while driving may interfere with the primary task of safely controlling the moving vehicle.

It is surprising to find that, although there is an extensive body of evidence on concurrent performance of two tasks, little research has been done directly into the question of whether driving skills are affected by the concurrent task of telephoning. There is one published study, however, which specifically addressed this question. This was by Brown, Tickner and Simmonds (1969) who carried out their investigation in anticipation of a likely upsurge of use of car-phones. They identified two aspects of the telephoning task that could interfere with driving. The first is having to make manual actions to operate the telephone to make or receive a call. Brown and his colleagues considered that the first problem, the possible impairment of the control skills of driving by a simultaneous manual task, was likely to be obviated by technological developments. In fact almost 20 years later, the 'hands-free' facility is still only a 'recommended option' according to the glossy brochures for mobile telephones.

The second potential source of interference arises from having to pay attention to the call. Brown and his colleagues pointed to the need to switch attention 'between the informational demands of the two tasks' as possibly leading to interference with driving, for example, by the disruption of visual scanning, or the impairment of the judgement of relative velocity. This is an analysis guided by the assumption of single channel theory, which has been seriously questioned as we have seen. Whether the same prediction can be derived from an account such as that of multiple resource theory is not clear. The telephone task would seem to be rather well-chosen from this perspective, with auditory input and vocal output. Driving principally relies on the input of visual information, and the control activities are manual. What can be said about the central coding involved in the two tasks is less clear. Presumably this would be verbal coding for the telephone task (though this would depend on the nature of the problem being discussed, and one could not preclude verbally posed problems evoking the use of spatial imagery, for instance). What complex central processes are involved in driving is not clear, but it is a task which requires fine judgements and control actions made at speed, based on perceptual data about the environment, and in anticipation of the actions of other road users.

The task which Brown, Tickner, and Simmonds (1969) used in combination with driving was a logical reasoning task (Baddeley 1968). In this task the subject has to make a series of true-false decisions about simple sentences purporting to describe the sequence of a pair of letters. Thus to the sentence 'B precedes A' paired with the letter sequence BA, the subject should give the response 'true'. Similarly for the sentence 'B is followed by A' paired with the letters AB, the correct response would be 'false'. The time taken to decide, and the accuracy of the decisions are used to describe the subject's performance. The sentences were presented auditorily via a radio-telephone headset, and the driver subject's spoken responses were tape-recorded. The task otherwise was to drive a car around a circuit on an unused airfield on which had been placed a sequence of wooden obstacles, set at varying distances apart, to present a graded series of gaps from some 3 inches less than the vehicle's width to some 9 inches more than it. The driver thus had to judge whether or not to pass through each gap, or to go around the obstacle. The driving task was done both with the reasoning task, and again without it.

The drivers tended to drive rather slower when doing the reasoning task than when not doing it. Despite this decrease in speed, more errors were made on the smallest gaps when concurrently doing the telephone task, drivers tending to attempt the 'impossible' gaps. There were no differences in the number of control actions, such as gear-changes, use of foot controls, and so on. (As to the reasoning task, responses were slower and more mistakes were made while driving than when not). Brown and his colleagues concluded that while the most practised or 'automatized' components of the driving skill may be unaffected by the secondary task, 'some perceptual and decision skills may be critically impaired'. It is clear that a theoretical characterization of driving should take heed of these findings, since in terms of multiple resource theory, this complex skill seems to call on the same central resources used in the logical reasoning task. As to the practical implications, it is not surprising that the British 'Highway Code' recommends that mobile telephones should be used only when the user is stationary. Whether this should be a compulsion rather than a recommendation is not clear, but it is certainly regrettable that current practice should have developed in the face of so little evidence.

Summary

The starting point for this chapter was the problem of operator overload, and the observation that the nature of workload is changing with the advent of new technologies. This is reflected in a change in the allocation of responsibilities between people and machines, with an increasing perceptual/cognitive component to the mental load on operators as they take an increasing responsibility for monitoring and supervising tasks. Methods of measuring mental workload were reviewed, including primary-task, secondary-task, physiological, and subjective measures. Differences in their sensitivity to load variations, and differences in their intrusiveness relative to the operator's principal task, were noted. The importance of the underlying assumptions regarding the nature of the processing resources drawn upon (especially the contrast between undifferentiated or general resources and differentiated or specific resources) was established. We also saw that operators may modify their goals and performance strategies, and hence affect the load experienced.

One aspect of task design that may cause difficulty for the operator is having to do more than one thing at a time. Dealing with this problem successfully may be seen as a matter of skilful time-sharing, or alternatively of the allocation of limited mental resources simultaneously. The prospect of selecting people with a high degree of the relevant ability was considered. Laboratory tasks of selective and divided attention, and of concurrent performance, have been used with some limited success.

Turning to basic research, the measurement of the time to switch attention was briefly reviewed to illustrate the possibility of examining the detailed temporal structure of attentional performance. Studies of the concurrent performance of two tasks were discussed, showing that high degrees of practice are advantageous.

Careful selection of the means of presenting task information (preferably by different input modalities), and of the means by which the actions required are carried out (by different response modalities), are ways to minimize the interference between two tasks. Progress in the theoretical analysis of human performance has emphasized the modular nature of the information-processing system, and this has been supported by studies of concurrent-task performance. One prominent line of theorizing considers the joint-performance problem in terms of the allocation of processing resources. While support has built up for a multiple-resources model, there is also an accumulating body of evidence indicating the shortcomings of such an account. As to the basic information-processing model of Chapter 2 (Fig 2.4), the interest in this chapter has not been in the basic processing stages, but has centred on the nature of the attentional system. In any event, applied and basic research on the problems of workload, attention, and performance are closely intermeshed, and seem to be progressing in a productive and mutually informative way.

6 VISUAL AND COGNITIVE ASPECTS OF READING

Reading: general introduction

Reading is a familiar but complex skill in which perceptual and cognitive processes are interwoven. It is representative of the practically important behaviours studied by cognitive psychologists. The growing understanding of this complex skill is symptomatic of cognitive psychology's successful commitment to matters of everyday interest and practical significance. It also demonstrates the close analysis that such matters must receive in the pursuit of insight and understanding. This chapter is devoted to an examination within the information-processing framework of some of the processes involved in reading.

Because a reader's objectives relative to the printed page often concern the reception of the thoughts and ideas of the writer, it is easy to overlook the contribution of the visual system to this process. But although reading emphatically is to do with knowing and understanding, it depends on the proficient use of a complicated and mobile visual apparatus, and so a complete model of reading must include an account of this aspect of the skill. The first part of this chapter deals with research on the contribution of eye movements to reading. The second part, recognizing the importance of comprehension and knowledge, considers the influence of contextual factors in reading. The third section of the chapter examines the impact of the new information technology for the practice and theoretical study of reading, with particular reference to eye-movement behaviour, and comprehension processes.

Practical issue I: eye movements in speed reading

Various commercial courses have been available over the years offering to 'increase your reading speed'. One of the techniques advocated for rapid or speed reading depends on learning a new style of eye-movement behaviour in which the eyes are moved down the page rather than along the lines from left to right. Moving the eyes back to parts of the page already seen is considered inefficient, and groups of words corresponding to whole ideas are to be read at a glance. In addition the hand may be used to pace the passage of the eyes over the page. The goal may be to increase reading speed by a factor of four or five, so the average reader may be expected to deal with the pages in this book at a rate of something in the region of four per minute (and hence the whole book in an hour or so's reading!). There have been investigations assessing the efficacy of speed-reading courses and their conclusions are generally not very favourable (see Gibson and Levin 1975). The skill they seem to encourage is closer to the reading style known as 'skimming', in which the reader is concerned to gain a rapid overview of the text without a concern for detail, or a useful or significant degree of comprehension. The likely consequences of attempting to streamline the eye-movement behaviour of a normal reader will become apparent from the research described in this chapter.

Eye movements and reading: basic issues

This section reviews some findings about eye movements in relation to reading, one of the richest sources of insights and discoveries about reading. The fundamental issues regarding the visually mediated guidance of the eyes in reading (Rayner 1978) include: what readers look at when reading; how much information can be picked up in a single fixation; and how eye movements are guided. The rationale for examining the relation between eye movements and reading is that the pathway followed by the eyes over the printed page – that is, how the text is scanned by the eyes – is evidence of how it is processed by the brain (Levy-Schoen and O'Regan 1979). But McConkie (1979) has stressed that the region of the visual field being used in language processing is not known despite knowledge at any instant, via a record of eye movements, of what the eye is fixated on. This caveat should be borne in mind, as a reminder of the inherent uncertainty of a discipline that can only ever achieve an indirect view of its subject matter.

Eye-movement activity during reading

Recordings of the eye movements of skilled readers show that the eyes are fixated about 90 per cent of the time. The rest of the time is occupied by 'saccadic' eye movements (or 'saccades' as they are known), the abrupt movements whereby the eyes shift from place to place when a stationary object is being scanned. Saccadic suppression, a reduction in visual sensitivity principally during but also just prior to and after an eye movement (Matin 1974), probably means that information is efficiently picked up only while the eyes are stationary. Saccades in reading involve fixation shifts of about 2 degrees; this is about 8–9 character spaces on average, though Rayner and McConkie (1976) reported a range of saccade lengths of 2–18 character spaces. They last about 20 to 30 msec, and the ensuing fixation is for about 250 msec on average. There is nevertheless considerable variation both within and between individuals, particularly in relation to fixation durations; most of them last 150–350 msec although a range of 100–500 msec was reported by Rayner and McConkie (1976).

A majority of eye movements (excluding return sweeps to the beginning of the next line) are progressive (from left to right), but regressive eye movements are not uncommon. Fixations resulting from forward eye movements take in every word or so in normal fluent reading, adults dealing with about 1.2 words at a glance. Regressive movements are about half the size of progressive movements and occur about once a line (Levy-Schoen and O'Regan 1979). Indeed there is something of a myth about the infrequency of regressions on the part of fluent readers, who according to the myth are not supposed to make them at all; in fact, although a high incidence of these right-to-left or bottom-to-top shifts in fixation may well be symptomatic of a poor reader, they do occur relatively frequently also in proficient readers, one study recording up to 20 per cent of all movements as regressions. The reading speed of an adult is about 250–300 words per minute, the latter figure being characteristic of a rather easy non-technical text. Children appear to take in about half a word per fixation (Levy-Schoen and O'Regan 1979). As the age of the child increases, progressive eye movements decrease in overall number, saccade length increases, and regressive movements become less frequent. The developmental picture is one of increasing efficiency in the use and deployment of resources of the eye-movement system, and in particular of more rapid and effective pick-up of information.

Perceptual span in reading

The question of how much information can be picked up at a single glance, referred to as the perceptual span, has been tackled by a variety of methods (Rayner 1975). Among the most recent methods are dynamic-display techniques, in which what is presented to the eye is contingent on the position currently fixated. For instance, in a study by McConkie and Rayner (1975) a systematically altered version of the text was presented to all but a region centred about the fixation point. As the eye moved to a new location, the text in the fixated region assumed its proper appearance, so that only a 'window' of correct text could be seen at any moment. The size of the window was varied, and the effect on saccade length and fixation time of the window size was noted. In addition the effects of various ways of changing the text in the area outside the clear window were investigated. Some examples of the experimental conditions studied are illustrated in Figure 6.1a. Studies of the effect of window size show a progressive improvement in reading time, increasing saccade length, and increasing fixation durations as window size increased.

A similar but less drastic method of altering the text was studied by Rayner (1975). Subjects read short paragraphs each of which contained a simple grammatical sentence in which a single word had been changed. As the reader's eyes passed an invisible boundary just before the critical word, that word reverted to its normal appearance. A simple memory test was used to ensure that the sentences had been read, a common precaution in this research. The material used in this investigation is illustrated in Figure 6.1b.

Figure 6.1 Examples of stimulus conditions investigated in studies using dynamic displays with eye-movement-contingent presentation techniques

(a) Dynamic window display technique (McConkie and Rayner 1975). Example with window size 13, showing the material outside the window replaced by 'x's, but retaining the correct spacing between words.

Original text with four successive fixations shown by the dots underneath the words:

```
This is what experimenters can dream up if they try.
     .      .        .     .
```

What the reader would see given the fixations indicated above:

```
xxxs is what expxxxxxxxxxx xxx xxxxx xx xx xxxx xxx.

xxxx xx xhat experimenxxxx xxx xxxxx xx xx xxxx xxx.

xxxx xx xxxx xxxerimenters cax xxxxx xx xx xxxx xxx.

xxxx xx xxxx xxxxxxxxxnters can drexx xx xx xxxx xxx.
```

(b) Eye-movement contingent display (Rayner 1975).

Sample sentence showing base word 'heard' in position:

```
The owner heard the boys in the backroom.
```

Sentences showing alterations prior to fixation on base-word location:

```
W-ST   The owner hired the boys in the backroom.

N-ST   The owner hrvcd the boys in the backroom.

N-T    The owner hcbid the boys in the backroom.

N-S    The owner krvcb the boys in the backroom.
```

In W–ST, the replacement was a word (W) with the same shape (S) and identical terminal letters (T). In the other examples the replacement was a nonword (N), with a shape difference in N–T, and different terminal letters in N–S.

Extrafoveal information processing

Evidence from studies of this sort suggests some pick-up of semantic information from words from the fovea (the central region of the retina specialized for fine-detailed vision) outwards to a distance equivalent to some 6 character spaces. Shape and terminal-letter information is available from words beginning up to 12 letter spaces from the fovea, and information about word length at a distance of 15 character spaces. Moreover the span is asymmetrical, extending some distance further to the right than to the left. One way of viewing these findings is to suppose that there is not a single perceptual span, but a variety of spans, corresponding to different kinds of information available in the text, serving different purposes in reading. In any event, information seen extrafoveally appears to influence the course of reading.

It is not unusual, however, for the conclusion to be made that for the purposes of exerting a serious influence on the course of visual perceptual activities such as reading, 'the retina is inactive' for angles greater than some 4 or 5 degrees from the centre of the fovea (Fisher and Lefton 1976). However, this conclusion may be overstated, since in spite of its limited resolving ability, the peripheral retina is quite well-equipped to do certain jobs that may be useful in reading. Evidence on the visual competence of the periphery includes the finding by Menzer and Thurmond (1970) that the gross outline of forms may be effectively resolved at retinal positions well outside the fovea; performance at discriminating between random geometric shapes did not fall to a chance level until the presentation angle was as large as 80 degrees. Performance held up much better for filled shapes than for unfilled outlines. Menzer and Thurmond's findings may therefore reflect the property of retinal summation, in which the outputs of several rods map onto a single cell at the next stage in the visual-processing sequence, as if gathering information pooled over a small region in space.

Evidence more directly concerned with the guidance function of the peripheral retina was reported by Williams (1966), whose findings were replicated in most essentials by Luria and Strauss (1975). Williams required his subjects to search in a cluttered visual field for numbers contained by geometric figures varying in colour, shape, and size. In addition to the target number, one or more of its other incidental characteristics might also be specified. When the colour was also given (e.g. 'look for the 63-red') subjects tended to fixate on red figures. This was not so when shape was given (e.g. 157-circle), and only to a limited extent for size (e.g. 35-very large). The selection of figures sharing the specified incidental attribute of the target must have been done on the basis of peripheral vision. On the basis of such studies it appears that the extrafoveal retina can provide useful data about movement, brightness, colour, size, and orientation. In addition it can provide a rough and ready indication about the overall outline of an object but it is not well suited to the specifics of shape information.

Although the evidence does not support a clearcut dichotomy between processes served by the fovea and those served by the periphery, it is convenient for theoretical purposes to treat the retinal facility as bifunctional. We have identified a precision capability, suited to deal with the detail of print and optimized to deal with information over a highly limited region, and a cruder capability, providing a guidance system for the fine-grain mechanism and dealing with a larger region of the extrafoveal visual field. In practice there seems to be more graduation in performance across the retina than this suggests, and it should be underlined that this distinction is one of relative rather than absolute emphasis.

Acquisition of visual information in reading: eye-movement guidance

A theoretical standpoint directly committed to a psychologically significant functional difference between the fovea and the periphery was expressed by Hochberg (1970) in the distinction between cognitive search guidance (CSG) and peripheral search guidance (PSG). These are considered to be effective in visual attention in general but are especially relevant in reading. A central concern of the model is the nature of the guidance of the eyes in reading. Cognitive search guidance refers to the influence exerted by previous information adduced from the text, which suggests where it might be useful to look next. This form of influence is through the generation of hypotheses and expectations as to what is coming later in the text, and the next location on which to fixate is chosen to optimize the confirmation or rejection of these predictons. Peripheral guidance contributes via the pick-up of low-acuity information, and thereby supplies a preliminary hint about where potentially useful information may lie.

We shall consider below whether or not supporting evidence is forthcoming for the position proposed by Hochberg (1970) regarding the roles of CSG and PSG in the control of eye movements in reading. Evidence considered by Hochberg to support the PSG hypothesis included studies suggesting that the periphery is more sensitive than measurements of acuity alone might indicate. As noted above this evidence suggests that useful information about upcoming stimuli may be picked up peripherally. Hochberg also pointed to a parallel with the apparent anticipatory use of the 'non-reading' hand by braille readers as evidence of an advance-guidance mechanism. He also cited evidence from studies from experiments on the effects on reading of tampering with the spaces between words (which will be considered in the next section), and studies of the effects of allowing the reader only a limited window through which to inspect the text being read. As seen above, further evidence has accumulated from investigations using eye-movement-recording methods.

Peripheral guidance in reading

Hochberg (1970) used evidence on the effect of removing the spaces between words as support for his peripheral-guidance hypothesis. In particular he cited his own research in which good readers were more affected than poor readers by the elimination of spaces, or their replacement by a symbol such as a dollar sign. He inferred from this that good readers normally made the more effective use of cues about the upcoming text via peripheral vision than poor readers, and hence were more influenced when these cues were degraded in quality by tampering with the inter-word spaces. This evidence is consistent with the peripheral-guidance hypothesis, but studies in which the entire text is altered fail to separate effects on foveal and peripheral-information acquisition. The outcome could be due to the reduced quality of peripheral information or because foveal word identification is impaired.

.The dynamic-window technique used by McConkie and Rayner (1975) enables the foveal material to appear normal while the peripheral material is altered. With a variety of text-alteration conditions, they compared displays with and without inter-word spaces for a range of window sizes, and found that space-filled peripheral displays led to shorter saccades, longer fixation durations, and slower reading times overall. This more unambiguously supports the peripheral-guidance hypothesis. More particularly, it indicates the importance of word-length information in eye-movement guidance. O'Regan (1979), also using a window technique, examined the effect of replacing all nonfoveal words by strings of 'x's of the appropriate length, and found that fixation durations decreased and the largest saccades became shorter. In this study the baseline for comparison was normal unaltered text, so that word-length information was preserved, and the result therefore suggests that something about the individual letters or the overall appearance of the words was being used. It should be noted that Rayner (1975) showed that there was little influence of semantic information at a distance beyond 6 character spaces from the point of fixation, so O'Regan's data leave a question to be resolved.

A study that very carefully examined the location of eye fixations within words was reported by Rayner (1979). There was a marked tendency for fixations following progressive eye movements to fall on the intermediate letters of words regardless of length. This does not imply that readers failed to fixate initial and final letters, just that the tendency to fixate elsewhere was much stronger. In addition there was a tendency for forward saccades to land on earlier rather than later letters, while *regressive* eye movements were more likely to land on later letters rather than earlier ones. In general, saccades were adjusted in extent according both to the length of the word from which the eye was departing, and that of the word on which the eye was about to land. For a transition from a 3- to a 5-letter word the saccade size averaged 5.3 character spaces, from a 3- to a 10-letter word it averaged 7.6 spaces, and from a 7- to a 10-letter word it averaged 8.8. It can be seen from this that the jump from one word to the next was not adjusted with fine precision, but there was a systematic tendency to vary it in accordance with word length.

Subjects tend to avoid blank regions inserted in the text, and they tend not to fixate on the gaps between sentences; and if they do, they fixate on them for less time (Rayner 1978). Yet although word length and spacing, and perhaps other non-semantic information about words too, seem to be important in mediating peripheral guidance, it does not follow that the eyes are aimed at a particular location with any exactness. As noted when discussing the spatial-justification hypothesis, if a slight drift in the text occurs in mid-eye movement, the subject not only fails to notice the slippage, but also the fixation position is not immediately corrected (O'Regan 1981). Levy-Schoen and O'Regan (1979) concluded that the precise position on which the eye lands may be immaterial. However Rayner and Pollatsek (1981) have found effects in the form of increased fixation durations and adjusted saccade lengths for the next fixation.

The evidence in general supports the hypothesis of word-length control of eye movements. This is effectively a strategy of aiming for the middle of the nearest word in non-central vision (O'Regan 1980). It is consistent with the evidence that subjects tend to skip short function words. However, this effect seems to involve something stronger than length control because skipping is not dictated simply by the brevity of the upcoming word; its linguistic status seems to be critical too. For instance, 'the' is more prone to be skipped than a 3-letter verb like 'ate' or 'ran'. Word frequency is confounded in this comparison, and indeed has been shown to be a factor in the 'the'-skipping effect. O'Regan (1979) found the difference in the frequency of fixation was greater for 'the' relative to comparatively rare 3-letter verbs (ate, met, ran) than for 'the' relative to a more common verbs (had, was, are). Thus there appears to be a contribution due to familiarity, and the 'the'-skipping effect at least reflects something more complicated than control by word length. O'Regan (1980) concluded that what he termed linguistic control was possible up to 7 character spaces beyond the point of fixation, after which control of eye movements was mediated by word-length information. Linguistic control is based on information contained in the mental lexicon, and is a component of cognitive guidance based on the immediately viewable text. Control by word length is one manifestation of peripheral guidance.

Opposition to the peripheral-guidance hypothesis

Notwithstanding the support for the peripheral-guidance hypothesis, a simple alternative account may be consistent with the evidence. On this account the reader is assumed to pick up information as far into the periphery as possible (typically in a rightward direction), and when no more useful visual data are available because of acuity limitations, an eye movement is initiated to bring to the fovea the text just out of the field of useful view. All that has to be done is to work out how far from the centre of vision the information lies, and in what direction, then the eye may be shifted by the necessary distance in the requisite direction. Accounts of this kind are favoured by McConkie (1979) and Rayner (1978).

Can such a model account for the evidence which otherwise supports the PSG hypothesis? McConkie (1979) argued that factors like word length, grammatical pattern, and so forth would influence saccade length, and that 'the'-skipping is also explained on the alternative model. As to the last of thses, McConkie reasoned that language constraints would sometimes be sufficient for 'the' to be highly probable, and to be identified from gross visual detail, while on other occasions the constraints would be less and it would have to be fixated. The attraction of this alternative view is its evident parsimony, because it does away with the assumption of the PSG mechanism. It is arguable, however, that McConkie's proposal is most important as a reminder that alternative accounts need to be formulated. The principal difficulty is to identify the crucial test to distinguish between the two models. Since it is hard to decide between these two points of view (peripheral guidance vs direct foveal regulation of eye movements) the matter will be left unsettled here.

Most of the research considered in the section on eye-movement control demonstrates the influence on eye-movement parameters (fixation time, saccade size, frequency of regressions) of *immediate, local* perceptual factors. Thus it was noted that saccades are longer if towards a long word, and the ensuing fixation is protracted if the word is an unfamiliar one and will be centred toward the first half of the word. Moreover the length of the word may be such as to call for a second fixation. Such findings are well-established, and draw attention to the very short range influences that the eye-movement system is subject to. How immediate the effects are remains to be clarified by future research (see McConkie 1983), and it is sufficient for our purposes to interpret this evidence as support for an immediacy hypothesis, so long as it is clear that this means momentary influences, effective on a given fixation or the adjacent one(s). Later in the chapter we shall consider some factors that are thought to be operative over a considerably longer range, and are more 'global' in nature and effect.

Graphic attributes as psycholinguistic signposts

In the model proposed by Hochberg (1970), peripheral guidance entails the immediate use of peripherally available graphic attributes of the text, which may include factors like word length, spacing, and punctuation. Such factors perhaps serve as graphic signs of grammatical structure. It is also possible that sufficient information may be picked up, perhaps by virtue of distinctive word shape, to allow parafoveal identification of some words. Evidence has accumulated to reinforce and qualify the possibilities in this respect, some reviewed earlier in the chapter. But how text cues and patterns may be used has not always been made clear, and can be illustrated by considering the possible role of word length. This attribute of a word may be interpreted as one of the rudimentary and limiting aspects of the word's shape. Function words (articles, prepositions, conjunctions, etc.) may be contrasted with content words (nouns, verbs, adjectives, etc.) in terms of word length. The former are over-represented among the short words in English, and are among the most common words in the language. Hence early detection of a short word is a potentially useful linguistic cue as to the structure of the upcoming text.

An extension of this argument was proposed by Ranklin (1977) who drew attention to the possibility of the word length *sequence* as a potentially salient peripheral cue in reading. Ranklin found from an analysis of text samples that certain phrases have a characteristic word-length structure. Both noun and verb phrases tend to take the form of ascending word lengths (e.g., to the station, for good citizens, was relegated). This is far from a universal property but is sufficiently common for such linguistic units to be capable of being signalled via the peripheral appearance of the appropriate word-length pattern. Ranklin's next step was to show that readers could indeed detect word-length sequence information at quite large visual angles (e.g., at above chance levels at an angle of 12 degrees), corresponding to retinal positions well outside the fovea. Hence readers have the ability at least to pick up perceptual information in the visual periphery that has potential use in reducing the range of syntactic alternatives relative to the upcoming text.

In addition, Ranklin showed that readers could reliably pick up punctuation information at some distance into the periphery. The subject had simply to report whether or not punctuation (specified for instance as period/space/capital) was present in a line of text with the punctuation sequence beginning at an angle of 4–12 degrees from the fovea (this was equivalent to a distance of between 17 and 51 letter spaces). The ability to do this would provide a diagnostic signal about the sentence frame itself. Some theorists have postulated sentence 'wrap-up' processes, concerned with the integration of the individual meanings of the sentence components. Supporting evidence includes a study (Mitchell and Green, 1978) in which passages of text were presented a few words at a time, with the reader summoning the next 'frame' of words by pressing a key. The time to make each key press was recorded, and it was found that there tended to be a delay in dealing with the last frame for each sentence. Furthermore, fixation durations are prolonged for the final word (Just and Carpenter 1980). Advance information about the limits of the sentence frame would enable the final wrap-up process to be initiated at an advantageous point ahead of the punctuation itself. This pushes us into speculative territory because it is by no means clear that people do any of this when reading, and to show this is a necessary further step to establish the peripheral graphic patterns available to and used by the fluent reader.

Cognitive guidance of eye movements: global vs local control

In this section we consider the contribution to eye-movement control arising from slow-acting or global cognitive factors, which include the context supplied by the passage. This is not to say that cognitive factors cannot be immediately effective. Indeed there is evidence that they may be, exemplified by the finding that fixations on difficult or unfamiliar words are sometimes prolonged relative to easy ones. Since what is referred to as 'difficulty' in this case is not a perceptual variable, and because the effect is on the fixation(s) on particular words as they are fixated, this is best interpreted as an immediate cognitive effect. An account of reading which examines a range of immediate cognitive factors is given by Just and Carpenter (1980).

Here, however, we are concerned with what may be thought of as control via slow-acting global factors, contrasted with immediate local factors, a distinction made by a number of researchers (Levy-Schoen and O'Regan 1979; McConkie 1983; Shebilske and Reid 1979). The distinction between local and global control may be thought of as one contrasting the influence of the microstructure (e.g. individual words, detailed typographic factors, and so on) and macrostructure (e.g. phrases, sentences, syntactic forms, and ideas) of the text. The latter is determined by information units accumulated over a wider time and spatial span than the former. It seems appropriate to include as global factors aspects such as the reader's purpose, prior knowledge of the topic, and his or her knowledge in general (as in Hochberg's 1970 cognitive-guidance principle).

The effects of global factors are considered to be reflected in global-performance measures such as average fixation times, saccade lengths, and aggregated measures like the number of forward and backward eye movements. They may also include general performance measures such as reading times and comprehension test scores. A global-control mechanism is assumed in a number of models of reading (see Levy-Schoen and O'Regan 1979), including that of Shebilske (1975), who made the contrast between indirect and direct regulation of eye movements in reading. In Shebilske's account a buffer is assumed, whose complement of information at any moment is considered to influence reading speed. If the buffer is full, then a decrease in reading speed is called for, but if it is empty then reading speed will be increased. Because of this buffering capability there is generally a loose relation between text parameters and eye movements. This is indirect regulation. On occasions, however, as when a highly predictable word is encountered, the buffer may be bypassed. This is an instance of direct regulation, and is also used when comprehension fails, and a regression is required.

While the tradition of reading research was for many years dominated by paradigms employing global measures, the recent practice in the laboratories using eye-movement recording techniques has been to use detailed indices of reading that enable local control to be investigated. The research described in the previous sections of this chapter exemplify this approach. However, other researchers have begun again to examine eye-movement behaviour over a broader focus, and an interest in more global aspects of reading and eye movements is beginning to be expressed once more.

An example is the work by Shebilske and Fisher (1983) in which they manipulated the study context of students reading a passage. This entailed the simple device of requiring them to read it as if for a homework assignment, while their eye movements were recorded. The material, a 2,866-word excerpt from a textbook, was subjected to a textual analysis into 'meaning units', whose importance among other things was obtained independently. The reading rate in the context of the passage was slower for important meaning units than for unimportant units, there were more regressions on the former, and saccade lengths were shorter. These effects may arise because of relatively superficial factors like vocabulary and syntax, independently of the overall context. But Shebilske and Fisher ruled this out by asking a control group of subjects to read a sample of the material in isolation from the context provided by the passage. There was no difference between the reading rates for important and unimportant units (118.1 vs 118.5 words per minute) out of context, but they were read much slower than when part of the passage, where there was a marked important–unimportant difference in reading rate (213 vs 254 words per minute respectively).

In a previous study, two subjects were also told that they were to be tested as if for a homework task, but that they would have two opportunities to read the passage. On the first occasion there was no difference in the reading rate for important (280 words per minute) and unimportant ideas (288 words per minute), but on the second reading they slowed down on the important ideas (to 229 words per minute) and speeded up on the unimportant ones (to 372 words per minute). This was reflected in longer fixation durations, more regressions, and shorter saccades on the important information than on the unimportant information. Although this experiment only used two subjects, and clearly needs to be replicated, the findings are of particular interest. It seems that the subjects used the first reading to establish where in the passage the important information was located, without waiting to absorb it in detail, and this locational knowledge was used to guide the rate of scanning on the second reading. The other experiment shows that importance can be established and be immediately effective, since the effect of idea importance was apparent on reading times on the single reading allowed.

Practical considerations

Eye-movement training

The basic facts about eye movements should arouse suspicion regarding techniques intended to improve reading by training the reader to use patterns of eye movement purely aimed at exposing the text to the eye, particularly when as small a sample of the printed page is fixated as it is in some schemes. For example, the strategy of passing the eyes vertically down the centre of a page such as this will sample the content inefficiently, and even if a couple of fixations are devoted to each line much will be missed. It is a defensible view that the visual periphery enables the pick-up of useful information, but the signs are clear that this is partial information which is inadequate for full recognition of meaning, and it may be best thought of as serving a guidance role for ensuing fixations. Imposed eye-movement patterns designed to optimize the coverage of the text will override both perceptual and cognitive guidance functions and expose the reader's eyes to an unduly haphazard information sequence, not driven by understanding.

Previous approaches to improving reading have frequently concentrated on the efficiency of the reader's eye movements. An emphasis on regulating the speed of reading in terms of the level of understanding is to invert the emphasis of the attempt to improve reading, with the eyes being driven by considerations to do with comprehension, rather than the reverse. This is the view of Shebilske and Fisher (1983) who stressed the potential practical implication of the research outlined in the previous section. Flexibility in reading is apparent from the modulation in scanning that they demonstrated, and so training might be given to gear reading rate to the judged importance of the information and the level of understanding achieved. It should be noted in this connection that good readers have been found to adjust their reading to the task goal – for example, reading for the gist of a passage as compared to reading 'normally' (Anderson 1937). While good readers speeded up in general, making fewer regressions and briefer fixations when reading for gist, poor readers actually slowed down, made more regressions and more protracted fixations relative to the control condition, as if the additional mental effort to read selectively, or perhaps to monitor an aspect of their reading, was an excessive mental load. It seems that this flexibility is a component of the reading skill that is a mark of the good reader. To help people achieve a degree of flexibility, it is arguable that they need to learn to monitor their level of comprehension of the material being read and the momentary difficulty of the text. But more basic research is needed, particularly studies of the effectiveness of training programmes based on this general approach.

Eye movements and developmental dyslexia

Given the perspective on reading taken at the beginning of the chapter, it is reasonable to ask whether eye-movement studies can throw any light on the problem of reading retardation, a form of learning disability which can lead to great academic and practical problems. Severe reading difficulties of children who otherwise have normal levels of intelligence are sometimes referred to as developmental dyslexias. (The contrast with the acquired dyslexias, a class of disorders which are associated with brain damage caused by stroke, injury, or cerebral disease should be noted.) We shall see that the plural form – the dyslexias – is appropriate as a way of emphasizing that they should be thought of as a family of conditions with a variety of aetiologies. Hence the answer to the question – of whether or not eye-movement studies illuminate the problem of the dyslexias – is a very qualified one. It would be unwise and potentially damaging to assume that severe difficulty in learning to read is attributable to one factor, for example, to some incapacity in the use of the eyes. Substantiating the causes of reading difficulty proves to be fraught with uncertainties.

Nevertheless, a proportion of the population of dyslexic readers are found to have unusual eye-movement patterns and the view has been advanced by some authorities that faulty eye-movement behaviour may be causal in such cases. However, it is a view that has been refuted by others, their opposition resting on the point that no evidence has been found that directly supports the postulated causal link; indeed, the evidence can as well be interpreted in quite opposite terms, namely that eccentric reading processes cause abnormal eye-movement behaviour during reading. Such uncertainty about causality is possible despite a hundred years of research into the problem of developmental reading retardation (Pirozzolo 1983). Yet there is reason for increasing optimism since in the past fifteen years or so there has been a dramatic increase in the amount of relevant research, including the rapid accumulation of evidence about the eye-movement behaviour of both normal and retarded readers.

Interest has been re-aroused into the question of the possible association between disordered eye-movement processes and dyslexia by a number of recent studies. Notable among them is that of Pavlidis (1981) who has made the firmest of claims based on a study in which the eye movements of children were recorded while they fixated along a row of five lights illuminated in a sequence. Pavlidis reported that dyslexics made considerably more fixations than normal readers and – perhaps the most important finding – they made many more regressions. Pavlidis's argument is that dyslexics have a problem in oculomotor control, a central deficit in sequencing behaviour, or perhaps both. The consequences of either or both of these would be manifest not only in reading but in non-reading tasks too, such as the sequential lights test. It will be readily appreciated that as a non-reading task this test is applicable to pre-readers, and could have considerable potential as a prognostic and as a diagnostic device.

Pavlidis's work, however, has been controversial and several published studies have failed to replicate his basic finding of differences in the saccadic eye movements of dyslexic and normal readers in sequential tracking tasks (Black *et al.* 1984; Brown *et al.* 1983; Olson, Kliegl, and Davidson 1983; Stanley, Smith, and Howell 1983). What is to be made of this surge of negative reports? Pavlidis (1985) contended that failures to replicate his findings were attributable to methodological changes but it seems that at least one study, that by Olson, Kliegl, and Davidson (1983), implemented all the salient methodological features mentioned by Pavlidis. As to the possibility of differences in selection criteria, this too seems not to be critical since Olson, Kliegl, and Davidson (1983) adopted the usual criteria for selecting dyslexics and as applied by Pavlidis (1981). This leaves the possibility of differences in sampling procedures, a view put forward by Rayner (1986) based on the idea that there are two main forms of dyslexia, one sampled by the source study and the other by the replications. Rayner argued that the negative studies were based on samples of dyslexics with a language deficit, while Pavlidis had seen subjects, twelve in number, wih a visuo-spatial deficit. Media coverage of Pavlidis's work and his reputation for dealing with dyslexics with visual problems could account for the selective availability to him of visuo-spatial dyslexics (Pollatsek 1983; Rayner 1986). This is an *ad hoc* argument, but it leads to a testable prediction. The deliberate selection of two groups of dyslexics, distinguished in terms of the nature of their reading difficulties (linguistic vs visuo-spatial), but matched otherwise on relevant criteria, should be decisive in determining whether or not unusual eye movements are found in the sequential lights and other related non-reading tasks. There are some data suggesting that such subtypes of developmental dyslexia do exist, and it includes evidence of differentiated eye-movement behaviour during reading.

If the origin of eccentric eye movements during reading is simply associated with oculomotor control problems then the difficulty level of the text should not influence the absence/presence of abnormal eye movements. Readers with oculomotor problems should show eye-movement abnormalities for both easy and difficult text. On the other hand, readers whose unusual eye movements are secondary to linguistic or cognitive problems should show increasing signs of abnormal eye movements as text difficulty increases. By varying the difficulty level of the text to be read, Pirozzolo and Rayner (1978) were able to classify their reading-disabled subjects along these lines, supporting the view that there are at least two forms of developmental dyslexia. Pirozzolo (1979) subsequently found that linguistic and visuo-spatial dyslexics differed among other things in terms of the speed with which they moved their eyes to left and right. Normal readers moved their eyes faster to the right than to the left, and the linguistic dyslexics resembled them in this respect. The visuo-spatial dyslexics showed the opposite pattern. Furthermore, the visuo-spatial dyslexics made more inaccurate return sweeps to the beginning of a new line of print. Aside from supporting the notion of a visuo-spatial vs linguistic classification, this bears on the abiding controversy of whether or not the presence of abnormal eye-movement patterns is symptomatic of faulty eye-movement control, a reasonable provisional interpretation being that 'the eye movements are a reflection of an underlying spatial processing deficit' (Rayner 1986). No one seems any longer to hold the strong view that eye movements cause dyslexia, although a recent commentary by Pavlidis (1986) seems to be ambiguous about this. In any event there is a lack of convincing evidence on causality of any putative form, though the next and final study to be considered seems to point in the necessary direction.

A novel proposition about how faulty eye-movement control might be a factor in the causation of reading difficulties was advanced by Stein and Fowler (1982). There are several links in Stein and Fowler's reasoning, some quite speculative as they admitted. Their relatively uncontroversial starting point was that for most people the verbal processes involved in reading take place in the left cerebral hemisphere, while visual information can be delivered to either hemisphere depending on where the eye is pointing. For reasons which we shall not consider in detail, it is possible for information being transferred across from the right to the left hemisphere to be reversed. It is therefore important for the left hemisphere to be informed about which eye is pointing where, so that such reversals can be compensated for. Moreover, quite small variations in eye position can lead to shifts in which hemisphere is receiving the character or word being read. Hence eye-position control is very important in reading, enabling the information from the printed page to be consistently routed to and correctly encoded in the left hemisphere. The normal course of events seems to be for motor dominance of one eye to develop, that eye only having to be controlled. For most children this is the right eye, which is controlled from the left hemisphere, and this therefore has a full record of the positions and movements of the dominant eye, as well as serving as the locus for further verbal processing.

In short, the hypothesis regarding visual dyslexia is that it results from the failure of the child to develop eye dominance. To test the hypothesis Stein and Fowler (1982) assessed the eye dominance of two groups, one of eighty dyslexics and one of eighty controls, the latter being children with normal reading matched in terms of age and IQ. Of the dyslexic group, fifty children had an inconsistent pattern of eye dominance, compared with only one child in the control group. The dyslexic readers had been independently classified as having 'visual' or 'other' forms of reading difficulty, and fifty-two of them were in the 'visual' category. This turned out to include all fifty of those without consistent dominance.

To establish the causal status of any particular factor in developmental dyslexia is a difficult matter, and it is certainly necessary to proceed beyond the demonstration that an association exists between the presence of some attribute (like imperfect eye dominance, and hence faulty eye-position control) and severe reading retardation. To show the causal role of the factor requires the kind of manipulation used by Stein and Fowler (1982) in the next step in their research. They devised a simple remediation technique, designed to facilitate the acquisition of eye dominance and to help a group of dyslexics to improve their reading. This consisted of asking children to wear special glasses, for a period of six months, with an eye-patch blocking off the left eye whenever they were doing 'close' visual work, especially reading. This 'occlusion technique' was designed to simplify the visual dyslexic child's problems with eye positioning and promote the development of eye dominance. Some of the visual dyslexics were not given the experimental treatment. In addition groups of normal readers and non-visual dyslexics were used as controls, some of the latter group also being selected to wear the occluding glasses. The treated 'visual' dyslexics showed marked improvements in their reading; they improved on average by 13.44 months in reading age in the six months of the project, while the untreated group improved by only 4.15 months on the average. The improvements included reported decreases in reversal effects and other instabilities.

Some reservations about this study should be noted. The authors gave a reasoned basis for rejecting the possibility of a 'placebo effect' arising from the special treatment being received by the children. None the less it is striking that the average increase in reading age for all groups except the untreated visual dyslexics was close to twice what it would normally be. This seems to be a positive gain, something beyond a mere placebo effect. Since it even applied to the normal readers, it seems fair to conclude that a much more extensive study is needed. Details of the nature of the improvement in reading, particularly regarding the incidence of errors considered characteristic of visual dyslexia, would have been illuminating. It should, however, be underlined that this kind of study is important, and quite unusual. It did not stop short at establishing evidence of an association between visual dyslexia and eye dominance, but went on to examine an experimental manipulation relevant to the authors' proposed causes of reading retardation.

An interesting question raised by the earlier discussion is the relative frequency of different subtypes of dyslexia (if they can be identified reliably). Of particular interest is the proportion of dyslexic readers with oculomotor difficulties, with markedly conflicting claims in the literature. Some are particularly dramatic. Pavlidis's (1981) assertions about the eye movements of dyslexics as erratic and idiosyncratic appear to have been quite general and seem to constitute a view that dyslexia is a single class of disorder. Stein and Fowler's (1982) estimate in the study discussed above was rather less sweeping, referring to just over 60 per cent of their dyslexic subjects as having a 'visual' form of reading difficulty, almost wholly a matter of inconsistent eye-movement dominance. It should, however, be noted that Stein and Fowler's sample, like that of Pavlidis, is also likely to include a strong bias because they dealt with dyslexics referred to a hospital opthalmology department. Other authorities consider that there are relatively few disabled readers with serious difficulties associated with abnormal eye movements. Pirozzolo (1983) stated that there are two basic forms of developmental dyslexia, auditory-linguistic and visuo-spatial, the former occurring four times as often as the latter. According to Pirozzolo, the visuo-spatial condition is characterized by faulty eye movements during reading, possibly reflecting ill-aimed saccades arising from poor visuo-spatial organization. One research group estimated from the samples participating in Pavlidis's research and the replication studies it spawned that 'the incidence of gross oculomotor deficits in dyslexics is less than 1 per cent (Olson, Kliegl, and Davidson 1983). But the range of eye-movement behaviours is bemusingly wide (there are even normal readers with abnormal eye movements), and most of the basic issues concerning diagnosis, incidence of different disorders, and their explanation, are unresolved.

Indeed, the relative frequency of forms of dyslexia in which eye-movement abnormalities play a part is not clearly established, partly because different investigations employ different test batteries and monitor different aspects of the reading process with varying degrees of thoroughness and conviction. This is true of most characteristics, and is to be expected of an area of such complexity and incomplete understanding as reading. Its developmental course can go astray for many reasons, and many aspects of information processing can be at variance with how they might optimally be. It is obvious that if the eyes are directed at the wrong places, if they deliver uncoordinated signals, or signals in a disorderly manner, then the learner may have serious difficulties. But there are many other fundamental aspects of reading that can be troublesome, such as the process of assembling the individual letters into a whole word, that of converting the printed word into a sounded form, the process of understanding the individual words, of co-ordinating their meanings, of using contextual information, and so forth. Such considerations suggest that various specific kinds of reading difficulty – subtypes of developmental dyslexia – may be identified (paralleling the classi-fication of the acquired dyslexias; Harris and Coltheart 1986; Patterson 1981). There is no space for a comprehensive account here but it is clear that the causes and accompanying features of reading problems are many and varied. However, progress has been made; there is increasing acceptance that subtypes may be isolated and important central factors acting as impediments to the development of fluent reading have been recognized, including letter sequencing problems, deficiencies in auditory short-term memory, and problems with the recoding of words into sounds (Taylor and Taylor 1983).

Practical issue II: reading as a guessing game?

One important and well-publicized account treats reading as a matter of perceptual–cognitive hypothesis-testing. The approach is important because it is advocated as the basis of a method of teaching reading by some highly influential writers (Goodman 1965, 1970; Smith 1971, 1973). The emphasis in this account is on the reader's comprehension of the passage, rather than the identification of the sequence of words which it comprises. Reading depends on the reader's prior knowledge, and in particular on expectations deriving from a knowledge of language, and it proceeds via a constructive interaction with the graphic display. However the contribution of perceptual processes is played down, and reading is considered to be a 'psycholinguistic guessing game'. A cycle of guessing and checking is engaged as the reader proceeds through the text, and proficiency in reading is a matter of efficiency in sampling the display and making predictions on the basis of as little information as possible. The printed word and the reader's visual perceptual system seem to play but minor roles in this account. It is proposed that children should be taught to guess as a means of improving their reading. This assumes the validity of the hypothesis-testing model, which some have argued is not specified in adequate detail, and has not been subjected to crucial experimental testing.

Context effects and reading

This kind of account emphasizes the contribution of cognitive processes to reading. This brings us to the important distinction between 'bottom-up' processing and 'top down' processing, though this contrast is not easy to sustain as we shall see. Bottom-up processing refers to the influence of the stimulus itself – the printed word in reading – on the course of information processing, while top-down processing relates to the influence of higher-order conceptual properties of the input and more generally includes the influence of expectations, goals, and prior knowledge. In the present chapter this contrast is represented in the form of the perceptual vs cognitive guidance of reading, the study by Shebilske and Fisher (1983) providing a clear example of top-down processing. The next section will review evidence on the influence of context on reading. As an introduction to this section, consider Figure 6.2, in which 'context' in some sense induces most readers to overlook one or more of the 'printing errors' it contains. This suggests that visual analysis (from the bottom up) is not always complete, and the fact that some errors are easier to detect than others arguably serves to illustrate the mutual dependence of perceptual and cognitive factors in reading.

'Context' and reading – definitions

We begin by noting some of the distinctions that may be made relative to the term 'context', a favourite but overworked explanatory concept among cognitive psychologists. According to Shebilske and Fisher (1983) there are three 'contexts' that are considered by psychologists to be relevant to reading text. The first is the situational context, which refers to the set of non-linguistic stimuli acting on the reader, including task requirements, the reader's

Oversights on the part of proofreaders demonstate
the effects of context. We have included some
delibenate errors in this shgrt passage, some of
which are considearably easier than othes to
to spot. The idea is that quessing results from
strong expetations. Count them for yourself.
Their are nime, sorry, ten errors. Did you have
to retrace your steps to get them all?

Figure 6.2   A passage with typographic errors to illustrate the effect of context

purpose, and the physical mode of presentation. There is also the
conceptual context which is provided by what the reader knows,
about the world in general and the topic in particular, and the
general concepts acquired earlier from the text in question. Finally
there is linguistic knowledge, which is the orthographic, syntactic,
and semantic information in the text. The last of these, the
contribution to the meaning of a word from the surrounding text is
nearest to the formal dictionary sense of 'context'.

A further helpful distinction is made relative to this last meaning
of 'context' by Gough, Alford, and Holley-Wilcox (1981). It is
between global context, provided by the text itself, and local
context, which is the more circumscribed environment of words
given by the current phrase or sentence. They argued that global
context is semantic (relating to the vocabulary of terms and concepts
associated with the topic of the passage) and is therefore stable and
effective over words, sentences, and paragraphs. Local context is
considered to have an important syntactic component in addition to
any locally distinctive semantic contribution. Further, because local
context must in part mirror the changing syntactic alternatives as the
word sequence proceeds, its influence must be comparatively
momentary. This conceptualization, together with the suggestions
of Shebilske and Fisher (1983), and much narrower forms of context
used in the research on letter recognition referring to the environment
of letters in which a particular target letter sits (e.g. Rumelhart and
McClelland 1982), presents us with a multiplicity of contexts
associated with the text and the reader. While there is overlap
between these various ideas, it is clear that 'context' is not a simple
unitary factor. It seems that in principle a number of different
contextual constraints may be effective simultaneously on the

reading process, but their identificaiton as functional influences in reading has to be demonstrated empirically. We shall therefore turn to some illustrative experiments, and alternative theoretical approaches to reading which seek to accommodate the evidence on context effects.

Errors in oral reading

The kind of account which assumes the reader's expectations are paramount receives support most directly from studies which demonstrate that the kinds of errors readers make when reading aloud are syntactically or semantically appropriate to the context in which they occur. Weber (1970) found that about 90 per cent of the errors a group of beginning readers made as they read aloud were grammatically consistent with the preceding linguistic context. For the remainder there tended to be a strong graphic resemblance between the correct word and the word given. The grammatical acceptability of so many errors suggests that beginning readers are sensitive to the structure of the language and that the responses they give are sometimes in anticipation of the passage content rather than always being dictated by what is actually on the printed page. Errors were sometimes spontaneously corrected, but this depended on whether or not the error maintained the sentence as a grammatical string. If grammatical sense was preserved by the error then it tended to be disregarded (with only 30 per cent corrections), but when the error was inconsistent with the later context then it was likely to be corrected (61 per cent corrections). Poor and good readers alike showed a sensitivity to grammatical constraint in terms of the pattern of spontaneous errors they made, though it was the good readers who were more likely to correct ungrammatical errors. Blaxhall and Willows (1984) have confirmed this general pattern for beginning readers but they concluded that the outcome is strongly influenced by the difficulty of the text being read. As the material increased in difficulty, the children in their study increased their reliance on graphic cues, as indicated by the increasing incidence of graphically similar errors. Semantically and syntactically appropriate substitution errors decreased as text difficulty increased, possibly reflecting the decreasing availability of useful contextual constraints.

Kolers (1970) confirmed the general findings regarding substitution errors in a study using adult readers in which a high rate of errors in oral reading was induced by requiring the subjects to read text that had been subjected to geometrical transformations like those illustrated in Figure 6.3. Readers' substitution errors were highly consistent relative to the preceding context. If a word was spoken in error it was likely to have the same number of letters as the correct word. Moreover when a substitution was visually similar to the actual word then it was semantically or syntactically inconsistent with the context only 12 per cent of the time. Thus when a noun was misread, a noun tended to be substituted, a misread verb tended to be replaced by another verb, and so on. Kolers (1972) concluded that this evidence shows that readers proceed not on a letter-by-letter or even a word-by-word basis, but 'by generating internal grammatical messages'.

Letter orientation	Scanning order	
(a) Normal spacing:		
Normal	Normal N	* also yellow waste ask turn happen
Normal	Reversed rM	neppah nrut ksa etwas wolley osla *
Inverted	Reversed R	* also yellow waste ask turn happen
Inverted	Normal rI	* neppah nrut ksa etwas wolley osla
(b) Unspaced:		
Normal	Normal N	* alsoyellowwasteaskturnhappen
Normal	Reversed rM	neppahnrutksaetwaswolleyosla *
Inverted	Reversed R	* alsoyellowwasteaskturnhappen
Inverted	Normal rI	* neppahnrutksaetwaswolleyosla

Figure 6.3 Examples of simple geometrical transformations of word strings. The asterisk shows the direction of scan in each case (after Menzies 1985)

One prominent theory that makes great capital of the nature of the errors that spontaneously occur in oral reading is that of Goodman (1965, 1969), who referred to such errors as 'miscues' since he contended that to characterize them as errors is to overlook the fact that this is the way that an acceptable alternative response may be produced. The advantage of the Goodman model is that it deals with some of the broad facts about reading. It accounts for the effect of text difficulty on reading speed (i.e., hard text takes longer to read than easy text), in terms of the decreasing predictability of the text as difficulty level increases. It explains the effects of spontaneous errors in oral reading by the assumption that reading is driven by context-related predictions. There is some circularity about both these points. Predictability is high when difficulty level is low, but how is difficulty to be measured? In terms of reading speed? Reading errors are most likely when the text is predictable, but when is this? When errors occur? Clearly indices of predictability independent of reading performances are necessary to add conviction to the account.

Criticisms of the 'guessing-game' hypothesis

The Goodman model of reading is criticized by Gibson and Levin (1975) for failing to state how predictions are made, what they are about (letters, words, ideas, or whatever), and how they are tested. It is clear that the model fails to make clear predictions, and indeed predictions that are unique to itself, that other accounts would not be able to accommodate. The evidence of spontaneous errors in oral reading does seem unequivocally to reveal the influence of context, but on what process or processes is not clear. And this is hard to resolve in terms of the model precisely because it is not specific about what the reader is making predictions about. The thrust of the writings of Goodman (1965, 1967, 1969) and Smith (1971, 1973), another advocate of the hypothesis-testing approach to reading, is that the reader is dealing with meaning quite directly. Hence predictions may not be generated at a word level at all, the emphasis being on the extraction of the gist of the material. But this would be inconsistent with the nature of spontaneous oral errors in reading which seem to affect individual words, and do not entail the paraphrase of word sequences as might be expected if the predictions were driven at the gist level.

A reasonable doubt about the hypothesis-testing account of reading, and a good point from which to develop the discussion of context effects in reading, relates to the difficulty of making accurate and useful predictions on the basis of contextual information. Gough (1983) described a study in which 100 subjects were given the first eight words in a series of 100 sentences drawn from the *Reader's Digest*, and were asked to predict the ninth word in each case. The correct word in half the sentences was a function word (preposition, conjunction, article, etc.) and in the rest was a content word (noun, verb, adjective, adverb). Average predictability was 25 per cent, reflecting a considerable advantage for the prediction of function words (39 per cent correct) relative to content words (10 per cent correct). Similar findings were obtained by Gough, Alford, and Holley-Wilcox (1981) when a subject made predictions on the basis of continuous text, being supplied with 100 words of running text prior to the word to be predicted. If only one word in four could be anticipated accurately, few of these bearing on the content of the passage, then prediction would not seem to help fluent reading.

Other forms of contextual influence in reading

The idea that reading is a 'top-down' process in which word identification in particular is guided by the reader's expectations came to dominate psychological theorizing about reading in the 1970s. On such a view context is all-important and skill in reading came to be identified with the ability to use context. But the balance has subsequently shifted as evidence has accumulated and theoretical positions have been articulated with greater clarity and precision. A useful framework for discussing the issue was provided by Posner and Snyder (1975), in an account of priming effects obtained with a letter-identification paradigm. Their theory was extended to single words by Neely (1977), and subsequently to effects on word recognition in sentence contexts as discussed below. The basic framework will be described first, together with some of its supporting evidence, and this will be applied to contextual effects on word recognition.

The basic task used by Posner and Snyder (1975) was for the subject to make a same–different judgement about a pair of letters (e.g., RR, Rr, RN, nn, rN, etc.) presented tachistoscopically. The letter pairs were preceded by a 'priming stimulus' (or 'prime') to alert the subject to the impending presentation of a letter pair. The prime had another part to play, as a less than perfectly reliable indicator of the response to be given. One letter was chosen as the priming stimulus for the 'same' response, and a second as the prime for the 'different' response. The prime might be correct, and therefore potentially helpful, 80 per cent of the time, but incorrect, and potentially misleading, for the rest of the time. For baseline purposes (to ascertain whether effects on performance were facilitatory, inhibitory, or null) the letter pairs were sometimes preceded by an uninformative + sign, serving as a neutral 'priming stimulus'. Performance was affected by the frequency with which the prime correctly predicted the relationship of the target pair of letters, as well as by the interval between the prime and the target pair.

The key aspects of the data for present purposes are that when the prime was 80 per cent predictive of the target, subjects took less time to respond. Secondly, when the prime was only 20 per cent predictive of the target, response latency was speeded up for short intervals but delayed at longer intervals (i.e., facilitation followed by inhibition). In the terms used by Posner and Snyder (1975) there was a benefit (facilitation) due to the highly predictive prime, and in the low predictive condition there was benefit (facilitation) turning to cost (inhibition) as the interval increased. The existence of both costs and benefits was interpreted by Posner and Snyder as evidence for two processes, the first automatic and the second under attentional control. The automatic process is fast and unconscious, does not utilize processing resources, and cannot be controlled by the subject. The controlled process by contrast is slow, is capacity demanding, and is moderated by the subject's intentions and expectations.

The two-process theory has also been applied to a class of priming effects involving the influence of one word on another in various word-recognition tasks. It is well-established that the semantic context provided by one word can influence the processing of another. For example, Meyer and Schvaneveldt (1971) showed that a word like DOCTOR used as a priming stimulus gave rise to quicker lexical decision times to a related word like NURSE than to an unrelated word like BREAD. Further research using appropriate control conditions with neutral priming stimuli (like rows of 'x's) suggests that there are two effects here, facilitation resulting from related primes and an interference or inhibition effect attributable to unrelated ones (Neely 1976, 1977).

In fact much of the evidence was satisfactorily accounted for by an additive-factors model evolved by Meyer, Schvaneveldt, and Ruddy (1975), in which three stages of processing were assumed for the task of word recognition. The first stage encodes the stimulus into an internal representation, which may be visual, phonemic, or semantic.

The second stage of lexical retrieval is responsible for comparing the encoded stimulus with stored representations until a match is found. The outcome of this stage is passed to the third stage which produces the relevant response. A fairly simple pattern of results emerged from studies which examined appropriate factorial combinations of variables such as word frequency, stimulus quality, and contextual congruity (between the priming word and the target). This will be recognized as an application of the additive-factors method of Sternberg (1969) (see p. 33).

As an example of the findings, Becker (1976), using a lexical-decision task (deciding whether a letter string is a word or not), found that the contextual factor interacted with stimulus intensity (i.e. stimulus quality), while word frequency was additive with intensity. It was inferred that context and quality both influenced the encoding stage, and that word frequency affected the lexical-retrieval stage, common words being easier to locate than rare ones but not differing in terms of time needed to encode them. None the less, the pattern of other findings was difficult to accommodate in a serial-stages model. For example, Becker (1979) found that the size of the effect of semantic relatedness of the prime and the target depended on the frequency of the target, an interaction effect that suggests that frequency and context are involved at the same stage, in which case one would expect the frequency and quality factors in the previous studies also to have interacted. Furthermore the evidence of Neely (1976, 1977) that unrelated primes may lead to a lengthening of lexical decision times is also at odds with the sequential-stages model which has no mechanism for producing interference effects.

As an alternative to the simple sequential-stages account of the data from the single-word priming paradigm, two-process theory postulates an automatic process of spreading activation which produces facilitation for words related to the prime or context word. Unrelated words are unaffected by the automatic process. In addition there is an attentional process, with limited capacity, which may be directed to the context word and which is effective through the subject's context-based expectations. A target which is unrelated to the context takes longer to process because attention has first to be shifted to it, and this becomes more probable with an increasing context–target interval. Responses to words which are congruent with the context are increasingly facilitated as the time during which attention is devoted to the context increases. Neely's (1976, 1977) findings supported this analysis since the facilitation effect for related primes and the inhibition effect for unrelated primes both increased as the interval between the priming stimulus and the target increased.

Sentential context effects

It is a short procedural step for the word prime to be replaced by a sentential prime, but an important move towards a more natural reading situation. In all but a handful of the studies using this form of context, the sentence is presented complete but for the last word, and it is this that serves as the target item (for the subject to identify, read aloud, or whatever). Tulving and Gold (1963) were among the first to demonstrate effects analogous to those obtained with isolated word primes. They showed that sentence contexts facilitated the tachistoscopic recognition of words that made congruent endings and inhibited the recognition of words making incongruent endings. An example of the material used by Tulving and Gold is shown in Figure 6.4. The pattern of findings in Neely's (1977) isolated word paradigm – facilitation for related targets and inhibition for unrelated ones – was confirmed for a lexical-decision task with sentences providing the prior context by Schuberth and Eimas (1977). A very similar outcome was reported by Stanovich and West (1979) using a word-naming task.

Context	Target
	... **COLLISION**
THREE PEOPLE WERE KILLED IN A TERRIBLE HIGHWAY	
	... **RASPBERRY**

Figure 6.4 Examples of context with congruous and incongruous targets from Tulving and Gold's (1963) study of word recognition

A qualification of this pattern of results – facilitation for related words and inhibition for unrelated ones – is indicated in a study by West and Stanovich (1978) in which the subjects were fourth- and sixth-grade children and college students. Time to name the words decreased with increasing age, and there was a theoretically significant change in the pattern of facilitation and inhibition. All subjects showed facilitation by congruent cues but only the children showed inhibition for the incongruent cues. It seems that the adults processed words so fast that the slow-acting effects of expectancies did not have time to exert an influence.

More interesting details of the picture were supplied by Stanovich and West (1981) who compiled a pool of words differing in their ease of recognition when presented alone, and found that sentence context effects were greater for difficult words than easy words. This was confirmed by Stanovich and West (1983a) who additionally found in one set of experiments that the effect of sentence context was of facilitation by congruent material with little or no inhibition due to incongruent material. In another experiment they degraded the quality of the stimulus by reducing the stimulus–background contrast, and found that while this slowed down responses there was both facilitation for congruent words and inhibition for incongruent words. This is consistent with the view that when processing is delayed, conscious expectations may come into play and their confirmation and disconfirmation may thus be responsible for the observed pattern of contextual facilitation and inhibition effects.

But other findings by Stanovich and West suggest that it is not a simple matter of slowing down processing *per se*. In another of their experiments the letters of the target word were separated by an asterisk. As expected and intended this slowed down processing, but more importantly it gave rise to the facilitation of naming but no inhibition effect. So the effect of reduced contrast in the previous experiment may have been due to subjects' conscious use of expectancies to offset the reduced stimulus quality; it would of course be apparent to the subject from the poor contrast that the input was unreliable. But this does not apply to the asterisked display which delivers clearly legible letters, though difficult to disembed and so also slow to process. On the other hand, reading w*o*r*d*s p*r*i*n*t*e*d i*n t*h*i*s f*a*s*h*i*o*n is not an easy matter, and may call for a letter-by-letter strategy of reading, imposing a high perceptual processing load as the letters are assembled into words and a high memory load (for the context), and hence giving little scope for conscious use of contextual cues.

Yet much of the research seems to lead to the position that factors – such as word difficulty, stimulus quality, and reading skill – that affect the speed of reading may be linked with the use of context. It seems that a delay in lexical access may trigger conscious provision of extra information via contextually derived expectancies. The proposed optional nature of the use of expectancies is an interesting theoretical development, as is the reference to conscious expectancies. It is in the spirit of the original two-process account, in which the attentional component is linked with consciousness (Posner and

Snyder 1975), and is certainly a direct reflection of the possibility that readers are strategically engaged in their task. Conditions designed to encourage subjects to operate with conscious expectancies would include presenting a high percentage of trials in which the sentence context was helpful. This is a matter for further research to resolve since the existing evidence gives conflicting signs (Eisenberg and Becker 1982; Stanovich and West 1983a).

The contextual facilitation effects described by Stanovich and West (1983a), obtained when the displays were of good visual quality, were considered by them to be accountable in terms of an automatic process of 'spreading activation' as a consequence of which there is enhanced lexical access to words related to the context. Thus this form of context effect is considered to be 'bottom-up' in nature. The effects induced when processing is slowed down to an extent that invites the use of expectancies and strategies are of a 'top-down' type.

An interesting speculative point made by Stanovich and West (1983a) is that although single word paradigms may give evidence of conscious strategies, such strategies may not be engaged in normal reading due to the continuous processing demands of sentence comprehension. Other experimental findings add to the reservations about the possibility of using predictions, conscious or otherwise, in normal reading. In a study by Fischler and Bloom (1979) using the RSVP technique (see p. 179) it was found that at rates of presentation approximating normal reading speed, there was only a marginal facilitation of naming by sentential context, and that at very high rates there was none. More important, however, it was found that there was facilitation only when the predictability of the target word was very high (averaging 90 per cent). Mitchell and Green (1978), using a self-paced presentation method in which the subject triggered the display of successive phrase-sized frames of the text, found no effect of context building up through the sentence. It is therefore interesting that the large number of experiments on sentence-context effects on word recognition almost invariably involve placing the target in the terminal position of the sentence. When the target occupied the penultimate position the effect of the preceding context was much reduced relative to those in earlier studies (Stanovich and West 1983b). Finally, evidence from studies like that of Mitchell and Green (1978; see also Just and Carpenter 1980) that more time is devoted to the last word in a sentence is accountable in terms of the integrative processes associated with comprehension. But it should be emphasized that this finding is just the opposite to what might be expected from an accumulating contribution from context.

Context and fluent reading

It would of course be incautious to equate the sort of manipulations described above with what fluent readers encounter in their normal reading. There are two more studies to discuss that allowed freer rein to the subjects' normal reading styles, although because the use of eye-movement recording was involved there may still be doubts about how natural was the behaviour observed. The first is a study of the effects of local context by Zola (1984) who presented pairs of paragraphs identical apart from the contextual constraint on certain words. Thus in a piece of text about the cinema the word 'popcorn' was preceded either by the adjective 'buttered' or 'adequate', for the high and low constraint conditions respectively. The strength of the constraint manipulation was confirmed by using an independent group of subjects to guess the target in the two contexts, a success rate of 83 per cent being achieved for the high constraint material and only 8 per cent for the low constraint material. Other subjects had their eye movements recorded while silently reading the passages. An additional feature of the experimental procedure was that the target word was misspelled on some occasions, to see whether high constraint led subjects to process the target less thoroughly. In the event the target word was fixated as frequently in the low-constraint condition as in the high (97 per cent in both cases). Although fixations on the target were prolonged when one of its letters had been changed to produce a printing 'error', this delay was independent of the contextual constraint. There was an overall effect of context, however, since fixations on the targets were 16 msec shorter when there was high as opposed to low local constraint (221 vs 237 msec respectively).

Global context was manipulated by Ehrlich and Rayner (1981), the overall sense of the text affording either a high or a low constraint context for a critical set of words. As in the Zola study the critical items were sometimes subjected to letter substitutions. In the high-constraint paragraphs, the critical words were mentioned directly, or were implicitly needed to understand the passage, so that their role and relevance throughout the paragraph was established. There was a strong effect of context on eye movement and performance measures. Probability of fixating the target was lower, fixation durations were shorter when the target was fixated, and probability of recalling the letter substitutions was lower, given the high-constraint condition rather than the low one. This clearly demonstrates a quite durable facilitatory effect of global context, possibly acting through a saving on the amount of visual feature-processing needed. At the same time it should be noted that there were longer fixation durations for the misspelled words, indicating that the visual input is subject to immediate monitoring and that eye-movement control may be exercised very promptly. Despite the possibility of immediate effects such as this, Zola's (1984) study suggests that local context does not exert a major short-range influence. Indeed it would appear from the findings of Ehrlich and Rayner (1981) that the contribution from semantic contextual information in normal reading may be at a quite general level, taking time to build up and possibly corresponding to the gist of the material. Clearly the relative contributions of the two sources of contextual constraint investigated in these two studies merit further research and need to be assessed in a single experiment.

For skilled readers, then, a clearer but by no means wholly consistent picture based on a growing base of hard evidence exists for a facilitatory influence of context in normal reading. It is unlikely given the timing considerations that the short-range effects are other than 'automatic' (i.e. not under conscious control). The evidence of a facilitatory effect from global context is more in accord with the idea of the development of generalized and relatively durable expectancies, relating to the general sense of the material being read. There is a body of evidence that supports this possibility in a general way, such as the unsurprising fact that it takes more time to read effectively randomly ordered passages than a passage in the correct word order (Morton 1964). Miller and Coleman (1967) reported that the accuracy of subjects' performance on a cloze task (supplying the words omitted from a passage) tended to increase over the length of a sentence, but not to extend beyond the sentence boundary. Prediction of the missing word seems to improve with the increasing amount of contextual information, but this only operates within each sentence frame, as if the contribution from context to this task is reset to zero at the end of each sentence. Such effects do not, as we have seen, materialize in fluent reading. Moreover there appear to be no inhibition effects in normal fluent reading, though the studies of congruous and incongruous contexts need to be replicated with continuous text and the use of eye-movement recording. On the other hand less proficient readers do exhibit inhibition effects. Conceivably their normal reading speed is slow enough to permit conscious expectancies to be developed on the basis of context, and for these expectancies to affect the course of reading. The conclusion must therefore be that the use of context partly depends on reading skill. But degree of skill must be related to the task in hand, and the most experienced and skilled adult reader must from time to time encounter material (e.g. in illegible handwriting, or expressed in unfamiliar terminology) that is so difficult as to enforce the use of context. Highly difficult material will slow down the skilled reader in his or her normal mode of operation and in that respect use of context may be seen to depend on reading speed. The conclusion otherwise is that the skilled reader in a normal mode of reading is to a degree influenced by but does not consciously utilize context.

When the context is such as to encourage false predictions (e.g. the sentence is completed by an unlikely word) little penalty is incurred in terms of delayed responding on the completion task (Fischler and Bloom 1979). Maybe it is as simple as that predictions are not made. Or perhaps they relate not to specific items but to a broad class of words (Mitchell 1982). As we have seen, Stanovich and West (1983a) found that the inhibitory effects of an unhelpful sentence context were small and relatively elusive, and were outweighed by the more regular and evident signs of beneficial effects from a helpful context. As Mitchell (1982) observed, the interval between presentation of the context and the 'target' word may be critical, and inhibitory effects arising from the short-range generation and disconfirmation of conscious expectancies may take rather more time than is allowed by the pace of normal fluent reading.

The signs are that interactive processes, analogous to those postulated by McClelland and Rumelhart (1981) in their account of context effects on letter identification, may be involved in sentence processing, although the facilitatory effects seem well and more simply characterized by the 'bottom-up' concept of automatic spreading activation. However, it is unlikely that fluent reading gives much scope for a conscious regulatory form of top-down influence of the sort that beginning readers are sometimes taught to use, and which even skilled readers deploy when challenged by obscure expression or illegible text. It seems fair to conclude with Mitchell (1982) who, following a comprehensive and careful review of the evidence on context effects in reading, asserted that top-down processing 'plays a very limited role in fluent reading'. This view contrasts sharply with earlier views, especially that of Smith (1973), who considered that fluent reading depended on the minimal use of visual cues to confirm predictions based on syntactic and semantic information. Mitchell (1982) contended that such views were based on studies using stimuli of an impoverished or degraded nature, thereby emphasizing the contribution of top-down processing. From a position in the early 1970s that reading proceeded so rapidly that it had to be under contextual control and expressed in a predictive sequence of guessing and checking, today's dominant view is that it is probably so rapid that it cannot be.

Practical implications

The effects of context and the reader's expectations are sometimes considered to direct the course of reading as a form of top-down processing, implying an influence from relatively high-order processes. The kind of errors people make when reading aloud tend to be syntactically or semantically congruent with the text, suggesting a dependency on contextual information. Indeed such evidence has been cited in support of the view that fluent reading is based on a form of hypothesis testing with the minimal use of visual cues from the text. Counter-evidence was considered suggesting that the capability of the reader to guess on the basis of contextual cues is limited and slow-acting relative to the pace achieved when reading fluently. Further evidence from priming studies with single words and sentences suggests that the beneficial influence of context is better interpreted in passive activational terms rather than as evidence of complex cognitive control of the course of reading. A hypothesis-testing mode of processing may intervene, however, when the reader has to abandon the fluent mode on encountering unfamiliar concepts, an ambiguous misprint, or illegible printing. The rationale for the proposal that children should be instructed to rely on a guess-and-check style of reading seems more tenuous than it did when first advanced. It is not a major aspect of the target skill of fluent reading, though it may be a means whereby the target may be reached, and so it remains to determine whether the acquisition of reading is facilitated by such an emphasis.

New reading technology

The influence of recent technological developments on the study of reading has been quite profound because of the possibilities they offer to record the visual behaviour of the reader as discussed early in this chapter. In addition new technologies for displaying information, such as computer-driven screens of various sorts, videotape and videodisc, have given researchers tremendously enhanced facilities for probing and manipulating the circumstances under which reading proceeds. Information can be displayed on computer-generated displays, including the familiar video display unit (VDU), that is more or less immediately contingent on what the reader has just done as in the dynamic display techniques (p. 141).

Necessarily, too, the ubiquity of the computer display in business, industrial, military, medical, and educational environments has raised questions of the comparability of the reading processes used for conventional and computerized methods of presentation. Perhaps the most intriguing development, from both practical and theoretical points of view, is the emergence of novel forms for presenting material to the reader, including some which ostensibly serve to bypass the eye-movement system. In this section we examine some of the evidence on the new technology of reading and the issues it raises and illuminates.

Practical issue III: reading computer-generated displays

The advent of computer-driven displays for the purposes of interactive computing, word processing, videotex, typesetting, and so forth, has often involved the replacement of the printed page as the means whereby the reader gets the relevant information. A sensible question to be asked, especially in light of the expense of electronic devices, is whether reading is affected by the display medium. Some features of the first generation of computer-text displays, such as the poor resolution of fine detail, might reasonably lead to the suspicion that reading would be adversely affected. Display technology has subsequently advanced considerably, and contemporary displays are perceptibly improved relative to the early ones, though there are many features that remain to be optimized in terms of human performance studies. For example, most screens continue to employ the reverse of the customary black-on-white style used for the printed page. Moreoever the spacing of the lines, the size of the characters, the typeface, the contrast ratio between the characters and the background, the line length, the viewing distance, and the problem of flicker effects are all factors that have to be taken into account in a comparison between methods of presenting text. And of course the computer screen is not manipulable in the way that a book or newspaper is. There has been research which has concentrated on the perceptual limitations of VDU technology, since these are clearly linked with the processes of extracting information from displays. This includes the design of character sets with improved legibility and the selection of character–background contrast levels on which legibility depends (see Van Nes 1984), the effect of screen resolution which affects image quality (Harpster and Freiwalds 1984), the choice of repetition rates so that flicker is not apparent (Bauer 1984), and the potential benefits for legibility arising from contrast reversal (i.e., dark characters on a light screen) (Bauer and Cavonius 1980; Van Nes 1984).

Moreover a number of studies have shown that reading is slower from computer screens, though which of the many differences between conventional and computerized forms of presentation is responsible is often not clear. Gould and Grischkowsky (1984) found that subjects doing a proofreading task on a computer screen one day and on 'hard copy' on another day worked about 20–30 per cent faster from hard copy than from the computer screen. Another study of proofreading by Wright and Lickorish (1983) confirmed this disadvantage to the computerized version of the task in terms of speed and accuracy of work, and found in addition that fast subjects were delayed more (46 per cent) than slow subjects (24 per cent). A similar outcome was reported for silent reading by Muter *et al.* (1982), who found that reading text on a television screen was 28.5 per cent slower than reading from a book. Kruk and Muter (1984) noted that this could reflect a number of uncontrolled differences and in a follow-up study found that the reduced reading speed from a video screen was partly attributable to the short-line/small-page format of the video condition used and the use of single spacing. While it is doubtless important to pinpoint the factors which facilitate and those which impair reading speed, it is as well to remember that the essence of reading is normally to understand, and the investigation of electronic presentation methods must naturally be complemented by measurement of comprehension (as well as the non-negligible matter of user-acceptability). Muter *et al.* (1982) in fact found that although reading from the video display was slower than from the printed version, there was no difference in comprehension.

The effect of 'scrolling' the display, in which the display is moved line by line up the screen, was studied by Kolers, Duchnicky, and Ferguson (1981). They found that comprehension of text was about the same for a static and a scrolled display, but the static version was preferred by the subjects. Another presentation technique called 'leading' was studied by Granaas *et al.* (1984). This involves moving the text in jumps of one or more characters at a time from right to left. The reader always saw a 'window' of 30–40 characters-worth of text (see Figure 6.5) which was subject to jumps of between 1 and 10 spaces in a variety of experimental conditions. The pause times between jumps were adjusted to produce a presentation rate around 300 words per minute for a paragraph of text, which corresponds to a quite respectable reading speed for non-technical information. Comprehension depended on jump size, being lowest for jump sizes of 1 and 2 (when the display would be least often at rest), and being at a more or less constant level for jump sizes between 4 and 10. For a presentation rate of 300 words per minute, comprehension was some 8 per cent poorer for the leading format than for a conventional

```
The reader might see a display

might see a display that unfo

a display that unfolded like

that unfolded like this in th

lded like this in the six-char

this in the six-character jump

e six-character jump condition

acter jump condition in a matt

condition in a matter of 3 or

in a matter of 3 or so second

er of 3 or so seconds.
```

Figure 6.5   A display of text in the 'leading' style. Each line would appear in the same place on the video screen, pausing for 370 msec

whole-page format. Displays of this sort in which a moving window of information is seen are most useful where space is at a severe premium, and have long had a place in shop-window advertising displays and in locations like Times Square and Piccadilly Circus for the presentation of stop-press news.

Some techniques have yet to be brought into effective contact with an applications context, but their potential can be anticipated. For instance, when concentration on single words is an integral feature of the performance of the task, as in proofreading, dynamic techniques which emphasize each word in turn would seem to be well chosen. This kind of performance would perhaps be facilitated by the unfolding display method used by Just, Carpenter, and Woolley (1982) in which successive words were revealed in their correct spatial position as the subject pressed a bar. Options such as reducing the brightness of words already viewed, or replacing them by length-matched strings of some neutral character, could also be considered as variations on this kind of presentation. Although it is not unknown for observers engaged in a target search or visual monitoring task to look at objects in the visual field without recognizing that they are targets (e.g. Snyder 1973), dynamic methods of highlighting would seem to engage the subject's attention effectively. Whether proofreading in particular would be facilitated in practice is a matter for empirical investigation. It nevertheless serves to underline the possible scope of the new reading technologies.

Psychological and practical opportunities of the new display technology

An interesting distinction may be drawn between many of the improvements in screen technology related to legibility and those technical possibilities that new technology offers to present text in novel formats. The former can be seen as part of a concern to emulate the high standards of graphic communication that the art of the printer has achieved since the time of Gutenberg. Display variables like resolution, contrast ratio, type size, and so on have thus been brought to such a point of technical advancement that they serve as fair approximations to the standards of the printed page. The point has arguably been reached at which further improvements will not be psychologically interesting in the sense that they will potentiate only marginal changes in the efficiency with which information can be picked up from the screen. Consider screen resolution, for example, which if sufficiently low can impair legibility so much that comprehension processes are disrupted, and the reader has sometimes to rely on guesswork. The current state of screen technology is such that resolution should no longer cause serious problems to the reader, and in general it seems that good image quality on a computerized display is achievable as a matter of routine.

By contrast those presentation techniques which are due to the new technology, like scrolling (which, incidentally, is more often than not still an inadvertent consequence of the screen hardware) and leading, constitute manipulations of the display that may impinge in much more radical ways on the reading process. As such they are of more interest to the psychologist because they may potentiate or interfere with the extraction of information, the control processes that serve to guide the eyes, and integration of information acquisition, working memory and comprehension processes. From an applied point of view, they are of some significance because, for instance, they offer a means of aligning presentation techniques and task demands, as was suggested above in the instance of 'unfolding' and proofreading.

Rapid serial visual presentation (RSVP)

To illustrate the psychological scope of the new reading technology, we shall examine the work on rapid serial visual presentation that goes under the acronym of RSVP. This was coined by Forster (1970), and entails the simple device of displaying letters or words one after another, typically in very quick succession, to the same spatial position. The reader as a result does not have to make eye movements from word to word, although it is arguable that this would harm the act of reading by denying access to the anticipatory processes mediated by parafoveal vision. It would certainly destroy the rescue facility provided by regressive eye movements, and at moderately fast presentation rates the intraword fixation adjustments that are commonly made in inspecting long words (O'Regan 1981) would be precluded. Notwithstanding these likely penalties, a potential benefit could accrue from the elimination of the processing load imposed in controlling the eye-movement system. This would, for example, potentially release time and resources normally needed to programme and execute eye movements.

The RSVP technique is of special interest because most of the effort at improving reading speed has hitherto concentrated on characteristics of the reader. Thus people are advised to tailor their *reading* strategy to the task in hand, for example 'skimming' when only the gist of the text is needed. Similarly 'speed-reading' courses advocate various ways in which the reader should deal with the text, including instruction about how to pass the eyes over the printed page. In contrast with this kind of emphasis, we find in RSVP a focus on the means whereby the information is presented to the reader. By displaying the information to be read in one limited region and at a sufficiently high rate, the limitations on information input which appear to be imposed by the speed of operation and the control processes of the eye-movement system are circumvented. That at any rate is the prospect, though whether or not comprehension is impaired in these unnatural viewing conditions is a matter for experiment to determine. It is also an empirical question whether readers can sustain reading in RSVP conditions for extended passages.

Recall and RSVP

Interest in the RSVP technique was stimulated by a study by Forster (1970) who used it to display strings of words for subjects to recall, with a presentation rate equivalent to 960 words per minute. Recall was possible at this rate for about half the words in a string of six. A finding of particular theoretical importance is that recall was better if the word sequence was an intact sentence rather than a scrambled version of one. A related finding was described by Juola, Ward, and McNamara (1982) who presented nine-word sequences in RSVP format for subjects to scan for letter targets or for words belonging to particular categories such as food or clothing. Presentation rates of 600 and 1,200 words per minute were used and, as in Forster's study, the word sequences were intact or scrambled sentences. Performance was better for the slower rate but was at a level in excess of 80 per cent correct for even the 1,200 wpm rate. Forster's finding that performance was improved when syntactic information was available was confirmed using a search task instead of a recall task, with a systematic advantage when the word strings formed sentences.

Many variations and developments on this general theme have been reported, the most important for our purposes being studies of readers' abilities to read sentences and paragraphs in RSVP format for comprehension. Theoretical interest in the RSVP technique lies in the connection postulated in various accounts (e.g. Just and Carpenter 1980; McConkie 1983) between eye-movement behaviour and the internal processes of comprehension. If reading speeds of 300 words per minute are characteristic of competent readers dealing with non-technical material presented in a conventional printed form, it is a matter of some interest to determine how they would cope with RSVP rates of twice, and even three or four times, their normal reading rate. Even if in such circumstances recall of the material is possible, the possibility that comprehension processes might be swamped by this bombardment of words remains, and will be considered next.

Reading text in RSVP

Potter, Kroll, and Harris (1980) extended the RSVP paradigm to the presentation of paragraphs, focusing on the question of whether text was capable of being remembered and understood in this form. Subjects were shown paragraphs, one at a time, and had to write down immediately what they could remember. The paragraphs were rather disjointed and ambiguous in the absence of a key 'topic sentence'; for the purpose of the study, performance was compared when this sentence was situated at the beginning, in the middle, or at the end of the paragraph, and when it was omitted. One such paragraph, specially composed for the investigation, is shown in Figure 6.6.

The topic sentence for the paragraph in the figure was 'I was hungry, but the pizza was hot' and is omitted to show the consequent ambiguity of the passage in its absence. Spontaneous mention of the topic scarcely ever occurred if the critical sentence had not been included, whereas the probability of reporting it if it was present was over 0.80. This finding was obtained regardless of RSVP rate (equivalent to between 240 and 720 words per minute, with a brief gap between sentences), even when the sentence appeared in the middle or at the end of the paragraph. Potter, Kroll, and Harris concluded that subjects comprehended a majority of the sentences even at the highest rates of presentation. By contrast recall of the sentence content as a whole (measured in terms of idea units remembered) declined as presentation rate increased. Performance was also better in the RSVP conditions than in conventional conditions matched for total display time, forcing the subject to 'skim' if the whole passage was to be viewed. The inference was

---

It seemed like hours since I had called. Finally it
arrived, richly coloured but a little thin. I wondered
if it was too hot to touch. The smell was so strong
that I couldn't help but try. I pulled at one section,
but it was difficult to remove, so I tried another.
Elastic fibres developed, attaching it to the rest.
I exerted more force. As I pulled, however, droplets
of hot oil splashed one side, burning my hand. I dropped
it. Perhaps I could last a couple more minutes. I was
impatient, but it was very hot.

Figure 6.6   Example of paragraph used in the RSVP studies of Potter, Kroll, and
Harris (1980)

made that while memory processes were overloaded by the rapid
presentation rate, it was none the less possible for those processes
responsible for comprehension to keep pace with the input.

It has been concluded, for example by Juola and his associates
(Juola, Ward, and McNamara 1982; Ward and Juola 1982), from
this kind of evidence that the comprehension processes involved in
RSVP and conventional reading are similar and that they are
essentially independent of presentation method. In particular it is
justifiable to use data from RSVP studies to generalize about normal
reading comprehension. Paragraphs were presented in a variety of
formats by Juola, Ward, and McNamara (1982) with comprehension
probed by a series of multiple-choice questions immediately each
paragraph had been read. Presentation rates were equivalent to
reading rates of between 200 and 700 words per minute, and whole-
page format was compared with various RSVP conditions, with an
average window size varying from 5 to 15 (adjusted so that the
sequence viewed always consisted of intact words). Comprehension
was no better for normal page format than for RSVP. Juola, Ward,
and McNamara emphasized that this applied despite the fact that
the subjects had less than 30 minutes' experience reading in RSVP
mode compared with a lifetime of reading in normal formats.

A subsequent study by Masson (1983) throws doubt on the

validity of those findings suggesting the equivalence of comprehension performance under RSVP and matched conventional whole-
page conditions. Indeed Masson found that comprehension of short
passages, probed by question-answering or by the requirement to
write a single sentence summary of them, was poorer for RSVP than
for the whole passage format. Why, in the face of the previous
evidence, did this reversal in the outcome of experimentation occur?

The major difference between Masson's (1983) series of RSVP
studies and the previous ones seems to be whether or not there was a
pause between sentences. This has typically amounted to a blank
interval lasting for about one or two words' worth of RSVP time,
and is a reflection of the investigator's concern to allow comprehension and memory processes associated with the end of sentences
to be concluded before the new information from the next sentence
begins to arrive. This seems to reflect a conviction that comprehension
(and/or possibly the capacity to retain information in working
memory) is not a matter of a smooth and continuous flow, and that
integration of information within a sentence frame may take an
appreciable amount of time, and moreover be phased to occur
between sentences. Masson (1983) reported two experiments in
which RSVP sentences were read with or without an inter-sentence
pause, and found that performance was substantially better for
RSVP with pauses. Unfortunately the question of whether whole-
page presentation produces better performance than RSVP with
pauses is not clearly answered by this study. Although an experimental comparison was made of the two conditions, and the deficit
due to the RSVP condition was reduced to about 3 per cent by the
provision of pauses, it seems possible that a more searching study,
which attempted to optimize RSVP performance, might change the
picture further. What readers might achieve given extended RSVP
practice (or for that matter practice at skimming) is unknown, but it
is plain that the whole-page format stands at a considerable
advantage because of the amount of experience that readers have of
it, and because it offers the possibility of reviewing text already seen.

Conclusions: bypassing eye movements?

There seems considerable scope in general for the investigation of
conditions which optimize performance with the novel methods of
presenting material, and for these methods to be suitably matched to
the reader's task. The theoretical implications of this research will

continue to be clarified, but some useful insights have emerged. There is comfort for almost all sides in the theoretical debate from the accumulated evidence. Abbreviating the exposure of the words in a sentence or passage to a level well below that of eye fixation durations (e.g., less than 100 msec for RSVP compared with 250–300 msec for normal reading) does not prevent the reader from picking up information about the gist or the detail of the text. Ward and Juola (1982) contend that the main limitation on comprehension in RSVP studies is the overall rate of presentation, and that comprehension is essentially independent of the variables which influence gaze duration in normal reading. It is indisputable that the evidence shows that comprehension declines as the presentation rate increases, and it seems that comprehension is sufficiently protracted and flexible to overcome the restricted processing opportunity offered when display times are fixed, and not under the reader's control. The effect of pausing between sentences seems to place some limit on this, and to reflect on the need for the comprehension processes to 'catch up', when there is a mounting debt of unprocessed conceptual inputs at fast RSVP rates. The trade-off between the gains in processing resources made available when RSVP inputs eliminate the need to control the eye-movement system, and the losses incurred when control is lost over what is seen and dwelt on, have not been fully elucidated, and the comparability of comprehension in RSVP and conventional reading remains to be determined.

One intriguing question that the RSVP experiments raise is to resolve the discrepancy between the time needed to process a word in a RSVP sequence (as little as 50–100 msec) and the time needed for a fixation in reading (250–350 msec). A pointer is provided by a study from the eye-movement literature (Rayner et al. 1981) in which a foveal window of text was masked (by replacing the letters and spaces by an unbroken row of 'x's) a short interval after the beginning of the fixation. The text only needed to be visible for the first 50 msec of the fixation interval for the words presented to be accurately identified. This is consistent with the performance achieved with RSVP. Rayner et al. proposed that the initial 50 msec or so are used for extracting information from the foveal region, and parafoveal/peripheral guidance is mediated later in the fixation interval.

Basic questions about the comparability of conventional and electronic displays have to be answered, and studies have to be made which seek to optimize the new displays and their conditions of use. Aside from this fundamental human factors research, which we have reviewed briefly, we have identified some intriguing novel opportunities to adapt the presentation of information to the reader's needs and skills using the new technology. This partly depends on the continuing development of electronic hardware but will also increasingly depend on the development of 'intelligent' software which is used to capitalize on the new display facilities. For example, the technique of leading could conceivably be modified to work with a variable window size, to enable the presentation of idea units. Leading could alternatively be operated with pacing by the reader (via a control button) and window size could be adjusted to maximize reading rate for the individual.

Summary

This chapter has dealt with a mixed set of aspects of reading, ranging from eye behaviour to cognitive processes. Basic data on eye movements during reading were described, data that are used to make inferences about the mental operations and processes thought to underly reading. The question was considered of what is picked up from the text that is used to guide the eyes in reading. Evidence from studies of visual discrimination and search suggest that while the fovea is responsible for the pick-up of detail, the competence of the visual periphery as a provider of pertinent information for the reading process should not be ignored. The quality of the information supplied peripherally – grossly characteristic of the scene and its constituent objects – possibly serves a 'local' guidance function for the eye-movement system with a direct and short-range effect. Supporting evidence from eye-movement studies of reading was reviewed, with the caveat that the peripheral-guidance hypothesis is not a theoretical position that is universally accepted. The relation between severe reading retardation, or developmental dyslexia, and unusual eye-movement patterns was discussed. No basis was found for considering developmental dyslexia as a unitary disorder, and certainly not one in which the difficulties are attributable to faulty eye movements. However there is a significant minority of children with reading difficulties whose problems may have a visuo-spatial origin, and failure in particular to develop eye dominance may be one factor.

Evidence was also reported for a slower acting form of control of eye movements, reflecting the influence of 'global' contextual factors. The situation regarding the contribution of context is also unfolding, and in a way that has raised doubts about the nature and force of top-down influences in fluent reading. It is plain that some effects which may be attributed to contextual information are not achieved in a deliberative mode, simply because there is not time in fluent reading for deliberative or predictive processes, certainly of a conscious kind. They may be better thought of as effects achieved with a minimum of monitoring, characterized in the literature as automatic-spreading activation. There appear to be no costs associated with these fast-acting processes in fluent reading. Benefits and costs, possibly on the basis of conscious prediction, occur when the reader is confronted by unfamiliar words or text which is deficient from a perceptual point of view. It is then that the process of fluent reading appears to revert to the ponderous, more nearly conscious, form of puzzle-solving that may be its developmental precursor. Arguably the clearest evidence of benefits arising from use of context is from eye-movement studies which show small but reliable improvements in the rate at which information is processed.

Conditions *precluding* the use of eye movements, or at least subjecting them to extreme limitations, may be contrived using computer-driven displays, the text being presented segmentally at a very rapid rate. The ability of readers to read in RSVP conditions was assessed. The conditions that optimize comprehension under these conditions, when rates considerably in excess of the reader's normal reading rate may be used, have still to be determined. This is one instance of new technology opening up novel ways of presenting information to the reader, and which may be tailored to special circumstances and needs, enabling performance to be improved or remediated. Research using these new display techniques was described, including studies in which the computer screen serves as a replacement for the conventional printed form. Other practical issues implicating the eye movement system and its control were discussed. The evidence on eye movement behaviour during reading was considered to cast doubt on certain speed-reading techniques involving eye-movement training and control. It is apparent that what the reader achieves is a smooth 'automatic' use of the perceptually definitive aspects of words and continuous text. So while the reflective use of perceptual cues may sometimes be beneficial – as when one puzzles over a strange word, or unfamiliar handwriting – the goal for the reader is the unconscious employment of these subtle perceptual/linguistic skills. In Chapter 5 it was seen that extended amounts of practice are necessary to achieve the seeming effortlessness of so-called automatic skills, and this must surely be a necessary condition for fluency in reading.

7 APPLICATIONS, IMPLICATIONS, AND CONCLUSIONS

In this book I have tried to put an emphasis on the application of cognitive psychology in the foreground of the discussion – instead of the more usual textbook approach of proceeding from theory to application. This was intended to recognize and highlight the importance to psychology of the applicability problem in general, and of applied research in particular. Hence in Chapters 3–6 practical problems were used to initiate the discussion, broadening out to more general theory-orientated material in each case. This served to particularize the general discussion relative to 'real-world' situations, and to illustrate the potential of psychology as a means of understanding everyday human activities. In this final chapter I want to take a brief final look at matters on either side of the theory–practice divide.

First, and most radically, there is the possible theoretical inadequacy of information processing as a paradigm for supplying insight into human performance. I have not intended, given the space available, to evaluate the paradigm (nor even to defend it), but to exemplify it in a small number of representative contexts. It has shortcomings, most obviously in the original form of Figure 2.4, and an expanded and elaborated version of that model is the least that the foregoing discussion calls for, and some particularly important implications for the model are summarized below. Notwithstanding the need for modification, the general analytical approach – of describing the underlying processing structures and their inter-connections – does provide a useful perspective from which to give a rough characterization of performance across a range of circum-stances. And it represents a way of conceptualizing performance which is easy to communicate to and share with other people.

Secondly, on the applications side there is the question of how to use information-processing psychology. It is not simply drawn by magic to the appropriate problems, bathing them in a glow of insight. It is applied by practising psychologists, and we need to understand how this is done; the problem is briefly considered in the section below.

Theoretical implications

Some of the implications of Chapters 3–6 for the outline infor-mation-processing model of Figure 2.4 have been noted in the respective chapters. We could replace the model by one which gave a more elaborate specification of basic processes, but this would submerge it in detail. The more important modifications that seem to be needed for a more complete model include the need to expound the structural components in more detail, for instance to take account of the evidence on early visual processes and the nature of the stored representations of visual stimuli. This was illustrated in Chapter 3 for the rather special case of face perception. We should have to examine a wider literature, dealing with the perception of a greater range of visual stimuli, to warrant general conclusions about early visual processing, but the evidence considered provides a useful starting point. There were implications about the nature of information-processing operations in Chapter 4, where the assump-tion of a strict sequential flow of information was questioned, with the possibility of stages operating in an overlapped manner. And in Chapters 3 and 6 there was evidence that late stages in (and to one side of) the flow may exert an influence on the course of information processing at early stages. Hence the components of the model may effectively be connected in a leapfrogged (feedforward) or a retroactive (feedback) fashion.

One feature of the tasks to which the outline model in Chapter 2 most directly applies is that the sequence from input to output takes very little time to complete, as is epitomized by the traditional reaction-time task. Tasks involving a more complex flow of information, and taking place over a more extended interval of time, not surprisingly call for models of greater complexity than the basic model of Chapter 2. An example of this is the psychological analysis of reading, which has accumulated a range of models, most of which deal with limited aspects of this important skill. Some researchers have chosen to focus on the performance of readers presented with one word at a time. The task may be to read each word aloud, or to make a decision about a property like the word's membership of some category. Comparatively simple tasks like these have commonly led to complex models, characterized, for example, by alternative information pathways by which the central set of representations of words – the mental lexicon – may be reached. Yet more complicated models are needed to begin to handle more 'natural' reading tasks, including the kinds of tasks discussed in Chapter 6. The time-span of the kind of performance involved here is much more protracted than that of the single word paradigms, and many cycles of input and output typically occur. Nevertheless some of the implications of Chapter 6 for the form of the basic model are worth recalling. For instance, the possibility was noted of 'top-down' processing in reading. In addition, reading a piece of text may be viewed as being jointly directed by information extracted from the centre of the visual field, and from the visual periphery. Moreover, as well as being subject to the co-ordination of these two sources of information, the course of reading may be steered by the contextual inputs derived from the printed page.

Other implications for the basic model emerged in Chapter 5 which dealt, among other things, with the subject of attention. This was represented in the original model as an amorphous system exerting its influence on any one or more of the central information processing stages, hence affecting their efficiency and rate of operation by the supply or withholding of 'resources'. Much of the research intended to throw light on the mode of operation of this system places a high workload on the subjects, commonly by requiring them to do two tasks at once. One popular account (Wickens 1984) maintains that the processing resources available to the human operator in such situations are separable in terms of the input modality, the central coding used, and the output modality. Tasks which call on different processing resources (e.g. different input modalities) can be done without mutual interference, whereas this is not generally so for tasks calling on the same resource (e.g. the same input modality). While much of the evidence favours this kind of account, there are signs that human performance may rely also on a general-purpose undifferentiated resource, used perhaps in the monitoring of multiple activities. This may be recruited on an all-or-none basis regardless of the nature of the modalities and codes, and regardless of the complexity of the tasks involved, showing up as a small deficit in performance when a task is done in tandem with another as opposed to being done alone.

In addition to these general indications for an information processing model, many other theoretical questions were touched on. The research inputs to the discussion from applied psychology are profitable in two ways. At their best and most rigorous this research supplies a complementary, frequently converging, and occasionally original line of evidence to inform and qualify the more academic research effort undertaken within mainstream cognitive psychology. And applied research typically aims for an ecological representativeness that preserves a connection with real-world issues and environments, without which the mainstream effort may drift into artificiality and irrelevance.

Applied cognitive psychology

The bridge between theory and application seems likely to be cemented as information-dependent tasks become increasingly prominent in the workplace. However on the evidence we have considered psychology is not as removed from the 'real world' as critics have asserted. It has in many cases – as illustrated in Chapters 3–6 – already achieved 'ecological validity', a representativeness in its research methods and procedures of the circumstances of everyday behaviour. In other cases what may seem most unpromising psychological raw material, not always thought of as having ecological validity, is found capable of throwing light on serious problems. As an example, Smith and Langolf (1981) used the Sternberg memory-scanning task as an index of the neurotoxic effect of mercury on certain US chemical-industry workers. No effects on the performance of these workers of their day-to-day tasks have been reported, perhaps because the possible measures for this purpose were simply too gross and insensitive, or because the workers adjusted their ways of working to offset any deficits. But the much-used and well-understood memory-scanning task revealed clear signs of increasing performance impairment as the amount of mercury in the worker's urine increased. Smith and Langolf therefore argued for the use of precision performance-measures as highly sensitive indicators of the impairment of mental functioning.

Guidelines for the application of cognitive psychology

Finally in this chapter we turn to a question that seems to have had little direct attention from those concerned with the application of cognitive psychology. This is the apparently simple question of *how* to apply psychology. Considering the apparent absence of any commentaries on this question, it might appear that the matter is so simple that we need not concern ourselves with it. Perhaps the application of psychology requires no guidance, perhaps it is just a matter of intuition and confidence!

Yet because numerous criticisms are levelled at psychology (concerning its 'relevance', its practical failings, its lack of external validity, etc.), we are alerted to a variety of cautions pertaining to its practical use. We could infer from the fact that the critics have felt it necessary to make these observations that some ways of applying psychology may be ineffective, some counter-productive, and some possibly even hazardous. For example, Chapanis (1967) made a series of critical comments about the 'laboratory model' in psychology. An interpretation of his concern is that the business of bridging the distance between the pure and applied worlds of psychology needs careful consideration and analysis, and that existing practices leave room for improvement. We may reasonably conclude that the identification of such 'malpractices' is tantamount to the specification of negative guidelines for the application of psychology. It follows moreover that there exist some bridging operations which psychological practitioners use, which are equivalent to procedures for the application of psychological knowledge. Although we cannot hope to formulate a set of *positive guidelines* for applications of psychology in the confines of an introductory text, we can perhaps make a start by noting the need to analyse what is involved in the application of psychology, and to formulate an agenda for further action.

Two broad aspects of this merit further discussion. There is first what can be called the *perspective problem*, which is in effect bound up with the differing viewpoints of those involved in the practical problem in hand. It includes the need for the psychological applications effort to take these perspectives into account; to incorporate an analysis of the problem from the user's standpoint, and to gear the communication of the proposed solution to the participants and decision-makers of the problem situation. Of course this issue also affects participants from other disciplines, but seems a particular responsibility for the psychologist, partly because of a vested professional interest in matters of communication, but more particularly because of the care that is needed over the expression of psychological terms and proposals. This is a difficulty that seems to be unique to psychology because of its use of and reliance on concepts and terms that are part of the natural currency of everyday language. Far from making psychological statements, conclusions, and recommendations more accessible to the non-specialist, it may be that this gives rise to special difficulties because of the unwanted nuances of everyday usage to which the nonspecialist is sensitive. This is compounded by the sometimes circumscribed and specialized constructions which psychologists put on their borrowed terminology. Examination of the psychological use in standard textbooks of terms like 'attention', 'reinforcement', 'processing', and many others amply illustrate the point.

The second aspect of the 'guidelines' issue is the *mapping problem*, which is the matter of relating the research effort to the operational and functional details of the problem situation. The research may or may not be empirical, and may range from custom-designed experimentation to a mere review of the psychological and other literature bearing on the problem. What the problem itself consists of will include whether the information and inputs the person requires for the performance of the task need to be reorganized or supplemented, how the task(s) might be restructured, whether (and how) feedback about performance should be supplied, how training could be given, whether (and how) conditions of overload and stress could be obviated, whether incentives would be beneficial, and much more. In all cases the application will have to consider what is the isomorphism (in the sense of what connections may be identified) between the parameters and the overall environment of the target problem (i.e. its realization in the real world) and the research model of it (i.e. its psychological scientific representation).

To analyse the material covered in this book in this way would require another chapter or two at least, putting into place a framework for the kind of problem and task analysis needed. Interestingly, this issue does not seem to have been addressed by the research or practitioner communities, and it will be regrettable if the rush to apply psychology (and science in general) is not accompanied by a considered attempt to analyse just what this basic activity consists of. It should not be supposed that psychology is peculiarly deficient among the sciences because its applications guidelines do not exist. On the contrary, these are general questions that may be raised about the application of scientific knowledge which do not seem to have been widely discussed in the philosophical and scientific literature. The analysis of disasters sometimes attributes responsibility to engineering-design failures, and painful lessons about the application of science may be learned from such incidents, a characteristic of which is that they continue to occur in environments which are generally well understood due to centuries of scientific scrutiny and insight. One difficulty for the application of psychological knowledge lies in the highly complex, incompletely understood environment in which people live, work, and act. To take due account of the range of factors that influence human decisions, actions, and performance in general is an immense task, and potentially a very serious one when the target environment is hostile.

I have not attempted to examine the mapping problem because of its sheer scope and complexity. It will, however, help to illustrate what is at stake. In the study of Smith and Langolf (1981) cited earlier in the chapter, a laboratory task, memory scanning, was used as an indicator of a particular neurotoxic effect. Smith and Langolf recognized that there is a question of how performance on this task is paralleled in the working environment. In this particular instance we may readily accept that a deficit of the kind they reported is justification in its own right for concern about the damage that may be occasioned by exposure to mercury. However, the connection between memory scanning and performance at work is unclear, although as Smith and Langolf pointed out a connection between memory scanning and the capacity of short-term memory has been postulated. On this basis it would be reasonable for further research to test whether the holding capacity of memory is affected by exposure to mercury as predicted, and to look for possible decrements in performance on tasks in the workplace (and in the everyday world) which would be affected by a reduced short-term memory. The potential importance of Smith and Langolf's findings is further underlined by evidence of a strong relationship between speed of performance on tasks like the memory-scanning task and performance on traditional cognitive tests like the IQ test (Vernon 1986). The thrust of most applications research would be more likely to be in the reverse direction, taking the workplace problem as the starting point, and from an analysis thereof to construct a basic psychological representation for further examination and research. The recommendations flowing therefrom would have a known field of reference, since the mapping between the target problem and the researchers' instantiation of it would have been established in advance. Taking tasks directly from the experimenter's shelf may not be the best way of proceeding, and tasks modelling the real-world situation may be needed. The evidence we have reviewed in Chapters 3–6 is an indication of how well (or badly) activities in the everyday world are modelled by the researchers, and perhaps may give some clues about how they implicitly resolve the mapping problem.

REFERENCES

Ackerman, P.L., Schneider, W., and Wickens, C.D. (1984) 'Deciding the existence of a time-sharing ability: a combined methodological and theoretical approach', *Human Factors* 26: 71–82.

Aitkenhead, A.M. and Slack, J.M. (eds) (1985) *Issues in Cognitive Modelling*, London: Lawrence Erlbaum.

Allport, D.A. (1975) 'The state of cognitive psychology: a critical notice of Chase, W.G. (ed.) *Visual Information Processing*, New York: Academic Press', *Quarterly Journal of Experimental Psychology* 27: 141–52.

Allport, D.A. (1980) 'Attention and performance', in G. Claxton (ed.) *Cognitive Psychology: New Directions*, London: Routledge & Kegan Paul.

Allport, D.A., Antonis, B., and Reynolds, P. (1972) 'On the division of attention: A disproof of the single channel hypothesis', *Quarterly Journal of Experimental Psychology* 24: 225–35.

Anderson, I.H. (1937) 'Studies in the eye movements of good and poor readers', *Psychological Monographs* 48: 1–35.

Anderson, J.R. (1980) *Cognitive Psychology and its Implications*, San Francisco: Freeman.

Attneave, F. (1959) *Applications of Information Theory to Psychology*, New York: Holt, Rinehart & Winston.

Baddeley, A.D. (1983) 'Working memory', *Philosophical Transactions of the Royal Society* Series B, 302: 311–24.

Baddeley, A.D. and Hitch, G. (1974) 'Working memory', in G.H. Bower (ed.) *The Psychology of Learning and Motivation*, 8, New York: Academic Press.

Bakan, D. (1980) 'Politics and American psychology', in Rieber, R.W. and Salzinger, K. (eds) *Psychology: Theoretical–historical perspectives*, New York: Academic Press.

Ballantine, M. (1983) 'Well, how do children learn population stereotypes?', in K. Coombes (ed.) *Proceedings of the 1983 Ergonomics Conference*, 1, London: Taylor & Francis.

Barber, P.J. and Legge, D. (1976) *Perception and Information*, London: Methuen.

Barnard, P.J., Hammond, N.V., Morton, J., Long, J.B., and Clark, I.A. (1981) 'Consistency and compatibility in human-computer dialogue', *International Journal of Man–Machine Studies* 15: 87–134.

Bateson, P.P.G. (1977) 'Testing an observer's ability to identify individual animals', *Animal Behaviour* 25: 247–8.

Bauer, D. (1984) 'Improving VDT workplaces in offices by use of a physiologically optimized screen with black symbols on a light background: basic considerations', *Behaviour and Information Technology* 3: 363–9.

Bauer, D. and Cavonius, C.R. (1980) 'Improving the legibility of visual display units through contrast reversal', in E. Grandjean and E. Vigliani (eds) *Ergonomic Aspects of Visual Display Terminals*, London: Taylor & Francis.

Becker, C.A. (1976) 'Allocation of attention during visual word recognition', *Journal of Experimental Psychology: Human Perception and Performance* 2: 556–66.

Becker, C.A. (1979) 'Semantic context and word frequency effects in visual word recognition', *Journal of Experimental Psychology: Human Perception and Performance* 5: 252–9.

Benton, A.L. (1980) 'The neuropsychology of facial recognition', *American Psychologist* 35: 176–86.

Bertelson, P. (1961) 'Sequential redundancy and speed in a serial two-choice responding task', *Quarterly Journal of Experimental Psychology* 12: 90–102.

Bertelson, P. (1963) 'S–R relationships and response times to new versus repeated signals in a serial task', *Journal of Experimental Psychology* 65: 478–84.

Bertelson, P. (1965) 'Serial choice reaction-time as a function of response versus signal-and-response repetition', *Nature* 206: 217–18.

Black, J.L., Collins, D.W.K., DeRoach, J.N., and Zubrick, S. (1984) 'A detailed study of sequential saccadic eye movements for normal and poor-reading children', *Perceptual and Motor Skills* 59: 423–34.

Blaxhall, J. and Willows D.M. (1984) 'Reading ability and text difficulty as influences on second graders' oral reading errors, *Journal of Educational Psychology* 76: 330–41.

Bradshaw, J.L. and Nettleton, N.C. (1981) 'The nature of hemispheric specialization in man', *Behavioural and Brain Sciences* 4: 51–91.

Bradshaw, J.L. and Wallace G. (1971) 'Models for the processing and identification of faces', *Perception and Psychophysics* 9: 443–8.

Broadbent, D.E. (1958) *Perception and Communication*, London: Pergamon.

Broadbent, D.E. (1980) 'The minimization of models', in A.J. Chapman and D.M. Jones (eds) *Models of Man*, Leicester: British Psychological Society.

Broadbent, D.E. (1982) 'Task combination and selective intake of information', *Acta Psychologica* 50, 253–90.

Broadbent, D.E. (1984) 'The Maltese cross: a new simplistic model for memory', *Behavioural and Brain Sciences* 7: 55–94.

Brown, B., Haegerstrom-Portnoy, G., Adams, A.J., Yingling, D.D., Herron, J., and Marcus, M. (1983) 'Predictive eye movements do not discriminate between dyslexic and control children', *Neuropsychologia* 21: 121–8.

Brown, E., Deffenbacher, K., and Sturgill W. (1977) 'Memory for faces and the circumstances of an encounter', *Journal of Applied Psychology* 62: 311–18.

Brown, I.D. (1978) 'Dual task methods of assessing work-load', *Ergonomics* 21: 221–4.

Brown, I.D., Tickner, A.H. and Simmonds, D.C.V. (1969) 'Interference between concurrent tasks of driving and telephoning', *Journal of Applied Psychology* 53: 419–24.

Bruce, V. (1979) 'Searching for politicians: An information-processing approach to face recognition', *Quarterly Journal of Experimental Psychology* 31: 373–95.

Bruce, V. (1983) 'Recognizing faces', *Philosophical Transactions of the Royal Society of London* Series B, 302: 423–36.

Bruce, V. and Valentine, T. (1986) 'Semantic priming of familiar faces', *Quarterly Journal of Psychology* 38A: 125–50.

Bruce, V. and Young, A.W. (1986) 'Understanding face recognition', *British Journal of Psychology* 77: 305–27.

Buckhout, R., Figueroa, D., and Hoff, E. (1975) 'Eyewitness identification: effects of suggestion and bias in identification from photographs', *Bulletin of the Psychonomic Society* 6: 71–4.

Card, S., Moran, T.P., and Newell, A. (1983) *The Psychology of Human-Computer Interaction*, Hillsdale, NJ: Lawrence Erlbaum.

Carey, S. (1980) 'Maturational factors in human development', in D. Caplan (ed.) *Biological Bases of Mental Processes*, Cambridge, Mass.: MIT Press.

Carey, S. (1981) 'The development of face perception', in G. Davies,

H. Ellis, and J. Shepherd (eds) *Perceiving and Remembering Faces*, London: Academic Press.

Casali, J.G. and Wierwille, W.W. (1984) On the measurement of pilot perceptual workload: a comparison of assessment techniques addressing sensitivity and intrusion issues, *Ergonomics* 27: 1033–50.

Chance, J.E., and Goldstein, A.G. (1976) 'Recognition of faces and verbal labels', *Bulletin of the Psychonomic Society* 7: 384–6.

Chapanis, A. (1967), 'The relevance of laboratory studies to practical situations', *Ergonomics* 10: 557–77.

Chapanis, A. and Lindenbaum, L.E. (1959) 'A reaction time study of four control-display linkages', *Human Factors* 1: 1–14.

Christie, D.F.M. and Ellis, H.D. (1981) 'Photofit constructions versus verbal descriptions of faces', *Journal of Applied Psychology* 66: 358–63.

Çlark, W.C. (1969) 'Sensory-decision theory analysis of the placebo effect on the criterion for pain and thermal sensitivity (d′)', *Journal of Abnormal Psychology* 74: 363–71.

Cohen, M.E. and Nodine, C.F. (1978) 'Memory processes in facial recognition and recall', *Bulletin of the Psychonomic Society* 12: 317–19.

Conrad, R. and Hull, A.J. (1968) 'The preferred layout for numeral data-entry sets', *Ergonomics* 11: 165–73.

Cooper, G.E. and Harper, R.P. (1969) 'The use of pilot ratings in the evaluation of aircraft handling qualities' (NASA Ames Technical Report, NASA TN–D–5153), Moffett Field, Calif.: NASA Ames Research Centre.

Cooper, W.E. (ed.) (1983) *Cognitive Aspects of Skilled Typewriting*, New York: Springer-Verlag.

Craft, J.L. and Simon, J.R. (1970) 'Processing symbolic information from a visual display: interference from an irrelevant directional cue', *Journal of Experimental Psychology* 83: 415–20.

Crowder, R.G. (1982) 'The demise of short-term memory', *Acta Psychologica* 50: 291–323.

Damos, D. and Wickens, C.D. (1980) 'The acquisition and transfer of time-sharing skills', *Acta Psychologica* 46: 569–77.

Damos, D., Smist, T., and Bittner, A.C. (1983) 'Individual differences in multiple task performance as a function of response strategies', *Human Factors* 25: 215–26.

Davies, G.M. and Christie, D.F.M. (1982) 'Face recall: an examination of some factors limiting composite production accuracy', *Journal of Applied Psychology* 67: 103–9.

Davies, G.M., Shepherd, J.W., and Ellis H.D. (1979) 'Similarity effects in face recognition', *American Journal of Psychology* 92: 507–23.

Deffenbacher, K.A. and Horney, J. (1981) 'Psycho-legal aspects of face identification', in G. Davies, H. Ellis, and J. Shepherd (eds) *Perceiving and Remembering Faces*, London: Academic Press.

Dember, W.N. and Warm, J.S. (1979) *Psychology of Perception*, 2nd edn, New York: Holt, Rinehart & Winston.

Deutsch, J. and Deutsch, D. (1963), 'Attention: some theoretical considerations', *Psychological Review* 70: 80–90.

Dodd, D.H. and White, R.M. (1982) *Cognition: Mental Structures and Processes*, Boston: Allyn & Bacon.

Dodds, A.G., Clark-Carter, D., and Howarth, C.I. (1986) 'The effects of precuing on vibrotactile reaction times: implications for a guidance for blind people', *Ergonomics* 29: 1063–71.

Donders, F.C. (1969) 'On the speed of mental processes', trans. by W.G. Koster in W.G. Koster (ed.) *Attention and Performance II*, Amsterdam: North Holland.

Dretske, F.I. (1983) *Knowledge and the Flow of Information*, Cambridge, Mass.: MIT Press.

Duncan, J. (1979) 'Divided attention: the whole is more than the sum of its parts', *Journal of Experimental Psychology: Human Perception and Performance* 5: 216–28.

Dyer, F.N. (1973) 'The Stroop phenomenon and its use in the study of perceptual, cognitive and response processes', *Memory and Cognition* 1: 106–20.

Egan, D., Pittner, M., and Goldstein, A.G. (1977) 'Eyewitness identification – Photographs vs. live models', *Law and Human Behaviour* 1: 199–206.

Ehrlich, S. and Rayner, K. (1981) 'Contextual effects on word perception and eye movements during reading', *Journal of Verbal Learning and Verbal Behaviour* 20: 641–55.

Eisenberg, P. and Becker, C.A. (1982) 'Semantic context effects in visual word recognition, sentence processing, and reading: evidence for semantic strategies', *Journal of Experimental Psychology· Human Perception and Performance* 8: 739–56.

Ellis, H.D. (1975) 'Recognizing faces', *British Journal of Psychology* 66: 409–26.

Ellis, H.D. (1981) 'Theoretical aspects of face recognition', in G. Davies, H. Ellis, and J. Shepherd (eds) *Perceiving and Remembering Faces*, London: Academic Press.

Ellis, H.D., Davies, G.M., and Shepherd, J.W. (1978) 'A critical examination of the Photofit system for recalling faces', *Ergonomics* 21: 297–307.

Ellis, H.D., Shepherd, J.W., and Davies, G.M. (1975) 'An investigation of the Photofit technique for recalling faces', *British Journal of Psychology* 66: 29–37.

Eysenck, M.W. (1984) *A Handbook of Cognitive Psychology*, London: Lawrence Erlbaum Associates.

Fischler, I. and Bloom, P.A. (1979) 'Automatic and attentional processes in the effects of sentence contexts on word recognition', *Journal of Verbal Learning and Verbal Behaviour* 18: 1–20.

Fisher, G.H. and Cox, R.L. (1975) 'Recognizing human faces', *Applied Ergonomics* 6: 104–9.

Fisher, D.F. and Lefton, L.A. (1976) 'Peripheral information extraction: a developmental examination of reading processes', *Journal of Experimental Child Psychology* 21: 77–93.

Fitts, P.M. and Jones, R.E. (1961) 'Analysis of factors contributing to 460 "pilot errors" experiences in operating aircraft controls', in H.W. Sinaiko (ed.) *Selected Papers on Human Factors in the Design and Use of Control Systems*, New York: Dover.

Fitts, P.M. and Posner, M.I. (1967) *Human Performance*, Belmont, Calif.: Brooks Cole.

Fitts, P.M. and Seeger, C.M. (1953) 'S–R compatibility: spatial characteristics of stimulus and response codes', *Journal of Experimental Psychology* 46: 199–210.

Flin, R.H. (1980) 'Age effects in children's memory for unfamiliar faces', *Developmental Psychology* 16: 373–4.

Forster, K.I. (1970) 'Visual perception of rapidly presented word sequences of varying complexity', *Perception and Psychophysics* 8: 215–21.

Galper, R.E. (1970) 'Recognition of faces in photographic negative', *Psychonomic Science* 19: 207–8.

Garner, W.R. (1962) *Uncertainty and Structure as Psychological Concepts*, New York: Wiley.

Garner, W.R. (1974) *The Processing of Information and Structure*, Hillsdale, NJ: Lawrence Erlbaum.

Gerver, D. (1974) 'Simultaneous listening and speaking and retention of prose', *Quarterly Journal of Experimental Psychology* 26: 337–41.

Ghiselli, E.E., Campbell, J.P., and Zedeck, S. (1981) *Measurement Theory for the Behavioural Sciences*, San Francisco: Freeman.

Gibson, E.J. and Levin H. (1975) *The Psychology of Reading*, Cambridge, Mass.: MIT Press.

Goldstein, A.G. and Chance, J.E. (1971) 'Visual recognition memory for complex configurations', *Perception and Psychophysics* 9: 237–41.

Goldstein, A.G. and Chance, J.E. (1981) 'Laboratory studies of face recognition, in G. Davies, H. Ellis, and J. Shepherd (eds) *Perceiving and Remembering Faces*, London: Academic Press.

Goldstein, A.J., Harmon, L.D., and Lesk, A.B. (1971) 'Identification of human faces', *Proceedings of the IEEE* 59: 748–60.

Goldstein, A.J., Harmon, L.D., and Lesk, A.B. (1972) 'Man–machine interaction in human-face identification', *The Bell System Technical Journal* 51: 399–427.

Goodman, K.S. (1965) 'A linguistic study of cues and miscues in reading', *Elementary English Journal* 42: 39–44.

Goodman, K.S. (1967) 'Reading: a psycholinguistic guessing game', *Journal of the Reading Specialist* 6: 126–35.

Goodman, K.S. (1969) 'Analysis of oral reading miscues: applied psycholinguistics', *Reading Research Quarterly* 5: 9–30.

Goodman, K.S. (1970) 'Reading: a psycholinguistic guessing game', in

H. Singer and R.B. Ruddell (eds) *Theoretical Models and Processes of Reading*, Newark, Del.: International Reading Association.

Gopher, D. (1982) 'A selective attention test as a prediction of success in flight training', *Human Factors* 24: 173–84.

Gopher, D. and Kahneman, D. (1971) 'Individual differences in attention and the prediction of flight criteria', *Perceptual and Motor Skills* 33: 1335–42.

Gough, P.B. (1983) 'Context, form, and interaction', in K. Rayner (ed.) *Eye Movements in Reading: Perceptual and Language Processes*, New York: Academic Press.

Gough, P.B., Alford, J.A., and Holley-Wilcox, P. (1981) 'Words and contexts', in O.L. Tzeng and H. Singer (eds) *Perception of Print: Reading Research in Experimental Psychology*, Hillsdale, NJ: Lawrence Erlbaum.

Gould, J.D. and Grischkowsky, N. (1984) 'Doing the same work with hard copy and with cathode-ray tube (CRT) computer terminals', *Human Factors* 26: 323–37.

Granaas, M.M., McKay, T.D., Laham, R.D., Hurt, L.D., and Juola, J.F. (1984) 'Reading moving text on a CRT screen', *Human Factors* 26: 97–104.

Green, D.M. and Swets, J.A. (1966) *Signal Detection Theory and Psychophysics*, New York: Wiley.

Green, E.J. and Barber, P.J. (1983) 'Interference effects in an auditory Stroop task: congruence and correspondence', *Acta Psychologica* 53: 183–94.

Greene, J.M. (1987) *Cognitive Psychology*, London: Methuen.

Greenwald, A.G. (1972) 'On doing two things at once: Time sharing as a function of ideomotor compatibility', *Journal of Experimental Psychology* 94: 52–7.

Gregg, V.H. (1986) *Introduction to Human Memory*. London: Routledge & Kegan Paul.

Hamilton, P., Mulder, G., Strasser, H., and Ursin H. (1979) 'Final report of physiological psychology group', in N. Moray (ed.) *Mental Workload: Its Theory and Measurement*, New York: Plenum.

Hammond, N. and Barber, P.J. (1978) 'Evidence for abstract response codes: Ear–hand correspondence effects in a three-choice reaction-time task', *Quarterly Journal of Experimental Psychology* 30: 71–82.

Harpster, J.L. and Freiwalds, A. (1984) 'VDT screen resolution and operator performance', *Proceedings of IFIP Conference on Human–Computer Interaction*, Amsterdam: Elsevier.

Harris, M. and Coltheart, M. (1986) *Language Processing in Children and Adults: An introduction*, London: Routledge & Kegan Paul.

Hartzell, E.S., Dunbar, S., Beveridge, R., and Cortilla, R. (1982) 'Helicopter pilot response latency as a function of the spatial arrangement of instruments and controls', *Proceedings of the 18th Annual Conference on Manual Control*, Dayton, Ohio: Wright Patterson Air Force Base.

Hay, D.C. and Young, A.W. (1982) 'The human face', in A.W. Ellis (ed.) *Normality and Pathology in Cognitive Functions*, London: Academic Press.

Hécaen, H. (1981) 'The neuropsychology of face recognition', in G. Davies, H. Ellis, and J. Shepherd (eds) *Perceiving and Remembering Faces*, London: Academic Press.

Hick, W.C. (1952) 'On the rate of gain of information', *Quarterly Journal of Experimental Psychology* 4: 11–26.

Hicks, T.G., and Wierwille, W.W. (1979) 'Comparison of five mental workload assessment procedures in a moving-base driving simulator', *Human Factors* 21: 129–43.

Hochberg, J. (1970) 'Components of literacy: speculations and exploratory research', in H. Levin and J.P. Williams (eds) *Basic Studies in Reading*, New York: Basic Books.

Hochberg, J. and Galper, R.E. (1967) 'Recognition of faces, 1: An exploratory study', *Psychonomic Science* 9: 619–20.

Hockey, R. (ed.) (1983) *Stress and Fatigue in Human Performance*, Chichester: Wiley.

Homa, D., Haver, B., and Schwartz, T. (1976) 'Perceptibility of schematic face stimuli: evidence for a perceptual Gestalt', *Memory and Cognition* 4: 176–85.

Hull, C.L. (1943) *Principles of Behaviour*, New York: Appleton-Century-Crofts.

Hyman, R. (1953) 'Stimulus information as a determinant of reaction time', *Journal of Experimental Psychology* 45: 188–96.

Isreal, J.B., Wickens, C.D., Chesney, G.L., and Donchin, E. (1980) 'The event-related brain potential as an index of display-monitoring workload', *Human Factors* 22: 211–24.

John, B.E., Rosenbloom, P.S., and Newell, A. (1985) 'A theory of stimulus-response compatibility applied to human–computer interaction', *CHI '85 Conference Proceedings* 213–19, New York: Association for Computing Machinery.

Juola, J.F., Ward, N.J., and McNamara, T. (1982) 'Visual search and reading of rapid, serial presentations of letter strings, words, and text', *Journal of Experimental Psychology: General* 111: 208–27.

Just, M.A. and Carpenter P.A. (1980) 'A theory of reading: from eye fixations to comprehension', *Psychological Review* 87: 329–54.

Just, M.A., Carpenter, P.A. and Woolley, J.D. (1982) 'Paradigms and processes in reading comprehension', *Journal of Experimental Psychology: General* 111: 228–38.

Kahneman, D. (1973) *Attention and Effort*, Englewood Cliffs, NJ: Prentice Hall.

Kahneman, D., Ben-Ishai, R., and Lotan, M. (1973) 'Relation of a test of attention to road accidents', *Journal of Applied Psychology* 58: 113–15.

Kerr, N.H., and Winograd, E. (1982) 'Effects of contextual elaboration on face recognition', *Memory and Cognition* 10: 603–9.

Klapp, S.T. (1969) 'Doing two things at once: the role of temporal compatibility', *Memory and Cognition* 7: 375–81.

Klapp, S.T. (1979) 'Doing two things at once: The role of temporal compatibility', *Memory and Cognition* 5: 375–81.

Klapp, S.T. (1981) 'Temporal compatibility in dual motor tasks II: Simultaneous articulation and hand movements', *Memory and Cognition* 9: 398–401.

Klapp, S.T., Hill, M.D., Jagacinski, R.J., Tyler, J.G., Martin, Z.E., and Jones, M.R. (1985) 'On marching to two different drummers: perceptual aspects of the difficulties', *Journal of Experimental Psychology: Human Perception and Performance* 11: 814–27.

Kolers, P.A. (1970) 'Three stages of reading', in H. Levin and J.P. Williams (eds) *Basic Studies in Reading*, New York: Basic Books.

Kolers, P.A. (1972) 'Experiments in reading', *Scientific American* 227: 84–91.

Kolers, P.A., Duchnicky, R.L., and Ferguson, D.C. (1981) 'Eye movement measurement of readability of CRT displays', *Human Factors* 23: 517–28.

Kristofferson, A.B. (1967) 'Attention and psychophysical time', *Acta Psychologica* 27: 93–100.

Kruk, R.S. and Muter, P. (1984) 'Reading of continuous text on video screens', *Human Factors* 26: 339–45.

Laberge, D., VanGelder, P., and Yellott, S. (1971) 'A cueing technique in choice reaction time', *Journal of Experimental Psychology* 87: 225–8.

Langan-Fox, C.P. and Empson, J.A.C. (1985) ' "Actions not as planned" in military air-traffic control', *Ergonomics* 28: 1509–21.

Laughery, K.R. and Fowler, R.F. (1980) 'Sketch artist and Identikit procedures for recalling faces', *Journal of Applied Psychology* 65: 307–16.

Laughery, K.R., Rhodes B.T., and Batten, G.W. (1981) 'Computer-guided recognition and retrieval of facial images', in G. Davies, H. Ellis, and J. Shepherd (eds) *Perceiving and Remembering Faces*, London: Academic Press.

Legge, D. and Barber, P.J. (1976) *Information and Skill*, London: Methuen.

Leonard, J.A. (1959) 'Tactual choice reaction: I', *Quarterly Journal of Experimental Psychology* 11: 76–83.

Levison, W.H. (1979) 'A model for mental workload in tasks requiring continuous information processing', in N. Moray (ed.) *Mental Workload: Theory and measurement*, New York: Plenum.

Levy-Schoen, A. and O'Regan, K. (1979) 'The control of eye movement in reading', in P.A. Kolers, M.E. Wrolstad and H. Bouma (eds) *Processing of Visible Language*, 1, New York: Plenum.

Light, L.L., Kayra-Stuart, F., and Hollander, S. (1979) 'Recognition memory for typical and unusual faces', *Journal of Experimental Psychology: Human Learning and Memory* 5: 212–28.

Long, J.B. (1975) 'Reduced efficiency and capacity limitations in multi-dimensional signal recognition', *Quarterly Journal of Experimental Psychology* 27: 599–614.

Loveless, N.E. (1962) 'Direction of motion stereotypes: a review', *Ergonomics* 5: 357–84.

Lovie, A.D. (1983) 'Attention and behaviourism – fact and fiction, *British Journal of Psychology* 74: 301–10.

Luria, S.M. and Strauss, M.S. (1975) 'Eye movements during search for coded and uncoded targets', *Perception and Psychophysics* 17: 303–8.

Mackworth, N.H. and Morandi, A.J. (1967) 'The gaze selects informative details within pictures', *Perception and Psychophysics* 2: 547–52.

Maslow, A.H. (1946) 'Problem-centring vs. means-centring in science', *Philosophy of Science* 13: 326–31.

Masson, M.E.J. (1983) 'Conceptual processing of text during skimming and rapid sequential reading', *Memory and Cognition* 11: 262–74.

Matin, E. (1974) 'Saccadic suppression: a review and an analysis', *Psychological Bulletin* 81: 899–917.

Matthews, M.L. (1978) 'Discrimination of Identikit constructions of faces: evidence for a dual processing strategy', *Perception and Psychophysics* 23: 153–61.

McClelland, J.L. (1979) 'On the time relations of mental processes: an examination of systems of processes in cascade', *Psychological Review* 86: 287–330.

McClelland, J.L. and Rumelhart D.E. (1981) 'An interactive activation model of context effects in letter perception: Part 1. An account of basic findings', *Psychological Review* 88: 375–407.

McConkie, G.W. (1979) 'On the role and control of eye movements in reading', in P.A. Kolers, M.E. Wrolstad, and H. Bouma (eds) *Processing of Visible Language*, 1, New York: Plenum.

McConkie, G.W. (1983) 'Eye movements and perception during reading', in K. Rayner (ed.) *Eye Movements in Reading: Perceptual and Language Processes*, New York: Academic Press.

McConkie, G.W. and Rayner K. (1975) 'The span of the effective stimulus during a fixation in reading', *Perception and Psychophysics* 17: 578–86.

McCormick, E.J. and Sanders, M.S. (1982) *Human Factors in Engineering and Design*, New York: McGraw Hill.

McKelvie, S.J. (1976). 'The role of eyes and mouth in the memory of a face', *American Journal of Psychology* 89: 311–23.

McKenna, F.P., Duncan, J., and Brown, I.D. (1986) 'Cognitive abilities and safety on the road: a re-examination of individual differences in dichotic listening and search for embedded figures', *Ergonomics* 29: 639–63.

McLeod, P. (1977) 'A dual task response modality effect: support for multiprocess models of attention', *Quarterly Journal of Experimental Psychology* 29: 651-67.

Menzer, G.W. and Thurmond, J.B. (1970) 'Form identification in peripheral vision', *Perception and Psychophysics* 8: 205-9.

Menzies, S.A. (1985) 'Perceptual and psycholinguistic units in reading processes', unpublished Ph.D. thesis, University of London.

Meyer, D.E. and Schvaneveldt, R.W. (1971) 'Facilitation in recognizing pairs of words: evidence of a dependence between retrieval operations', *Journal of Experimental Psychology* 90: 227-34.

Meyer, D.E., Schvaneveldt, R.W., and Ruddy M.G. (1975) 'Locus of contextual effects in visual word recognition', in P.M.A. Rabbitt and S. Dornic (eds) *Attention and Performance*, V, New York: Academic Press.

Miller, G.A. (1956) 'The magical number seven plus or minus two: some limits on our capacity for processing information', *Psychological Review* 63: 81-97.

Miller, G.R. and Coleman, E.B. (1967) 'A set of thirty-six prose passages calibrated for complexity', *Journal of Verbal Learning and Verbal Behaviour* 6: 851-4.

Mitchell, D.C. (1982) *The Process of Reading: A Cognitive Analysis of Fluent Reading and Learning to Read*, Chichester: Wiley.

Mitchell D.C. and Green D.W. (1978) 'The effects of context and content on immediate processing in reading', *Quarterly Journal of Experimental Psychology* 30: 609-36.

Moray, N. (1959) 'Attention in dichotic listening', *Quarterly Journal of Experimental Psychology* 11: 56-60.

Moray, N. (1967) 'Where is capacity limited? A survey and a model', *Acta Psychologica* 27: 84-92.

Moray, N. (1982) 'Subjective mental workload', *Human Factors* 23: 25-40.

Moray, N., Fitter, M., Ostry, D., Favreau, D., and Nagy, V. (1976) 'Attention to pure tones', *Quarterly Journal of Experimental Psychology* 28: 271-85.

Morin, R.E. and Grant, D. (1955) 'Learning and performance on a key-pressing task as a function of the degree of spatial stimulus-response correspondence', *Journal of Experimental Psychology* 49: 39-47.

Morton, J. (1964) 'The effects of context upon speed of reading, eye movements and eye-voice span', *Quarterly Journal of Experimental Psychology* 16: 340-54.

Morton, J. (1979) 'Facilitation in word recognition: experiments causing change in the logogen model', in P.A. Kolers, M.E. Wrolstad, and H. Bouma (eds) *Processing of Visible Language* 1, New York: Plenum.

Mowbray, G.H. and Rhoades, M.V. (1959) 'On the reduction of choice reaction times with practice', *Quarterly Journal of Experimental Psychology* 11: 16-23.

Muter, P., Latremouille, S.A., Treuniet, W.C., and Beam, P. (1982) 'Extended reading of continuous text on television screens', *Human Factors* 24: 501–8.

Navon, D. (1977) 'Forest before trees: the presence of global features in visual perception', *Cognitive Psychology* 9: 353–83.

Navon, D. and Gopher, D. (1979) 'On the economy of the human processing system', *Psychological Review* 86: 214–55.

Neely, J.H. (1976) 'Semantic priming and retrieval from lexical memory: evidence for facilitatory and inhibitory processes', *Memory and Cognition* 4: 648–54.

Neely, J.H. (1977) 'Semantic priming and retrieval from lexical memory: the roles of inhibitionless spreading activation and limited-capacity attention', *Journal of Experimental Psychology: General* 106: 226–54.

Neisser, U. (1967) *Cognitive Psychology*, New York: Appleton-Century-Crofts.

Neisser, U. (1976) *Cognition and Reality*, San Francisco: Freeman.

Newell, A. (1973) 'You can't play 20 questions with Nature and win', in W.G. Chase (ed.) *Visual Information Processing*. New York: Academic Press.

Newman, E.B. (1966) 'Speed of reading when the span of letters is restricted', *American Journal of Psychology* 79: 272–8.

Norman, D.A. (1968) 'Toward a theory of memory and attention', *Psychological Review* 75: 522–36.

Norman, D.A. and Bobrow D.G. (1975) 'On data-limited and resource-limited processes', *Cognitive Psychology* 7: 44–64.

Olson, R.K., Kliegl, R., and Davidson, B.J. (1983) 'Dyslexic and normal readers' eye movements', *Journal of Experimental Psychology: Human Perception and Performance* 9: 816–25.

O'Regan, J.K. (1979) 'Moment to moment control of eye saccades as a function of textual parameters in reading', in P.A. Kolers, M.E. Wrolstad, and H. Bouma (eds) *Processing of Visible Language* 1, New York: Plenum.

O'Regan, K. (1980) 'The control of saccade size and fixation duration in reading: the limits of linguistic control', *Perception and Psychophysics* 28: 112–17.

O'Regan, J.K. (1981) 'The convenient viewing position hypothesis', in D.H. Fisher, R.A. Monty, and J.W. Senders (eds) *Eye Movements: Cognition and Visual Perception*, Hillsdale, NJ: Lawrence Erlbaum.

Pachella, R. (1974) 'The use of reaction time measures in information processing research', in B.H. Kantowitz (ed.) *Human Information Processing*, Hillsdale, NJ: Lawrence Erlbaum.

Palmer, S., Rosch, E., and Chase, P. (1981) 'Canonical perspective and the perception of objects', in J.B. Long and A.D. Baddeley (eds) *Attention and Performance* IX, Hillsdale, NJ: Lawrence Erlbaum.

Parks, T.E. (1966) 'Signal-detectability theory of recognition memory performance', *Psychological Review* 73: 44–58.

Patterson, K.E. (1981) 'Neuropsychological approaches to the study of reading', *British Journal of Psychology* 72: 151–74.

Patterson, K.E., and Baddeley, A.D. (1977) 'When face recognition fails', *Journal of Experimental Psychology: Human Learning and Memory* 3: 406–17.

Patterson, K.E. and Bradshaw J.L. (1975) 'Differential hemispheric mediation of non-verbal visual stimuli', *Journal of Experimental Psychology: Human Perception and Performance* 1: 246–52.

Pavlidis, G.T. (1981) 'Do eye movements hold the key to dyslexia?' *Neuropsychologia* 19: 57–64.

Pavlidis, G.T. (1983) 'The "dyslexia" syndrome and its objective diagnosis by erratic eye movements', in K. Rayner (ed.) *Eye Movements in Reading: Perceptual and Language Processes*, New York: Academic Press.

Pavlidis, G.T. (1985) 'Erratic eye movements and dyslexia: Factors determining their relationship', *Perceptual and Motor Skills* 60: 319–22.

Pavlidis, G.T. (1986) 'The role of eye movements in the diagnosis of dyslexia', in G.T. Pavlidis and D.F. Fisher (eds) *Dyslexia: Its Neuropsychology and Treatment*, New York: Wiley.

Peters, M. (1977) 'Simultaneous performance of two motor activities: the factor of timing', *Neuropsychologia* 15: 461–5.

Peterson, L.R. and Peterson, M.J. (1959) 'Short-term retention of individual verbal items', *Journal of Experimental Psychology* 58: 193–8.

Petropolous, H., and Brebner, J. (1981) 'Stereotypes for direction-of-movement of rotary controls associated with linear displays: the effects of scale presence and position direction, of pointer direction, and distances between the control and the display', *Ergonomics* 24: 143–51.

Pheasant, S.T. (1986) *Bodyspace: Anthropometry, Ergonomics and Design*, London: Taylor & Francis.

Pirozollo, F.J. (1979) *The Neuropsychology of Developmental Reading Disorders*, New York: Praeger.

Pirozzolo, F.J. (1983) In K. Rayner (ed.) *Eye Movements in Reading: Perceptual and Language Processes*, New York: Academic Press.

Pirozollo, F.J. and Rayner, K. (1978) 'Disorders of oculomotor scanning and graphic orientation in developmental Gerstmann syndrome', *Brain and Language* 5: 119–26.

Pollatsek, A. (1983) 'What can eye movements tell us about dyslexia?', in K. Rayner (ed.) *Eye Movements in Reading: Perceptual and Language Processes*, New York: Academic Press.

Posner, M.I. (1980) 'Orienting of attention', *Quarterly Journal of Experimental Psychology* 32: 3–25.

Posner, M.I. and Keele, S.W. (1968) 'On the genesis of abstract ideas', *Journal of Experimental Psychology* 77: 353–63.

Posner, M.I. and Snyder, C.R. (1975) 'Attention and cognitive control', in R.L. Solso (ed.) *Information Processing and Cognition: The Loyola Symposium*, Hillsdale, NJ: Lawrence Erlbaum.

Potter, M.C., Kroll, J.F., and Harris, C. (1980) 'Comprehension and memory in rapid sequential reading', in R.S. Nickerson (ed.) *Attention and Performance*, VIII, Hillsdale, NJ: Lawrence Erlbaum.

Price, R.H. (1966) 'Signal-detection methods in personality and perception', *Psychological Bulletin* 66: 55–62.

Rabbitt, P.M.A. (1967) 'Signal discriminability, S–R compatibility and choice reaction time', *Psychonomic Science* 7: 419–20.

Ranklin, J.E. (1977) 'Psycholinguistic cues in peripheral vision during reading', unpublished Ph.D. thesis, University of London.

Ray, R.D. and Ray, W.D. (1979) 'An analysis of domestic cooker control design', *Ergonomics* 22: 1243–8.

Rayner, K. (1975) 'The perceptual span and peripheral cues in reading', *Cognitive Psychology* 7: 65–81.

Rayner, K. (1978) 'Eye movements in reading and information processing', *Psychological Bulletin* 85: 618–60.

Rayner, K. (1979) 'Eye guidance in reading: fixation locations within words', *Perception* 8: 21–30.

Rayner, K. (1986) 'Eye movements and the perceptual span: Evidence for dyslexic typology', in G.T. Pavlidis and D.F. Fisher (eds) *Dyslexia: Its Neuropsychology and Treatment*, New York: Wiley.

Rayner, K. and McConkie, G.W. (1976) 'What guides a reader's eye movements?', *Vision Research* 16: 829–37.

Rayner, K. and Pollatsek, A. (1981) 'Eye movement control during reading: evidence for direct control', *Quarterly Journal of Experimental Psychology* 33A: 351–73.

Rayner, K., Inhoff, A.W., Morrison, R.E., Slowiaczek, M.L., and Bertera, J.H. (1981) 'Masking of foveal and parafoveal vision during eye fixations in reading', *Journal of Experimental Psychology: Human Perception and Performance* 7: 167–79.

Reason, J.T. (1979) 'Actions not as planned: the price of automation', in G. Underwood and R. Stephens (eds) *Aspects of Consciousness*, 1, London: Academic Press.

Remington, R. and Pierce, L. (1984) 'Moving attention: evidence for time-invariant shifts of visual selective attention', *Perception and Psychophysics* 35: 393–9.

Rizzollatti, G., Umilta, C., and Berlucchi, G. (1971) 'Opposite superiorities of the right and left cerebral hemispheres in discriminative reaction time to physiognomical and alphabetical material', *Brain* 94: 431–42.

Robertson, I.T. and Downs, S. (1979) 'Learning and the prediction of performance: development of trainability testing in the United Kingdom', *Journal of Applied Psychology* 64: 42–50.

Rollins, R.A. and Hendricks, R. (1980) 'Processing of words presented simultaneously to eye and ear', *Journal of Experimental Psychology: Human Perception and Performance* 6: 99–109.

Rosch, E., Mervis, C., Gray, W., Johnson, D., and Boyes-Braem, P. (1976) 'Basic objects in natural categories', *Cognitive Psychology* 6: 382–439.

Rumelhart, D.E. and McClelland, J.L. (1982) 'An interactive activation model of context effects in letter perception: Part 2. The contextual enhancement effect and some tests and extensions of the model', *Psychological Review* 89: 60–94.

Scharf, B. (ed.) (1975) *Experimental Sensory Psychology*, Glenview, Ill.: Scott, Foresman.

Schuberth R.E. and Eimas P.D. (1977) 'Effects of context on the classification of words and nonwords', *Journal of Experimental Psychology: Human Perception and Performance* 3: 27–36.

Seymour, P.H.K. (1977) 'Conceptual encoding and the locus of the Stroop effect', *Quarterly Journal of Experimental Psychology* 28: 245–65.

Shaffer, L.H. (1975) 'Multiple attention in continuous verbal tasks', in P.M.A. Rabbitt and S. Dornic (eds) *Attention and Performance*, V, London: Academic Press.

Shallice, T., McLeod, P., and Lewis, K. (1985) 'Isolating cognitive modules with the dual-task paradigm: Are speech perception and production separate processes?', *Quarterly Journal of Experimental Psychology* 37A: 507–32.

Shebilske, W.L. (1975) 'Reading eye movements from an information-processing point of view', in D.W. Massaro (ed.) *An Information-Processing Analysis of Speech Perception, Reading and Psycholinguistics*, New York: Academic Press.

Shebilske, W.L. and Fisher, D.H. (1983) 'Eye movements and context effects during reading of extended discourse', in K. Rayner (ed.) *Eye Movements in Reading: Perceptual and Language Processes*, New York: Academic Press.

Shebilske, W.L. and Reid, L.S. (1979) 'Reading eye movements, macro-structure and comprehension processes', in P.A. Kolers, M.E. Wrolstad, and H. Bouma (eds) *Processing of Visible Language*, 1, New York: Plenum.

Shepard, R.N. (1967) 'Recognition memory for words, sentences, and pictures', *Journal of Verbal Learning and Verbal Behaviour* 6: 157–63.

Shepard, R.N. and Metzler, J. (1971) 'Mental rotation of three dimensional objects', *Science* 171: 701–3.

Shepherd, J.W. and Ellis, H.D. (1973) 'The effect of attractiveness on recognition memory for faces', *American Journal of Psychology* 86: 627–33.

Shepherd, J., Davies, G., and Ellis, H. (1981) 'Studies of cue saliency', in G. Davies, H. Ellis, and J. Shepherd (eds) *Perceiving and Remembering Faces*, London: Academic Press.

Shinar, D. and Acton, M.B. (1978) 'Control-display relationships on the four-burner range: population stereotypes versus standards', *Human Factors* 20: 13–17.

Shulman, H.G. and McConkie, A. (1973) 'S–R compatibility, response discriminability, and response codes in choice reaction time', *Journal of Experimental Psychology* 98: 375–8.

Shulman, G.L., Remington, R.W. and McLean, J.P. (1979) 'Moving attention through visual space', *Journal of Experimental Psychology: Human Perception and Performance* 5: 522–6.

Simon, J.R. (1969) 'Reactions toward the source of stimulation', *Journal of Experimental Psychology* 81: 174–6.

Simon, J.R. and Small, A.M. (1969) 'Processing auditory information: interference from an irrelevant cue', *Journal of Applied Psychology* 53: 433–5.

Skinner, B.F. (1938) *The Behaviour of Organisms*, New York: Appleton.

Skipper, J.H., Rieger, C.A., and Wierwille, W.W. (1986) 'Evaluation of decision-tree rating scales for mental workload estimation', *Ergonomics* 29: 585–99.

Smith, E.E. (1968) 'Choice reaction time: an analysis of the major theoretical positions', *Psychological Bulletin* 69: 77–110.

Smith, F. (1971) *Understanding Reading*, New York: Holt, Rinehart and Winston.

Smith, F. (1973) *Psycholinguistics and Reading*, New York: Holt, Reinhart & Winston.

Smith, P.J. and Langolf, G.D. (1981) 'The use of Sternberg's memory-scanning paradigm in assessing effects of chemical exposure', *Human Factors*, 23: 701–8.

Smith, S. (1981) 'Exploring compatibility with words and pictures', *Human Factors* 23: 305–15.

Snyder, H.L. (1973) 'Dynamic visual search patterns', in *Visual Search*, Washington, DC: NAS–NRC Committee on Vision.

Solomons, L. and Stein, G. (1896) 'Normal motor automatism', *Psychological Review* 3: 492–512.

Spelke, E., Hirst, W., and Neisser, U. (1976) 'Skills of divided attention', *Cognition* 4: 215–30.

Sperandio, J.C. (1978) 'The regulation of working methods as a function of workload among air traffic controllers', *Ergonomics* 21: 193–202.

Standing, L. (1973) 'Learning 10,000 pictures', *Quarterly Journal of Experimental Psychology* 25: 207–22.

Standing, L., Conezio, J., and Haber, R.N. (1969) 'Perception and memory for pictures: single-trial learning of 2500 visual stimuli', *Psychonomic Science* 19: 73–4.

Stanley, G., Smith, G.A., and Howell, E.A. (1983) 'Eye movements and sequential tracking in dyslexic and control children', *British Journal of Psychology* 74: 181–7.

Stanovich, K.E. and Pachella, R.G. (1977) 'Encoding, stimulus-response compatibility, and stages of processing', *Journal of Experimental Psychology: Human Perception and Performance* 3: 411–21.

Stanovich, K.E. and West, R.F. (1979) 'Mechanisms of sentence context effects in reading: automatic activation and conscious attention', *Memory and Cognition* 7: 77–85.

Stanovich, K.E. and West, R.W. (1981) 'The effect of sentence context on ongoing word recognition: tests of a two-process theory', *Journal of Experimental Psychology: Human Perception and Performance* 7: 658–72.

Stanovich, K.E. and West, R.F. (1983a) 'On priming by a sentence context', *Journal of Experimental Psychology: General* 112: 1–36.

Stanovich, K.E. and West, R.F. (1983b) 'The generalizability of context effects on word recognition: a reconsideration of the roles of parafoveal priming and sentence context', *Memory and Cognition* 11: 49–58.

Stein, J.F. and Fowler, S. (1982) 'Towards the physiology of visual dyslexia', in Y. Zotterman (ed.) *Dyslexia: Neuronal, Cognitive and Linguistic Aspects*, New York: Pergamon.

Sternberg, S. (1967) 'Two operations in character recognition: some evidence from reaction measurements', *Perception and Psychophysics* 2: 45–53.

Sternberg, S. (1969) 'The discovery of processing stages: extensions of Donders' method', *Acta Psychologica* 30: 276–315.

Sternberg, S., (1975) 'Memory scanning: new findings and current controversies', *Quarterly Journal of Experimental Psychology* 27: 1–32.

Stroop, J.R. (1935) 'Studies of interference in serial verbal reactions', *Journal of Experimental Psychology* 18: 643–62.

Sutherland, N.F. (1973) 'Object recognition', in E.C. Carterette and M.P. Friedman (eds) *Handbook of Perception* III, New York: Academic Press.

Taylor, D.A. (1976) 'Stage analysis of reaction time', *Psychological Bulletin* 83: 161–91.

Taylor, I. and Taylor, M.M. (1983) *The Psychology of Reading*, New York: Academic Press.

Teichner, W.H. and Krebs, M.J. (1974) 'Laws of visual choice reaction time', *Psychological Review* 81: 75–98.

Theios, J. (1975) 'The components of response latency in simple human information processing tasks', in P.M.A. Rabbitt and S. Dornic (eds) *Attention and Performance* V, London: Academic Press.

Treisman, A.M. (1960) 'Contextual cues in selective listening', *Quarterly Journal of Experimental Psychology* 12: 242–8.

Treisman, A.M. and Geffen, G. (1967) 'Selective attention and cerebral dominance in perceiving and responding to speech messages', *Quarterly Journal of Experimental Psychology* 19: 1–17.

Treisman, A.M. and Riley, R.G. (1969) 'Is selective attention selective perception or selective response? A further test', *Journal of Experimental Psychology* 79: 27–34.

Tulving, E. and Gold, C. (1963) 'Stimulus information and contextual information as determinants of tachistoscopic recognition of words', *Journal of Experimental Psychology* 66: 319–27.

Underwood, G. (1974) 'Moray vs. the rest: The effects of extended shadowing practice', *Quarterly Journal of Experimental Psychology* 26: 368–72.

Valentine, E.R. (1982) *Conceptual Issues in Psychology*, London: Allen & Unwin.

Van Nes, F.L. (1984) 'Limits of visual perception in the technology of visual display terminals', *Behaviour and Information Technology* 3: 371–7.

Vernon, P.A. (1986) 'Speed of information-processing, intelligence, and mental retardation', in M.G. Wade (ed.) *Motor Skill Acquisition of the Mentally Handicapped: Issues in Research and Training*, Amsterdam: North Holland.

Walker-Smith, G.J., Gale, A.G., and Findlay, J.M. (1977) 'Eye movement strategies involved in face perception', *Perception* 6: 313–26.

Wallace, R.J. (1971) 'S–R compatibility and the idea of a response code', *Journal of Experimental Psychology* 88: 354–60.

Ward, N.J. and Juola, J.F. (1982) 'Reading with and without eye movements: reply to Just, Carpenter, and Woolley', *Journal of Experimental Psychology: General* 111: 239–41.

Weber, R.M. (1970) 'First graders' use of grammatical context in reading', in H. Levin and J.P. Williams (eds) *Basic Studies in Reading*, New York: Basic Books.

Welford, A.T. (1960) 'The measurement of sensory-motor performance: survey and reappraisal of twelve years' progress', *Ergonomics* 3: 189–229.

Welford, A.T. (1968) *Fundamentals of Skill*, London: Methuen.

Welford, A.T. (1976) *Skilled Performance*, Glenview, Ill.: Scot, Foresman.

Wells, G.L., Leippe, J.R., and Ostrom, T.M. (1979) 'Guidelines for assessing the fairness of a line-up', *Law and Human Behaviour* 3: 285–93.

West, R.F. and Stanovich K.E. (1978) 'Automatic contextual facilitation in readers of three ages', *Child Development* 49: 717–27.

Westland, G. (1978) *Current Crises of Psychology*, London: Heinmann.

Wewerinke, P.H. (1974) 'Human operator workload for various control conditions', *10th NASA Annual Conference on Manual Control*, Wright-Patterson Air Force Base, Ohio.

Whitaker, L.A. and Sommer, R. (1986) 'Perception of traffic guidance signs containing conflicting symbol and direction information', *Ergonomics* 29: 699–712.

Whiteley, A.M. and Warrington, E.K. (1977) 'Prosopagnosia: a clinical, psychological and anatomical study of three patients', *Journal of Neurology, Neurosurgery and Psychiatry* 40: 395–403.

Wickens, C.D. (1984) *Engineering Psychology*, Columbus, Ohio: Merrill.

Wickens, C.D., Mountford, S.J., and Schreiner, W. (1981) 'Multiple resources, task hemispheric integrity, and individual differences in time-sharing', *Human Factors* 23: 211–29.

Williams, L.G. (1966) 'The effect of target specification on objects fixated during visual search', *Perception and Psychophysics* 1: 315–18.

Woodhead, M.M., Baddeley, A.D., and Simmonds D.C.V. (1979) 'On training people to recognize faces', *Ergonomics* 22: 333–43.

Wright, P. and Lickorish, A. (1983) 'Proof-reading texts on screen and paper', *Behaviour and Information Technology* 2: 227–35.

Yin, R.K. (1969) 'Looking at upside-down faces', *Journal of Experimental Psychology* 81: 141–5.

Yin, R.K. (1970) 'Face recognition by brain-injured patients: a dissociable ability?', *Neuropsychologia* 8: 395–402.

Zola, D. (1984) 'Redundancy and word perception during reading', *Perception and Psychophysics* 36: 277–84.

NAME INDEX

Ackerman, P.L. 118
Acton, M.B. 77
Adams, A.J. 155
Aitkenhead, A.M. 68
Alford, J.A. 161, 165
Allport, D.A. 11, 122, 123, 129
Antonis, B. 122, 123
Anderson, I.H. 153
Anderson, J.R. 29, 30, 67, 68
Attneave, F. 16

Baddeley, A.D. 29, 36, 37, 40, 131
Bakan, D. 2
Ballantine, M. 73
Barber, P.J. 22, 28, 32, 91, 92
Barnard, P.J. 97
Bateson, P.P.G. 39

Batten, G.W. 48
Bauer, D. 176
Beam, P. 176
Becker, C.A. 167, 170
Ben-Ishai, R. 113
Benton, A.L. 55
Berlucchi, G. 55
Bertelson, P. 87
Bertera, J.H. 184
Beveridge, R. 77
Bittner, A.C. 116, 117
Black, J.L. 155
Blaxhall, J. 162
Bloom, P.A. 170, 173
Bobrow, D.G. 131
Boyes, Braem, P. 61
Bradshaw, J.L. 55–7
Brebner, J. 75

SUBJECT INDEX

accidents 73, 100, 113
additive factors logic 87–90,
    166–7
air-traffic control 100–1, 110–11
applying psychology, guidelines
    11, 191–4
applied psychological research 4,
    6–7, 50
attention 3, 24–7, 111, 112–15,
    118–20, 121–2, 134–5; capacity
    105, 118, 132–3; dichotic
    listening 25, 113–14;
    shadowing 25–6, 121–4, 127–8;
    spatial attention 118–19;
    theories 26; switching attention
    111, 113–15, 118–20; time-
    sharing 99, 111–20, 123, 130
automaticity 84, 120–1, 166–7

behaviourism 16, 24

carphones 133–5
choice reaction time 82–3, 87–8;
    repetition effect 87–8
compatibility: actions and effects
    68–71; conceptual compatibility
    95; direction of movement
    stereotypes 73–6; displays and
    actions 70–1, 79–82;
    expectations 95; ideomotor
    compatibility 84; locus of S–R
    compatibility effects 87–90;
    incidental compatibility effects
    90–3; mental models 68–9;
    population stereotypes 71–6,
    80, 85; spatial compatibility
    76–82, 91–2